THE BLOODAXE BOOK OF
CONTEMPORARY INDIAN POETS

THE Bloodaxe Book OF
CONTEMPORARY
INDIAN POETS

edited by JEET THAYIL

with photographs by
MADHU KAPPARATH

FULCRUM

BLOODAXE BOOKS

ISBN: 978 1 85224 801 7

First published 2008 by
Bloodaxe Books Ltd,
Highgreen,
Tarset,
Northumberland NE48 1RP,
IN ASSOCIATION WITH
Fulcrum: an annual of poetry and aesthetics,
421 Huron Avenue, Cambridge,
Massachusetts 02138, USA

www.bloodaxebooks.com
For further information about Bloodaxe titles
please visit our website or write to
the above address for a catalogue.

Bloodaxe Books Ltd acknowledges
the financial assistance of
Arts Council England, North East.

Cover design: Neil Astley & Pamela Robertson-Pearce.

Cover printing: J. Thomson Colour Printers Ltd, Glasgow.

Printed in Great Britain by
Bell & Bain Limited, Glasgow, Scotland.

This anthology is dedicated to the poets who died:
Kersy Katrak and Revathy Gopal in 2007;
Santan Rodrigues in 2006;
Arun Kolatkar, Dom Moraes and Nissim Ezekiel in 2004;
Gopal Honnalgere and Reetika Vazirani in 2003;
Agha Shahid Ali in 2001;
G.S. Sharat Chandra in 2000;
Srinivas Rayaprol in 1998;
Lawrence Bantleman in 1995;
A.K. Ramanujan in 1993.

CONTENTS

JEET THAYIL

Preface to this selection

Modernism arrived in India at roughly the same time as Independence, which is to say after it had already established itself as the new orthodoxy in other parts of the world. It came to some of the regional Indian languages before it came to English. In Marathi, to take one instance, in the years immediately following Independence, the modernist movement attempted to recast seemingly immovable social divisions, including those of caste and sex, in a literature that was nothing if not indigenous. These writers were in a hurry to overthrow the conventions of the Indian bourgeois as well as those of their once colonial masters. Later Marathi modernists such as Dilip Chitre and Arun Kolatkar owed their allegiance not to British but to European and American poetry, particularly to the surrealists and the Beats. Indian poetry in English took longer to emerge from the influence of 'English' poetry, by no means a situation peculiar to verse.

In the 60 years since Independence, in jurisprudence, on the stage, and in the media, British accents and honorifics have been commonplace. The most prominent Indian modernists of the 50s, Nissim Ezekiel and Dom Moraes, shaped the canon and cleared the way, but the sounds they made were British and they confined even their experimentation to the essential iamb. It wasn't until the 70s that Internationalism established itself on the English page in India, with the Clearing House editions of Adil Jussawalla, Jayanta Mahapatra, Arvind Krishna Mehrotra and Arun Kolatkar, and with the psychic weather that poets such as A.K. Ramanujan, Keki Daruwalla, Eunice de Souza and R. Parthasarathy brought to their lines. The next generation of Indian poets, the poets of the 80s and 90s in Bombay and other cities, were more conservative in some ways than their immediate forebears, and there was a return to the canonical influence of mid-20th century British poetry.

To demonstrate the range and variety among Indian poets since Independence, this anthology includes poets who live in places other than the urban centres of India, who trace their imaginative lineage to Ashbery, Brodsky, Szymborska and Walcott as much as to Larkin, Auden, Eliot and Pound. Also, it returns forgotten figures such as Lawrence Bantleman, Gopal Honnalgere, G.S. Sharat Chandra and Srinivas Rayaprol to the centre stage where they belong, and features poets who have never shared a stage together.

A chronological parade of poets can be as arbitrary as an alphabetical one. The arrangement in these pages bypasses those systems for the pleasures of unexpected juxtaposition. By placing Ezekiel beside Aimee Nezhukumatathil, born 50 years later and writing in a very different poetic and social environment, it is possible to see genetic connections not only in tone but in formal disposition. This system of placement may make it difficult to form a quick assessment of the literature's development, but it gives the reader something quite as important, a sense of how vast and riverine the poetry is, and a view of its undercurrents and vitality. While inclusiveness has been a point in my selection of poets and in the selection of a representative range of their work, in some cases, for instance with Ramanujan and Vikram Seth, I did not include the obvious, over-anthologised pieces, choosing instead the unfamiliar and the over-looked.

This selection grew out of the pages of *Give the Sea Change and It Shall Change: Fifty-Six Indian Poets* (1952-2005), which appeared as a special supplement in *Fulcrum* number four (2005). One of the developments between that anthology and this is the addition of four names – Kersy Katrak, Revathy Gopal, Santan Rodrigues, and Lawrence Bantleman – to the names of the dead on the dedication page. In my original headnote to Bantleman's poems I wrote that he had 'vanished so effectively that none of his friends knew what became of him'. Eunice de Souza, working from Bombay, on e-mail, made contact with a former colleague who confirmed what had been conjecture, that Bantleman moved to Vancouver and died there more than a decade earlier, that he had given up poetry, that he had given up writing altogether. He had a job in the department of social housing where he made affordable accommodation for the city's poor. He quit the post after a falling-out with a supervisor. 'Lawrence had developed an alcohol problem but he remained brilliant,' the colleague wrote. And there was a project named after him, the Lawrence Bantleman Court, and a handful of people who still remembered him, though not as a writer. In many ways, Bantleman's story is an Indian one. He produced first-rate work as a young poet, and then, because of financial anxiety and the lack of a sustained response to his poems, the usual dénoument occurred: flight, an end to the writing, a disappearance into alcoholism and obscurity. This anthology is a way of bringing him back.

Bangalore
December 2007

PUBLISHER'S NOTE
American spellings are retained in work by poets from the United States (or living there), except for *-ize* suffixes, which are modernised to *-ise*. Punctuation follows Bloodaxe's British house style (including single inverted commas for quotation, double for qualified expressions, punctuation outside quotation marks except where a whole sentence is quoted).

JEET THAYIL

One Language, Separated by the Sea:
INTRODUCTION

Here is M.K. Gandhi, at the age of 19, setting sail for England
with the idea of making himself into a gentleman and a barrister:

> I was quite unaccustomed to talking in English, and except for Sjt
> Majumdar, all the other passengers in the second saloon were English.
> I could not speak to them. For I could rarely follow their remarks
> when they came up to me, and even when I understood I could not
> reply. I had to frame every sentence in my mind before I could bring
> it out.

Gandhi's experiment with gentlemanliness was only partly suc-
cessful. He gave up English clothes, but he kept the language. When
he wrote in English, he wrote well enough, though it was never
an easy relationship: he could not help but see the language as a
vestigial implement of India's colonial legacy. This suspicion by
association still persists among many Indians today.

Those who write in English – a small, Westernised, middle-class
minority – are divided by more than language from other Indian
writers. Where a Malayalam poet has a distinct readership, English
language poets do not. They are known only unto themselves. This
has led to crises of identity, to a few inelegant labels for the writ-
ing – 'Indo-English', 'Indo-Anglian', 'Indian English' – and to a
charged debate that has carried on for at least 18 decades.

In this exchange, writers who work in English are held
accountable for nothing less than a failure of national conscience.
The harshest criticism comes from writers in regional languages
who preface their comments with assurances that jealousy has lit-
tle to do with the intensity of their opinions. It is instructive to
hear what they have to say, but it isn't illuminating. The only
illuminating point about the controversy is that it is conducted
entirely in English. And it's worth revisiting for an idea of the
context against which Indian poetry has, against all expectation,
grown into itself.

Rabindranath Tagore's *Gitanjali* was published in 1912 with a
celebratory introduction by W.B. Yeats, '[T]hese prose translations
from Rabindranath Tagore have stirred my blood as nothing has
for years.' Soon enough, Yeats would retract his opinion of India's
most famous poet and add an early comment to the debate about
writers who write in languages other than their mother tongue. In
a letter to his friend, William Rothenstein, Yeats wrote:

Damn Tagore. We got out three good books, Sturge, Moore and I, and then, because he thought it more important to see and know English than to be a great poet, he brought out sentimental rubbish and wrecked his reputation. Tagore does not know English, no Indian knows English. Nobody can write music and style in a language not learned in childhood and ever since the language of his thought.

The passage is striking for its self-assurance and for the fact that Yeats did not write his own poems – or indeed the letter to his friend – in the language he learned in childhood, Gaelic. But his argument found enthusiastic backers among India's regional language writers, and, puzzlingly, among those who wrote in English.

The Concise Encyclopaedia of English and American Poets and Poetry, edited by Stephen Spender and Donald Hall, carried an entry on Indian poetry by the poet and critic Buddhadeva Bose. Agreeing with Yeats that Indians should not write in English, Bose – more loyal than his master – took the argument further: 'As for the present-day 'Indo-Anglians', they are earnest and not without talent, but it is difficult to see how they can develop as poets in a language which they have learnt from books and seldom hear spoken in the streets or even in their own homes...' He added that English poetry written by Indians was 'a blind alley, lined with curio shops, leading nowhere'. Bose's encyclopaedia entry appeared in 1963. In the intervening years, the world has become a smaller place. English is a fact of life in many Indian homes and on many Indian streets; Indian movies and advertisements employ an energetic mix of Hindi and English; more Indians write English than ever before. But none of this makes a difference to the anti-English brigade, which insists that genuine expression is possible only in the vernaculars,

While this opinion may seem obsolete in today's India, it is useful – for perspective and context – to look at a small (very small) selection of the arguments marshalled against the use of English.

One critic said the language was part of a state ideology aimed at 'maximising the interests of a collaborationist minority vis-à-vis the vast native subaltern sector'. I quote from Ajanta Sircar's 'Production of Authenticity: The Indo-Anglian Critical Tradition' in *The Economic and Political Weekly*, a long-running Bombay journal of the left. English users, Sircar said, were perpetuating colonialism in a post-colonial era and doing so in a manner 'historically designed to impoverish both the land and the people'. This is a large claim – for any writing, anywhere – and an absurd one. Inevitably, in a nation where both largeness and absurdity are unremarkable, many Indians believe it.

They believe, too, that English is essentially a conjuror's trick. 'It doesn't upset me really that they make so much money out of their writing. They are such necromancers, creating something out of nothing,' Marathi author Balachandran Nimade told the newsweekly *Outlook* in a 2002 cover story titled 'Indian English writers are intellectual pygmies.' The Hindi writer Rajendra Yadav characterised his English-language compatriots as 'second-rate', then adjusted the ranking: they were really a 'third-rate serpent-and-rope trick.'

The most frequent question raised by these writers was one of authenticity, as if language were a kind of cuisine and for the real thing you must travel deep into uncharted native territory. A Kannada writer congratulated himself on the richness of his back yard – with its centuries-old folk tradition and village life – compared to the writer of English, who owned little more than a makeshift front yard. The Tamil novelist Ashokamitran said English users suffered from 'a sense of not belonging anywhere, their lack of emotive content [making] them prime candidates for a spiritual life, not writers'. Ashokamitran is an alumnus of the International Writing Program in Iowa, whose novel *Mole!* (Orient Longman, 2005) is an account of the seven months he spent in Iowa in the early 70s. He may not write in English, but his fiction grows out of a narrative tradition that is recognisably American and modernist. Nirmal Verma, the distinguished Hindi novelist who died in 2005, said Indian writers in English were unable to link themselves to 'the culture of their region, its real life, its metaphors and images'. He compared them, unfavourably, to writers such as himself whose 'language links me to a tradition of 5,000 years, to the medieval writers, the Bhakti poets, to the Sanskrit classics and also connects me to the philosophical texts of Indian culture'. This too is a large claim, impossible to substantiate. And Verma's own novels are fine character studies of not belonging anywhere: they mine not the arguable linear heritage of Indian literature, but the decade he spent in Prague in the 60s. Like Ashokamitran's, his books have been translated into English – for an Indian readership!

While these writers are novelists and their comments are aimed largely at other novelists, it is the poets who find themselves most vulnerable to this and other criticisms about authenticity and tradition. Unlike Indian novelists, poets receive no advances; their books are usually out of print; even the best-known among them have trouble finding publishers and are virtually unknown outside India. These are difficult conditions under which to write. That they continue to produce original work is nothing short of remarkable.

A convenient starting point for a look at modern Indian poetry is Independence, when His Majesty officially gave India back to the Indians. More convenient still, for this anthology, is the year 1952, when Nissim Ezekiel published his first book, *A Time to Change*, with the Fortune Press in London. Until Ezekiel, Indian poetry in English was a 19th-century product that had survived well into the

20th. A backward glance over the 150 years before Ezekiel turns up only four figures of note in English, three of them Bengali, all of them Calcutta-based: Tagore, Toru Dutt, Michael Madhusudan Dutt (no relation), and Henry Louis Vivian Derozio.

Whatever *Gitanjali*'s merits or demerits, for many years it was the standard volume in any discussion of Indian poetry; and despite good translations by William Radice and Ketaki Kushari Dyson, the best-known *Gitanjali* version – with its high 19th-century romanticisms – is still Tagore's.

Born in 1856 into a family of writers and Anglophiles, Toru Dutt's indifferent health and love of English literature dominated her life. Her father took the family to France, England, and Italy. On her return to India, she published her first, and only, collection of poems; some showed the influence of Keats.

> And oft at nights the garden overflows
> With one sweet song that seems to have no close
> Sung darkling from our tree

She was 20; she died soon after the book appeared, of Keats's malady; she would be unknown in India – and slightly less unknown in Europe – for a hundred years.

Michael Madhusudan Dutt (1824-73) saw himself as an English poet, and, in that mode, he converted to Christianity and produced two books, including *The Captive Ladie*. His blank verse sonnet 'Satan', in the manner of Milton's *Paradise Lost*, recast Satan as hero ('A form of awe he was – and yet it seemed / A sepulchre of beauty – faded, gone, / Mouldering where memory, fond mourner, keeps / Her lonesome vigils'). 'Satan' prefigured his Bengali epic *Meghnada Badha Kabya*, which derived a tragic hero from a villainous Ramayana figure. According to one version of Dutt's life, he switched to Bengali when told by a London poet that he would always be considered second rate in English – he might as well give his mother tongue a try.

Henry Derozio was born in 1809. He was Anglo-Indian, a school teacher, a journalist, and, briefly, an indigo planter. Below is a stanza from 'Ode – from the Persian of Half Queez', which may be the first instance of an Indian English poem in the literature. It appeared in 1827, four years before Derozio's death at the age of 22.

> Without thy dreams, dear opium,
> Without a single hope I am,
> Spicy scent, delusive joy;
> Chillum hither lao, my boy!

'Half Queez' is the poet we know as Hafiz. And it is the stanza's last, trochaic line that establishes a connection to the Indian English poems of the later Ezekiel, or the work of half a dozen novelists. The line has five words – two English, two Hindi, and one that belongs to both ('hither' in English, which incidentally derives from the Old English *hider*, implies Hindi's 'idhar' and means the same thing). The line is inaccurate (the chillum is not used to smoke opium), but it is recognisable colloquial speech. It could have been written, or spoken, yesterday, perhaps in a novel such as Upamanyu Chatterjee's *The Mammaries of the Welfare State*:

> 'Are you all right?' he asked in Hinglish – 'Aap all right hain?' While waiting for her to unwrap herself, he realised that he liked the rhythms of Hinglish. It was a genuinely national language, as truly mirroring the minds of the people as Benglish, Tamilish, Maralish, Punjlish and Kannalish. He told himself that when he returned to his boarded-up verandah, he should note in his diary the following items as food for thought: i) Why can't Hinglish be the Official Language of the Welfare State? and, ii) Why don't you translate into Hinglish or Benglish some of your favorite English poems? *The Alphred Pruphrock-er LaabhSong?* and *Shalott ki Lady?*

Chatterjee's novel – a sequel to his first, *English, August* – is a good example of the kind of Indian fiction seen as responsible for the 'chutnification' of English. *English, August* appeared in 1988; Salman Rushdie's *Midnight's Children* in 1981. Before novelists discovered Indian English, Derozio had already been there and so had Arun Kolatkar and Nissim Ezekiel. But the new ground they were instrumental in mapping ended up being claimed for fiction.

Tagore was the last important poet before Ezekiel, Derozio the first. After Ezekiel, the number of poets producing notable work in English increases by a startling number. They live not in Calcutta or Bombay, but throughout the world; what they have in common is English. To present them together in one volume requires more than an appreciation of the cartographer's instinct, it needs a rethinking of the enterprise.

Most anthologies of Indian poetry choose depth over breadth. Like small clubs that share membership and material, the same poems by a dozen or so poets have appeared in various anthologies. Important figures have been left out, and the perpetual reprinting of poets and poems leaves the reader with a sense of claustrophobia, of a narrow world defined by its own obsessions. The larger collections, on the other hand, tend to feature poets who hardly merit inclusion.

Indian poetry, wherever its writers are based, should really be seen as one body of work. Towards that ambition, this anthology includes poets who live in Denmark, France, Canada, Australia, the United States, China, the United Kingdom – and India.

(If India and the United States have the largest representation here, this is as it should be. The connection between the two countries goes back to Tagore, whose first appearance in the West was in *Poetry*, at the behest of Ezra Pound. Pound, John Berryman, Robert Lowell, Theodore Roethke and Allen Ginsberg, among

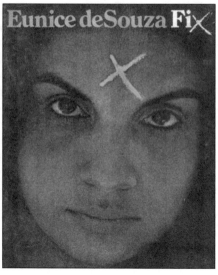

POETRY COLLECTIONS WITH COVER
DESIGNS BY ARUN KOLATKAR

TOP LEFT: Adil Jussawalla's
Missing Person
(Clearing House, 1976).

TOP RIGHT: Eunice de Souza's *Fix*
(Newground, 1979).

LEFT: Dilip Chitre's
Travelling in a Cage
(Clearing House, 1980).

others, influenced two generations of Indian poets. Srinivas
Rayaprol was a friend of William Carlos Williams. *East and West*,
the journal he founded on returning to India, included Indian and
American poets. The first book published by the Writers' Work-
shop in Calcutta was by an American, and the workshop's cata-
logue includes work by a number of others. Hanuman Press, by
Francisco Clemente and Raymond Foye out of Madras, published
prayer-book editions of Ginsberg, John Ashbery, Robert Creeley,
Gregory Corso, Richard Hell, Rene Ricard, William Burroughs.)

There are 72 poets in this anthology, selected from more than
100, presented not chronologically, but with a view to verticality.

Often there is synchronicity from far-flung places: Vijay Seshadri's mongrel dog in Brooklyn and Arun Kolatkar's pi-dog in Kala Ghoda (pivotal elements in both poets' retelling of the story of Yudhishthira and his dog from *The Mahabharata*); Vikram Seth's stray American cat and E.V. Ramakrishnan's stray Indian one; Nissim Ezekiel's Indian English and Daljit Nagra's. The selection misses certain poets who belong in these pages but were omitted either because copyright holders would not part with the necessary permissions or because their conditions of use are unacceptable. Otherwise the selection betrays only my own preference for craft. Against this, it links a community separated by the sea and it serves as an introduction to an undeservedly little-known literature.

EDITORIAL ACKNOWLEDGEMENTS

I wish to thank Molly Daniels-Ramanujan, Sarayu Srivatsa, Ashok Shahane, P. Lal, Ranjit Hoskote, E.V. Ramakrishnan, Bruce King, Ravi Shankar, and Arvind Krishna Mehrotra for advice and materials. Special thanks to Adil Jussawalla for the use of his archive, for editorial help, and for the uncollected Dom Moraes poem. I could not have completed this project without the help of my late wife, Shakti Bhatt. I would not have begun it without Philip Nikolayev, whose idea it was.

Nissim Ezekiel, PEN Centre, Bombay, 1995

NISSIM EZEKIEL

(1924-2004)

Nissim Ezekiel was born in Bombay in a tiny community of Marathi-speaking Bene Israeli Jews, descendants of Galilean oil pressers who were shipwrecked off the Maharashtra coast around 150 BC. His father was a professor of botany and his mother was the principal of a school. His first book of poems – with its premonitory title *A Time to Change* (Fortune Press, 1952) – signalled the arrival of modernism in Indian poetry, and a delayed post-Independence awakening to the possibilities of direct speech. His subjects were Bombay and himself, in iambic lines that charted marriage, adultery, and fatherhood. He wrote comic poems in exaggerated Indian English, 'latter day psalms' in a language influenced by the Bible, poems that made use of his experiments with spirituality, philosophy, and LSD, and a steady number of love poems. He became the face of Indian poetry both in the country and abroad, creating a model for the Bombay school with his urbanity and early use of form. He died in Bombay.

A Morning Walk

Driven from his bed by troubled sleep
In which he dreamt of being lost
Upon a hill too high for him
(A modest hill whose sides grew steep),
He stood where several highways crossed
And saw the city, cold and dim,
Where only human hands sell cheap.

It was an old, recurring dream,
That made him pause upon a height.
Alone, he waited for the sun,
And felt his blood a sluggish stream.
Why had it given him no light,
His native place he could not shun,
The marsh where things are what they seem?

Barbaric city sick with slums,
Deprived of seasons, blessed with rains,
Its hawkers, beggars, iron-lunged,
Processions led by frantic drums,
A million purgatorial lanes,
And child-like masses, many-tongued,
Whose wages are in words and crumbs.

He turned away. The morning breeze
Released no secrets to his ears.
The more he stared the less he saw
Among the individual trees.

The middle of his journey nears.
Is he among the men of straw
Who think they go which way they please?

Returning to his dream, he knew
That everything would be the same.
Constricting as his formal dress,
The pain of his fragmented view.
Too late and small his insights came,
And now his memories oppress,
His will is like the morning dew.

The garden on the hill is cool,
Its hedges cut to look like birds
Or mythic beasts are still asleep.
His past is like a muddy pool
From which he cannot hope for words.
The city wakes, where fame is cheap,
And he belongs, an active fool.

Night of the Scorpion

I remember the night my mother
Was stung by a scorpion. Ten hours
of steady rain had driven him
to crawl beneath a sack of rice.
Parting with his poison – flash
of diabolic tail in the dark room –
he risked the rain again.
The peasants came like swarms of flies
and buzzed the Name of God a hundred times
to paralyse the Evil One.
With candles and with lanterns
throwing giant scorpion shadows
on the sun-baked walls
they searched for him: he was not found.
They clicked their tongues.
With every movement that the scorpion made
his poison moved in mother's blood, they said.
May he sit still, they said.
May the sins of your previous birth
be burned away tonight, they said.
May your suffering decrease
the misfortunes of your next birth, they said.

May the sum of evil
balanced in this unreal world
against the sum of good
become diminished by your pain.
May the poison purify your flesh
of desire, and your spirit of ambition,
they said, and they sat around
on the floor with my mother in the centre,
the peace of understanding on each face.

More candles, more lanterns, more neighbours,
more insects, and the endless rain.
My mother twisted through and through
groaning on a mat.
My father, sceptic, rationalist,
trying every curse and blessing,
powder, mixture, herb and hybrid.
He even poured a little paraffin
upon the bitten toe and put a match to it.
I watched the flame feeding on my mother.
I watched the holy man perform his rites
to tame the poison with an incantation.
After twenty hours
it lost its sting.

My mother only said:
Thank God the scorpion picked on me
and spared my children.

Two Nights of Love

After a night of love I dreamt of love
Unconfined to threshing thighs and breasts
That bear the weight of me with spirit
Light and free. I wanted to be bound
Within a freedom fresh as God's name
Through all the centuries of Godlessness.

After a night of love I turned to love,
The threshing thighs, the singing breasts,
Exhausted by the act, desiring it again
Within a freedom old as earth
And fresh as God's name, through all
The centuries of darkened loveliness.

Goodbye Party for Miss Pushpa T.S.

Friends,
our dear sister
is departing for foreign
in two three days,
and
we are meeting today
to wish her bon voyage.

You are all knowing, friends,
what sweetness is in Miss Pushpa.
I don't mean only external sweetness
but internal sweetness.
Miss Pushpa is smiling and smiling
even for no reason
but simply because she is feeling.

Miss Pushpa is coming
from very high family.
Her father was renowned advocate
in Bulsar or Surat,
I am not remembering now which place.

Surat? Ah, yes,
once only I stayed in Surat
with family members
of my uncle's very old friend,
his wife was cooking nicely...
that was long time ago.

Coming back to Miss Pushpa
she is most popular lady
with men also and ladies also.
Whenever I asked her to do anything,
she was saying, 'Just now only
I will do it.' That is showing
good spirit. I am always
appreciating the good spirit.
Pushpa Miss is never saying no.
Whatever I or anybody is asking
she is always saying yes,
and today she is going
to improve her prospects
and we are wishing her bon voyage.

Now I ask other speakers to speak
and afterwards Miss Pushpa
will do the summing up.

The Patriot

I am standing for peace and non-violence.
Why world is fighting fighting,
Why all people of world
Are not following Mahatma Gandhi,
I am simply not understanding.
Ancient Indian Wisdom is 100% correct,
I should say even 200% correct,
But modern generation is neglecting –
Too much going for fashion and foreign thing.

Other day I'm reading newspaper
(Every day I'm reading *Times of India*
To improve my English Language)
How one goonda fellow
Threw stone at Indirabehn.
Must be student unrest fellow, I am thinking.
Friends, Romans, Countrymen, I am saying (to myself)
Lend me the ears.
Everything is coming –
Regeneration, Remuneration, Contraception.
Be patiently, brothers and sisters.

You want one glass lassi?
Very good for digestion.
With little salt, lovely drink,
Better than wine;
Not that I am ever tasting the wine.
I'm the total teetotaller, completely total,
But I say
Wine is for the drunkards only.

What you think of prospects of world peace?
Pakistan behaving like this,
China behaving like that,
It is making me really sad, I am telling you.
Really, most harassing me.
All men are brothers, no?
In India also
Gujaratis, Maharashtrians, Hindiwallahs

All brothers –
Though some are having funny habits.
Still, you tolerate me,
I tolerate you,
One day Ram Rajya is surely coming.

You are going?
But you will visit again
Any time, any day,
I am not believing in ceremony
Always I am enjoying your company.

Poet, Lover, Birdwatcher

To force the pace and never to be still
Is not the way of those who study birds
Or women. The best poets wait for words.
The hunt is not an exercise of will
But patient love relaxing on a hill
To note the movement of a timid wing;
Until the one who knows that she is loved
No longer waits but risks surrendering –
In this the poet finds his moral proved,
Who never spoke before his spirit moved.

The slow movement seems, somehow, to say much more.
To watch the rarer birds, you have to go
Along deserted lanes and where the rivers flow
In silence near the source, or by a shore
Remote and thorny like the heart's dark floor.
And there the women slowly turn around,
Not only flesh and bone but myths of light
With darkness at the core, and sense is found
By poets lost in crooked, restless flight,
The deaf can hear, the blind recover sight.

AIMEE NEZHUKUMATATHIL
(*b.* 1974)

Aimee Nezhukumatathil was born in 1974 in Chicago, Illinois. Her father is a Roman Catholic from Kerala and her mother a Methodist from the Philippines. The poems in *Miracle Fruit* (Tupelo Press, 2003) and *At the Drive-in Volcano* (Tupelo Press, 2007) are formally arranged, but they have the sound of intimate conversation. They celebrate language, taste, and touch as necessary pleasures, and – as with the work of Lawrence Bantleman – the poems are almost entirely contained in their last lines. Nezhukumatathil teaches at State University of New York at Fredonia.

Small Murders

When Cleopatra received Antony on her cedarwood ship,
she made sure he would smell her in advance across the sea:
perfumed sails, nets sagging with rosehips and crocus
draped over her bed, her feet and hands rubbed in almond oil,
cinnamon, and henna. I knew I had you when you told me

you could not live without my scent, bought pink bottles of it,
creamy lotions, a tiny vial of *parfume* – one drop lasted all day.
They say Napoleon told Josephine not to bathe for two weeks
so he could savor her raw scent, but hardly any mention is ever
made of their love of violets. Her signature fragrance: a special blend

of these crushed purple blooms for wrist, cleavage, earlobe.
Some expected to discover a valuable painting inside
the locket around Napoleon's neck when he died, but found
a powder of violet petals from his wife's grave instead. And just
yesterday, a new boy leaned in close to whisper that he loved

the smell of my perfume, the one you handpicked years ago.
I could tell he wanted to kiss me, his breath heavy and slow
against my neck. My face lit blue from the movie screen –
I said nothing, only sat up and stared straight ahead. But
by evening's end, I let him have it: twenty-seven kisses

on my neck, twenty-seven small murders of you. And the count
is correct, I know – each sweet press one less number to weigh
heavy in the next boy's cupped hands. Your mark on me washed
away with each kiss. The last one so cold, so filled with mist
and tiny daggers, I already smelled blood on my hands.

One Bite

Miracle fruit changes the tongue. One bite,
and for hours all you eat is sweet. Placed
alone on a saucer, it quivers like it's cold
from the ceramic, even in this Florida heat.

33

Small as a coffee bean, red as jam –
I can't believe. The man who sold
it to my father on Interstate 542 had one
tooth, one sandal, and called me

'Duttah, Duttah.' I wanted to ask what
is that, but the red buds teased me
into our car and away from his fruit stand.
One bite. And if you eat it whole, it softens

and swells your teeth like a mouthful
of mallow. So how long before you lose
a sandal and still walk? How long
before you lose the sweetness?

Making Gyotaku

In Osaka, fishermen have no use for the brag,
the frantic gestures of length, blocks of air

between their hands. They flatten their catch
halfway into a tray of sand, steady

the slick prize. The nervous quiver
of the artist's hands over the fish – washing it

with dark ink, careful not to spill or waste,
else feel the wrath of salty men long at sea.

If it is a good print, the curves and channels of each scale
will appear as tidy patterns to be framed and hung

in the hallway of his house. But perhaps the gesture
I love most – before the pressing of rice paper over

inked fish, before the gentle peel away of the print
to show the fish's true size – is the quick-light stroke

of the artist's thumb, how deftly he wipes away
the bit of black ink from the fish's jelly eye –

how he lets it look back from the wall at the villagers,
the amazed staring back at the amazed.

Dinner with the Metrophobe

Metrophobia is the fear of poetry

I could tell from our onion blossom
this was all a mistake. There was no
'flower' of fried petals, but a soggy mess
in a napkin-lined wicker basket instead,

a bad corsage at the end of prom night.
But at work he was kind – always had
an extra envelope, a red pen, offered
to get me coffee from the machine

downstairs. He was the only one
who didn't gasp when I cut eight inches
off my hair. There was no competition
over publications (he never even read

The New Yorker), and sometimes, he'd hold
my elbow as we climbed staircases.
So when he asked me out for dinner over
e-mail, I thought it was just his way.

I had to lower my silly poet-standards
of expecting roses with each question,
a clever note snuck in my coat pocket
about my eyelashes breaking his heart

or how he must see me right now. I never
expected this guy's hands to shake all over
our appetiser of clams casino – shook so hard
his shell spilled its stewy contents on his tie.

The clatter of his teeth on his sweaty
water glass as he dribbled. The hives.
All I said was Don't be too nice to me.
One day I might write this all down.

K.V.K. MURTHY

(*b.* 1950)

K.V.K. Murthy was born in 1950 in Proddatur, Andhra Pradesh, and educated in Secunderabad, Warangal, Ahmedebad and Jabalpur. His father was a government servant, in civil aviation, and the family moved around. At the age of 23, just out of college, Murthy joined the State Bank of India in Bangalore, where he continues to live and work. Despite his long residence in that town, in that job, there is little sense of place in his poems. Instead, there is old world courtliness and a wry awareness of neglect. In 1987 he took part in the British Council's All India Poetry Competition, in which he was shortlisted but failed to win. He continued to write though he did not publish, and his work escaped the attention of the usual anthologies and poetry publishers. This is an unfortunate obscurity, for Murthy's gift with rhyme and his elegant line should make him distinctive. He is among a handful of Indian poets whose influences can be traced to Dom Moraes, and through Moraes to the poets of the British mid-20th century.

Just Dead

So this is what it means to be dead.
Not much to it, save a certain lightness,
a vague nothing to get used to,
with the day a uniform whiteness
and nights not black but reduced to
a nondescript grey, the colour of lead.

But I know that's wrong, even as I use
the settled nomenclature of the living.
Those quotidian certitudes must yield
to softer lines, an idiom more forgiving
of imprecision: nascent word revealed
in inchoate thing. And so I cruise

in this otherworld where meaning
makes no sense, without a name –
for *ghost* after all is earthspeak
like all the rest, and it's not the same;
while time lies still over this bleak
landscape, beyond hope of a greening.

It suits me well, this strange vacuity
of place and purpose, my only quest
being one of definition: for words
are cognates no longer here, at best
fickle fingerposts pointing towards
a fooling spurious continuity.

Reason fails in this uncertain light,
and language gropes with tenuous roots.
And all the fixities that life defined
are no more than extinct truths,
an irrelevant construct of the mind –
and I'm not sure that mind is right.

Hospital Journal

It is possible, perhaps even reasonable
to tell oneself that this alone is real,
the one grim truth ineluctable.
Purgatory or hell, it's immaterial.

Not Dante but Bosch, this: the stylised fright
of ether, smells and swabs, and groans
punctuating the strip-lit night,
unspared by strident insistent phones.

Outside cars, neon, flights overhead –
the whole damn business of living in fact –
cavalcade past the varying dead
like dreams against this waking act.

Martyr

Silence descends like a curtain,
shrouding the land, inert in heat
and history. This is locust country,
no matter borne on wings or feet.
The river minds its inventory
of fable, back into the far uncertain.

Silence descends, its shadow swallowing
the skits and masques of earlier farce,
stage cleared of all but the man:
only the desert shifts in this sparse
theatre, wayward wind against sand.
The calm will herald the blowing.

Soon the horizon darkens, and a hum
or murmur gives life to cloud, dust
spangled with glints of steel, clock
racing with hooves: till a spear's thrust
makes mud of human rock.
And silence closes, till the armies come.

Bookmark

This I suppose is what endures:
The odd encounter like a sign.
This strand of hair must be yours:
It's much too long to be mine.

Exhibit

It was almost closing time, and the keeper
jangled his keys on his rounds.
Late afternoon shadows recessed deeper
into the gloom, and the night's first sounds

were tuning their pitches. I saw her enter,
uncertain in the light, or rather, lack
of it, walk down the centre
of the long marbled passage to the back,

where I was. 'Five minutes, lady!' I could hear
authority sing across the dark corridor,
as she stepped up closer to peer.
She caught her breath, though more

through beating the clock than awe,
I thought. She knit her brows, gazed intently,
and in the minutes given to her she saw
what the blind centuries had failed to see:

not love-light in a statue's eyes,
but history's finely sculpted lies.

Relocation

I step in, flick the light switch.
All as I'd left it, the still life
of a minor lifetime. On the sofa lie
unread papers in quiet reproach,

failed promises piled high.
Underneath, half-hidden, a few handy gods
in effigy, to bless the bare odds
and ends of litter, wry

remnants of a twilit faith.
Inside, my books in loving disarray
stand aside like retainers: even they
are mute witnesses to a death.

In the bathroom I check for leaks,
unplug the heater, clear the sill
of bits of soap, get on with the drill
of shutting down. It'll be weeks

before this dear derelict sprouts a soul
for someone else to call a home –
not long now before the packers come,
and make the deferred desolation whole.

Signature

A dateline leaps off the flyleaf, yellowed
with age: *Calcutta, '74*. Above it, like barbed wire
in faded royal blue, youth proclaims
its arrogance in points of fire.
Bend your mind, and they could be flames
licking the sky, pride unmellowed.

But that's a skyline thirty years old,
before Time worked on those ungainly spikes
with such tools as only he knows:
files for the pliant, rasps for the likes
of the obdurate and bellicose
before their stubborn ires went cold.

Look at it now, and you'll see little
of that awkward landscape. The horizon's free
of gawky pines, marked now by a few
troughs and slopes; vestigial anarchy
from some past ferment, beyond one's view.
And soon, very soon, this too must settle.

Life Stilled

In hindsight I sang too soon
of beauty surprised of an afternoon.

Today, spread-eagled on the final stair,
death mocks the intolerably bare

eaves where love had nested:
frame broken, wings untested.

KAZIM ALI
(*b.* 1971)

Kazim Ali was born in 1971 in Croydon, Surrey. His family emigrated to Canada in 1974, and, five years later, to the United States. He is the author of two volumes of poetry and a novel, *Quinn's Passage*. His poems limn the exquisite and the mystic even when they are talking about sex or the self – 'only the I-craft, swimming through the crazy water, / breathing it, being burned by it, thinking to walk on it' – and the unrhymed, sometimes unpunctuated couplets and one-line stanzas are studded with aphoristic phrases: 'all the points of passage from one body to another are points of danger'. He lives in Ohio and teaches at Oberlin College.

Gallery

You came to the desert, illiterate, spirit-ridden,
intending to starve

The sun hand of the violin carving through space
the endless landscape

Acres of ochre, the dust-blue sky,
or the strange young man beside you

peering into 'The Man Who Taught William Blake
Painting in His Dreams'

You're thinking: *I am ready to be touched now, ready to be found*
He's thinking: *How lost, how endless I feel this afternoon*

When will you know:
all night: sounds

Violet's brief engines
The violin's empty stomach resonates

Music a scar unraveling in four strings
An army of hungry notes shiver down

You came to the desert intending to starve   so starve

Renunciation

The Sailor cannot see the North — but knows the Needle can —

The books were all torn apart, sliced along the spines
Light filled all the openings that she in her silence renounced

Still: her handwriting on the papers remembered us to her
The careful matching of the papers' edges was a road back

One night Muhummad was borne aloft by a winged horse
Taken from the Near Mosque to the Far Mosque

Each book likens itself to lichen,
stitching softly to tree trunks, to rocks

what was given into the Prophet's ears that night:
A changing of directions — now all the scattered tribes must pray:

Wonder well foundry, well sunborn, sundered and sound here
Well you be found here, foundered and found

Prayer

Four green threads interrogate the wind.
Pilgrims tie them to the iron fence around the saint's tomb.

Each thread is a prayer. Each prayer is a chance to weave.
I do not want to return home without that which I came for.

The poet was here – but he's gone now –
you've missed him.

The river turns three times on the journey home.
I have to tie the thread around my own wrist bone.

Night

Up against the window, the fading sun.
In rags, Orion's notes appear against your skin.

Sparsely thrown across your chest.
Swathed in the folds of blankets.

Now you are luminous.
The bow no longer exists.

The star chart I traced into the palm of my hand.
Has smoke written all through it.

Are you terrified of absolute silence?
I drive miles into the country just to have a look at you.

You are no plagiarist of dusk.
Nothing in the sky equals itself.

All the stars have changed positions.
All the fortunes have been faked.

Charted against a lover who hasn't existed for a million years.

Speech

How struck I was by that face, years ago, in the church mural:
Eve, being led by Christ through the broken gates of Hell.

She's been nominated for the position of Featured Saint
on the Icon of Belief, up against the dark horse candidate –

me: fever-ridden and delirious, a child in Vellore, unfolding
the packet around my neck that I was ordered not to open.

Inside, a folk cure, painted delicately in saffron.
Letters that I could not read.

Why I feel qualified for the position
based on letters I could not read amounts to this:

Neither you nor I can pronounce the difference
between the broken gates and the forbidden letters.

So what reason do we need to believe in icons or saints?
How might we otherwise remember –

without an image to fasten in that lonely place –
the rock on which a Prophet flung himself into fever?

Without icon or church, spell 'gates of Hell'.
Spell 'those years ago unfolding'.

Recite to me please all the letters you are not able to read.
Spell 'fling yourself skyward'.

Spell 'fever'.

July

We lay down in the graveyard, hinged there.

Emerald moss growing thickly in the chiseled letters.

You're explaining how trees actually breathe.

When green in the names and trees went up to join gray in the sky.

And the gray-green sky came down in breaths to my lips and sipped me.

Vase

He wrote to you once, night's cold I,
storm-broken branches,

here in this room on the galaxy's edge.

He wrote to you twice, sun-yellow dusk,
midnight enameled vase,

snow-blue shelf in the sky.

He wrote to you three times,
and the nothing inside flew up,

a listless prisoner, tethered, a spy.

Flight

The clouds drop below us a hundred one meters,
a carpet of wavelets forgets to unravel,

we're spinning a shadow against the deflowered
historical blue, a tornado bequeathing

denuded arrangements, a hasty departure,
the conference fled, its message disbanded,

what widower bird could remain here against
the explicit commands of destructive rebellion?

the war is eternally on, the unmasking
complaint: though we cannot yet hear the recorder

of ravenous charms we still savor belief as
we fall from the sky with the slightest of prayers –

Two Halves

two halves circle each other
each aching for the other's arms

they're rent in their itching
to hit the ground at the speed of sound

the half of you is tone deaf
but the other half still sings

one half forgot the other's face
his 'collision or collusion with history'

the two lock now one to the other
sink blazingly below the clouds

surrendering the instinct to disfigure
the one's half mad by now, a curse-river

he's parched, strung out, devoured
unable to articulate how the other half felt

falling, shrieking, about to cut the sky in half
as for what they were holding when they fell

sun-spilled, thunderous, sundered
each can only remember

the lonely earth, an only child,
given to the mother who will let go

A Century in the Garden

It is hard not to know my death my nowhere trajectory

What is the difference between entity and eternity

I asked him the long syllableless afternoon

The ache a quench the eighty-ninth question

My disappeared friend a body I used to know

It doesn't need to know my death its dark current

Four o'clock

An old man with a bag of chocolates, lost on the sidewalk, on his way home
from the corner store.

He won't be missed until his granddaughter arrives home from school at four o'clock to an empty house.

A mouthful of chocolates, the recitation of a chapter – tangible and intangible ways of saying: 'God' or 'come home'.

Being borne up over elms and houses by waves of voices reciting saffron chapters written into the streets and sky.

Written onto the sheet that years later will be wrapped over him, around his forehead, folded over his mouth.

Illusion is the sheet and the thing lying under it.

Gone the streets he knows, unwritten the map of how to find him.

Dizzy with all the changing directions. It's a minute before four.

Where did I come from? Which way will I be borne?

SRIKANTH REDDY
(b. 1973)

Srikanth Reddy's parents emigrated from rural Andhra Pradesh to Chicago, where they still live and practise medicine. He was born in Chicago in 1973. His poems reconstruct history from debris and from the random texts of a collapsed world. They use a strange array of imagined source materials: outdated schoolbooks, whimsical instruction manuals, stray pages from sacred texts. His dry titles (*Facts for Visitors*, 'Fundamentals of Esperanto') do not hint at the dazzle, the emotion, and the narrative drive in the verse. He is the Moody Poet-in-Residence at the University of Chicago.

Burial Practice

Then the pulse.
Then a pause.
Then twilight in a box.
Dusk underfoot.
Then generations.

*

Then the same war by a different name.
Wine splashing in a bucket.
The erection, the era.
Then exit Reason.
Then sadness without reason.
Then the removal of the ceiling by hand.

*

Then pages & pages of numbers.
Then the page with the faint green stain.
Then the page on which Prince Theodore, gravely wounded, is thrown onto
    a wagon.
Then the page on which Masha weds somebody else.
Then the page that turns to the story of somebody else.
Then the page scribbled in dactyls.
Then the page which begins *Exit Angel.*
Then the page wrapped around a dead fish.
Then the page where the serfs reach the ocean.
Then a nap.
Then the peg.
Then the page with the curious helmet.
Then the page on which millet is ground.
Then the death of Ursula.
Then the stone page they raised over her head.
Then the page made of grass which goes on.

*

Exit Beauty.

*

Then the page someone folded to mark her place.
Then the page on which nothing happens.
The page after this page.

Then the transcript.
Knocking within.

Interpretation, then harvest.

*

Exit Want.
Then a love story.

Then a trip to the ruins.
Then & only then the violet agenda.

Then hope without reason.
Then the construction of an underground passage between us.

Corruption

I am about to recite a psalm that I know. Before I begin, my expectation extends over the entire psalm. Once I have begun, the words I have said remove themselves from expectation & are now held in memory while those yet to be said remain waiting in expectation. The present is a word for only those words which I am now saying. As I speak, the present moves across the length of the psalm, which I mark for you with my finger in the psalm book. The psalm is written in India ink, the oldest ink known to mankind. Every ink is made up of a color & a vehicle. With India ink, the color is carbon & the vehicle, water. Life on our planet is also composed of carbon & water. In the history of ink, which is rapidly coming to an end, the ancient world turns from the use of India ink to adopt sepia. Sepia is made from the octopus, the squid & the cuttlefish. One curious property of the cuttlefish is that, once dead, its body begins to glow. This mild phosphorescence reaches its greatest intensity a few days after death, then ebbs away as the body decays. You can read by this light.

Fundamentals of Esperanto

The grammatical rules of this language can be learned in one sitting.

Nouns have no gender & end in – o; the plural terminates in – oj (pronounced – oy) & the accusative, – on (plural – ojn).

Amiko, friend; amikoj, friends; amikon & amikojn, accusative friend & friends.

Adjectives end in – a & take plural & accusative endings to agree with things.

Ma amiko is my friend.

All verbs are regular & have only one form for each tense or mood; they are not altered for person or number. Mi havas bonajn amikojn is simply to say I have good friends.

Adverbs end in – e.

La bonaj amiko estas ie. The good friend is here.

*

A new book appears in Esperanto every week. Radio stations in Europe, the United States, China, Russia & Brazil broadcast in Esperanto, as does Radio Vatican. In 1959, UNESCO declared the International Federation of Esperanto Speakers to be in accord with its mission & granted this body consultative status. The youth branch of the International Federation of Esperanto Speakers, UTA, has offices in 80 different countries & organises social events where young people curious about the movement may dance to recordings by Esperanto artists, enjoy complimentary soft drinks & take home Esperanto versions of major literary works including the Old Testament & *A Midsummer Night's Dream*. Esperanto is among the languages currently sailing into deep space on board the Voyager spacecraft. William Shatner's first feature-length vehicle was a horror film shot entirely in Esperanto.

*

Esperanto is an artificial language
constructed in 1887 by L.
L. Zamenhof, a Polish
oculist. I first came
across Fundamento Esperanto, the text
which introduced this system
to the world, as I travelled abroad
following a somewhat difficult period
in my life. It was twilight & snowing on the
railway platform just outside
Warsaw where I had missed
my connection. A man in a crumpled track suit
& dark glasses pushed a cart
piled high with ripped & weathered volumes –

sex manuals, detective stories, yellowing
musical scores & outdated physics textbooks,
          old copies of *Life*, new smut,
               an atlas translated,
a grammar, *The Mirror*, Soviet-bloc comics,
          a guide to the rivers &
                    mountains, thesauruses, inscrutable

musical scores & mimeographed physics books,
defective stories, obsolete sex manuals –
          one of which caught my notice
(Dr Esperanto,
Zamenhof's pen name, translates as He Who Hopes) &
since I had time, I traded
my *Leaves of Grass* for a used copy.

*

Mi amas vin, bela amiko.
I'm afraid I will never be lonely enough.
There's a man from Quebec in my head,

a friend to the purple martins.

Purple martins are the Cadillac of swallows.
All purple martins are dying or dead.
Brainscans of grown purple martins suggest
these creatures feel the same levels of doubt

& bliss as an eight-year-old girl in captivity.
While driving home from the brewery
one night this man from Quebec heard a radio program
about purple martins & the next day he set out
to build a swallow house
in his own back yard. I've never built anything,
let alone a home,
not to mention a home
for somebody else.
I've never unrolled a blueprint onto a workbench,
sunk a post,
or sent the neighbor's kid pedalling off
to the hardware store for a paper bag full of black nails.

I've never waited ten years for a swallow.

Never put in aluminum floors to smooth over the waiting.
Never piped sugar water through colored tubes
to each empty nest lined with newspaper I didn't shred
with strong, tired hands.
Never dismantled the entire affair

& put it back together again.
Still no martins.
I never installed the big light that stays on through the night

to keep owls away. Never installed lesser lights,
never rested on Sunday

with a beer on the deck surveying
what I had done
& what yet remained to be done, listening to Styx

while the neighbor kids ran through my sprinklers.
I have never collapsed in abandon.
Never prayed.
Never did it in the back seat.

But enough about purple martins.

*

As we speak, Esperanto is being corrupted
by upstart languages such as Interlingua,
Klingon, Java & various cryptophasic tongues.

Our only hope of reversing this trend is to write
the Esperanto epic. Through its grandeur
& homegrown humility, it will spur men

to freeze the mutating patois so the children
of our children's children may dwell in this song
& find comfort in its true texture & frame.

It's worth a try. As I imagine it, it ends
in the middle of things. Every line of the work
is a first & a last line & this is the spring

of its action. Of course, there's a journey
& inside that journey, an implicit voyage
through the underworld. There's a bridge

made of boats; a carp stuffed with flowers;
a comic dispute among sweetmeat vendors;
the digression on shadows; men clapping

in fields to scare away crows; an unending list
of warships: *The Unternehmen, The Impresa,*
The Muyarchi, Viec Lam, The Przedsiebiorstwo,

The Indarka, The Enterprise, L'Entreprise,
Entrepreno... One could go on. But by now,
all the characters have turned into swallows

& bank as one flock in the sky – that is,
all except one. That's how we finally learn
who the hero was all along. Weary & old,

he sits on a rock & watches his friends
fly one by one straight out of the song,
then turns back to the journey they all began

long ago, keeping the river to his right.

Aria

The ending is sad if you think of it.
Portable castle, luna,

two singers pretending to kiss
for the mob. Ovation. The end

51

of applause, the sound of a fire
beginning to fail in the dark.

Somebody took down the bay
& left us to pick up the boats

in the pit. Rigging everywhere.
What stagecraft, what dripping

cathedrals. I sit on my rock
with a fistful of raisins

& listen. Sometimes an extra
dismantles a cloud. Sometimes

a whale remembers the spotlight.

SUDESH MISHRA

(*b.* 1962)

Born in Suva, Fiji, in 1962, and educated in Fiji and Australia, Sudesh Mishra is a fourth
generation descendant of indentured workers from India. In four books of poems and two
plays, he uses 'a mix of history and hyperbole' to write of dispersal by water. These maritime
narratives celebrate 'that grandmaster, the sea' as the true instrument of diaspora. He lives
in Melbourne, Australia, and teaches as Deakin University.

Joseph Abela

What does Joseph Abela, grandmaster
of the fishing village of Marsaxlokk,
dream of, asleep in a currachy chair,
his imitation bentwood cane bending
seawards like a ship's prow? A mountain girl
with mournful luzzu eyes he'd coveted
among the weathered stones of Haqar Qim,
who, at the hint of a kiss, had weathered
like a stone? Or perhaps he dreams of being
the crab St Paul shook out of his beard
after the discourtesy of his ship-
wreck, a detail no fresco remembers.
Maybe Joseph dreams of nothing at all,
or of everything at once: Odysseus
mouthing a lewd calypso on Mistra
rocks, the Phoenicians stuffing their bread

52

with undead squids, the Knights Hospitalliers
made invincible by a marvellous
rock fungus, laying rout to the chainmailed
Janissaries, and Napoleon en route
to Egypt, annexing the Maltese cross
with the sly delicate offhandedness
of a Bonaparte. What topsyturvydom?
What brainfever of magic and mishaps?
All this, however, is a ruse. Surely
Joseph dreams of our dream of him dreaming,
and wakes to find himself a boy again,
deft of eye and wrist, drawing a fishing
net with strokes finer than any Dürer
in earshot of that grandmaster, the sea.

Suva; Skye

A half-spent
mosquito coil
mounted on an upended fork
buoyed
inside a squat jar
brimming with smoky water
is nothing
like the swan
he saw
that neutral day
arching
its ancient ashen neck
upon the flood
of a loch
crammed with brilliant sky.
Nothing like.

Sea Ode

Although remoter than remotely
from this keyboard city
of tumescent skyscrapers
they call the medina
of bytebrats and cybercats,

I come across traces of you
(as one stumbling upon the perfume
of a fugitive era
is suddenly made fugitive) –
in the rinsed restless irises
of an oil-presser from Cadiz,
in the spiteful sibilance
of a St Kilda shipwreck,
in the Fraulines of a dowager
scandalised by a pissing cherub.
Morning and night, I sense
your sublunar passions
in the mournful heaving of tidal traffic
scoffed by exultant moons.
Outside Signor Montale's
vine-jibbed trattoria
your sad, jilted mermaids
daub their severed, writhing braids
in Sicily's sweetbitter sauces.
None but they can discern
(through garlic rosaries
swaying from waisted rafters)
why a swollen, gusting sheet –
revenant in sunlight –
sparks me up the mizzenmast
to bawl for roiling streetcars.
Strange blubber! Stranger Quaker
whose harpooned trophies
thrash about in seething wordhives.
Yet, since the wick of longing
battens on the fat
of your butchered leviathans,
poetry too is culpable,
just as this foul gargoyle
sneering from its voluted eyrie
in the Victorian quarter
is culpable in the pitiless history
that provoked the sneer.
But now that the sneered at,
scenting modernity,
ride with the sneering pack,
you alone remain guiltless.
And cast by traces
into your sacramental swells,
I'm the legendary drowned swimmer
astonished to discover
his lungs commending water.

Winter Theology

the lion-footed bathtub
is a beast
with the cloudy head
of a human being
– a sphinx, no less,
with a soul of clear water
or what passes for clear water.
thus when the divine portion
rejects the torso,
despite its sublime brutishness,
as the woman,
(we behold her now)
haunted by towels,
desquamates,
stepping out of her improbable loins,
into another,
more exalted afterlife,
the soul
(more water than soul)
exulting in baser things,
retreats further
into what's primal, mud-sullied,
and unfinished.

Pi-dog 4 (Reprise)
(in memoriam Arun Kolatkar)

Dog in tow,
Yudhishthira comes to rest
amid a pride of couchant rocks

about to roar off
into the shimmering sweet hereafter.
His kinsmen,

led by a draggle-tailed Draupadi,
have fallen by the Wayside Inn.
Between calculated gasps,

and with the deviousness
of a master mason from the Chandela days,
he chips away

at the legendary intransigence.
Brought to his wit's end
the gate-keeper chucks in the towel:

'Have it your way,' he growls,
and steps aside.
Overjoyed, Yudhishthira calls to his dog

but it plays deaf and won't budge.
The master begs, cajoles and hectors,
with the same result.

He tries a different tack.
He calls it names:
ass, cur, crackpot, and worse,

but the dog takes no notice.
When all fails,
he tries courting it with a juicy bone.

The brute lunges at a flea instead.
'Ingrate,' says Dharamraja,
'Know you not I lead us into paradise?'

'In that case,' says the dog,
'You had better press on without me.'
And that's how it came to pass

that my prickly ancestor
became the only mongrel in recorded history
to win heaven by losing it.

MUKTA SAMBRANI

(b. 1975)

Born in Pune in 1975, Mukta Sambrani's poems from *Broomrider's Book of the Dead* are
notable for their extreme strangeness. The book-length sequence is presented as the work-
ing manuscript of its fictional protagonist, Anna Albuquar, whose project is 'to renegotiate
the idea of authorship'. There are asides, hesitations, false starts, instructions to the reader,
and, throughout, a steady engagement with language. Her first book *The Woman in This
Poem Isn't Lonely* (Writers Workshop, 1997) was received in India with incomprehension
and admiration. She moved to the United States in 1999 and lives in Berkeley, California.

The Insurgence of Color, or Anna Thinks Anne Carson Is God, No Smaller than Marx

Anne Carson lives in Canada, in Greece, in Rome and in China.
Mothers of gods everywhere suffer prolonged pregnancy and unnatural labor.
In the hours following the bloodshed, the emperor mourned alone.
That he was always a pacifist in spirit did not go down in history.
The scholar, the scribe, the teacher, the writer and the world are one.
What is the language of mythology? What do gods say to each other?
Each petal gleams, enhances its hue on its way to her hair or his book.
When revolution came, it took everything and dyed the streets red.
The resurgence or movement led by quasi-militant forces will be crushed.
In the early hours of the morning, the following day, there will be executions.
In the debris of the aftershocks they recovered Brahma from Vishnu's navel.
The tropics are in the process of being cleansed so eternal power may prevail.
Mothers of gods everywhere suffer prolonged pregnancy and unnatural labor.
This poem is a compilation of issues it attempts to address through false starts.
When the poem found itself, the sky turned. Colors of empires come from blood.
The revolutionary in hiding clenches the future in his fist along with a hand
        grenade.
My mother and her mother and her aunt are one. They follow the sacrosanct.
I believe Anne Carson will prevail as the petals in this book begin to turn fire
        to light.

What is wrong with Anna? Oh she couldn't say. She has Marquis de Sade syndrome. She imagines she lives this life. It isn't real, you know. That is what they call it. It is a rare and protean disease although 'disorder,' she is told, is a better word for it. It is all about perspective like Ishmail says.

The mob did not stop hitting you till after you were dead. The moon sank to the bottom of the ocean and didn't rise for several nights. The mob left all the dead in shallow graves. The police had them thrown into the valley under the blue cliff. It turned red and then brown and then yellow and green from the festering. They planted a flag over the valley. The city filled with the dead. They kept walking round in circles in the night looking for home. Anna went looking for the driver. She had to borrow breathing apparatus from the fire department to step in. She lowered herself on a makeshift rope pulley. She stepped on something green. It was familiar. The driver hung by his arms from a yellowing tree. His shoulders had become dislocated but his hands remained firmly locked around the branch. He had made one last attempt to break his fall. Then she walked to his house. The family came to the door. There was no use cremating him. There are too many. The Broomrider stole a petrol truck that night. She drove it into the valley. Then she climbed out and threw her cigarette stub into the gorge. The Broomrider mourns the happy dead.

'Learn to drive trucks. Every talent counts,' – from *Broomrider's Guide to Broom-riding*.

The reader probably knows by now that Anna is attempting to write a book of books. Anna wants to know of any readers she may have confused. Has she? Are there many readers then and what do they think of her? Do they think she is in convalescence, emerging from ennui or trauma or both? What is this place she writes from? There is more than one place for sure. The writing is so different everywhere. Don't you feel like telling Anna a thing or two about consistent punctuation? This is what Anna wants. She wants to convey the splitting and she wants your participation.

Names Anna Forgets: Narayan, Vishwanath, Padmapani

Tell me the story of the swallowed plum pit or girl carried away to den of ants,
silence for breaking. Break it. Was it a boy imprisoned by carpenter birds?
Not woodpeckers. No. And was it a boy? Break. Who gets on the wrong train?
He is the ocean of love, ocean of compassion. Who puts her hand in the river?
He has many hands. In one he holds a lotus. Whose hand is taken by the
        crocodile?
He saves. Narayan, Padmanabh. His name is screaming ocean, screaming earth.
The perfect bow of his lips, lotus stems for wrists, his feet, wet lotus leaves,
        sinuous, his
spine, axis of the universe, Trivikram, master of the three worlds, lotus navel.
Conch shell and mace, the sun, his discus, spear and flute, accompaniment,
a carriage of horses, snake for bed. Vaikunth. Land unseen. A woman
soft as tendrils to stroke his feet and he hers, a woman lush. Padmapani.
What the child cannot see, hurled into the stars, the unfolding arms of the lotus.
For a dream to haunt her, is it a nightmare? You, which ocean are you?
In the placid, non murky plains, no arms, no blue god rising to pull or to
        embrace,
no ocean of constant reconciliation. But there it is. An ocean, isn't there?
A lotus rests in his right hand. But who is freed here? In what ocean?
After swallowed plum pit, nose turns to tree. Blue god sets elephant free,
crocodile redeemed as nightmare brings notice to pre dawn hazes and dry heat.
What lotus? Mendicant holds swapped child for one life, swapped child redeemed,
someone said life is cheap there because people are reborn. Who decides what
        price?
Padmapani. Lessons taught and learnt, the aesthetic of obedience, now full,
antiseptic darkness of closed doors, within every lotus petal, ocean of love.
From his navel emerges the creator, Anna shifts in the familiar discomfort of
        the atheist,

Anna sees him reclining, his name committed to amnesia like ocean, now empty.
He turns green leaf to morsels, much like any god, he eats, he drives, he sleeps,
he makes love, women love him, he charms, blue skin becomes him. Anna turns,
blue lotus stem under her tongue. Arms radiate symmetrical, hands of the tree,
in every compartment in the hexagonal arrangement, he encompasses encompass.
It is he, ocean. Padmapani sets down lotus stem, takes her face in blue hands,
and there he rests it, his benevolence, screaming ocean, blue burning.
My name is vestiges. Blue hands rest on her chest. Nothing escapes around
          culverts,
over the fine strain of instruments, my green hand embraces rubble and water,
I, vestiges of what is and what wasn't, take form in shapes you recognise as
          the world,
mystical as mountains, hidden as breath, you my point of squinting at the sun,
I am yours of what is left behind. Nothing escapes his eyes for he Jagadeesh,
Lord of the world and vestiges, plum pits and ant hills is nothing without her.

What the Postman Might Translate

I am thinking of you on the front steps, cleaning, always cleaning.
Ask the school master if he received the dictionaries I sent by airmail.
The children and I pray everyday and hope your knees are better.
This letter is short because you always say I write and talk too much.
And I am thinking of your eyes. Think nothing of the rumors mother.

Sashi, or How Moon Could Mean Sun

We've never met but I am writing to you from having known your son. He
was very gifted. I know you know this or perhaps don't believe me or don't
know what to think of this letter. We walked together he and I with many
other people, drunk and full of optimism. We talked. I was a hypocrite for
wearing leather while vegetarian. To rise fully, you must fall fully first. I know
that now. I hope someone reads this to you. I know you thought long and hard
before you named him.

G.S. SHARAT CHANDRA

(1935-2000)

Born in Nanjangud, Mysore, Sharat Chandra was raised there and in Bangalore. He was educated in India, Britain and the United States. His father was an attorney and advocate general, and Sharat Chandra would have become a lawyer if he had not, in the late 60s, decamped to the University of Iowa. He told his family he wanted 'to be a poet', and he wrote poetry and fiction that vary widely in subject matter and setting, turning from India to the West and back. There is a poignancy and urgency he seems able to summon at will, and an endearing oddness, 'My good shoe has run away / with the tacks / of its slutty twin.' Among American readers he is remembered for his short stories as well as his poetry. There is a short fiction prize named after him, and a book of his poems, *A Family of Mirrors* (BkMk Press, 1993), was nominated for a Pulitzer Prize. He was a professor of creative writing and English at the University of Missouri, a post he held for 17 years. He died in Kansas City.

Reasons for Staying

I am talking to the kitchen table
full of roses.
The language is my own,
I tell them
I own them.

There are roses because I say so,
the vase is mine,
so is the kitchen.
I like them red,
I pay for the water.

The chairs immediately respond,
the table,
the knives and plates,
the salt shaker,
join in.

Vendor of Fish

all night he waits at the harbor
his eyes the colour of the sea
the sea the colour of trawlers
he grabs the finest wipes them
on his shawl his shawl
the color of blood

fish the colour of rupees
he thinks of the meal he'll buy
the meal of chapattis and kurma
the fish in the smell of kurma
he packs them in the basket with ice
his hands the color of fire

he leaps on the tar road faster
than sweat can print his feet
the distance is the colour of dreams
the fish in the basket shine
sawdust daubs their fins
he sings in praise of their color

Consistently Ignored
(for my mother)

Consistently ignored in a family of ten
I asked mother, 'Am I your real son?'
She paused from grinding spice,
'No, I bought you from a beggar
For a bushel of rice!'
From behind, sisters giggled.

I matched features, spied on beggars,
Roamed the backyard thinking
Of distant huts, certain
My mother sat busy in one
Scheming to trade another son
For fish to add to that bushel.

I Feel Let Down

I feel let down when the birds
In the sky suddenly leave

At sundown and hide in the dark trees,
Paralysed by the terror

That sets into their eyes.
Birds are resting, we say,

And retire to our living rooms.
But out there beyond the lights,

The noisy highway and the airport,
The birds to not speak well

Of their condition.

Rule of Possession

My rule of possession is simple.
Let each man claim the part of a stone
He throws into a river.

The place shall be marked
As the measure of his holding,
A throwaway display of silver.

Those that see great wisdom in this
Shall sleep peacefully on any precipice.
Those that try it out shall have magnificent hands.

Those that laugh at this
Shall soon turn into stagnant ponds
Surrounded by men throwing stones.

Encircled

Always this circle
within which I seek those that are dear,
those that have gone ahead without me
to ride the carnival wheels,
hands clutched around radiant balloons,
heads vanishing into lights
as I grope for them.

And always this man,
not a stranger, not a friend,
someone even more intimate,
rows a rigged boat on a fake lake
beside the large blue canvas

of stars, moon, bleached clouds.
This man whom I also know
in my wakefulness,
whose name I can easily recall.
The fish swim below his sway
flapping their fins on the oars,
they're accustomed to his weight
above the crowd, above my anxious face.

Irreversible
even in these dreams where I've found
my wife, children adrift in high balloons,
in voices that swallow their dark heads.
I call, push bodies soft as pillows,
my friend who sees everything,
dips absurdly into the juggled air.

Friends

They're never there
when you describe them.

They're solid as oak
but bad weather gets in their way.

They need you as much
when you wish they were away.

Like stolen wives
they fit your life.

They're best scribbled on napkins
late at night.

Seeing My Name Misspelled, I Look for the Nether World

I wander like this
because they've taken my name
& misspelled it
with a tag that reads,
if not redeemed
sell as is.

A blank page crosses
the intersection,
I did not do it!
They say they're waiting
for me to begin.

I cannot cross,
the lights are against me,
stuck in their slots
like a gun in the holster,
the rose in my lapel.

My good shoe has run away
with the tacks
of its slutty twin
across the wheatfields
with all the money.

All I have is a dime
glinting in my palm,
someone's wrong number
with the shatter
of broken glass.

There's a key in a jar
in this part
we're about to resolve;
where we're headed for,
door to dark door,
we're all misspelled.

Brothers

Last night I arrived
a few minutes
before the storm,
on the lake the waves slow,
a gray froth cresting.
Again and again the computer voice said
you were disconnected,
while the wind rattled
the motel sign outside my room
to gather
its nightlong arctic howl,

like an orphan moaning in sleep
for words in the ceaseless
pelting of sleet,
the night falling
to hold a truce with the dark.
In the Botticellian stillness
of a clear dawn I drove
by the backroads to your house,
autumn leaves like a school of yellow tails
hitting the windshield
in a ceremony of bloodletting.
Your doorbell rang hollow,
I peered through the glass door,
for a moment I thought
my reflection was you
on the other side,
staring back,
holding hands to my face.
It was only the blurred hold of memory
escaping through a field of glass.
Under the juniper bush
you planted when your wife died,
I found the discarded sale sign, and looked for a window
where you'd prove me wrong
signaling to say
it was all a bad joke.
As I head back, I see the new
owners, pale behind car windows
driving to your house.
You're gone who knows where,
sliced into small portions
in the aisles of dust and memory.

MAMANG DAI

(*b.* 1959)

Mamang Dai was born in 1959 in Pasighat, Arunachal Pradesh, near the Siang River. Her poems are incantations to the rivers and mountains – the water and light – of her home state. They are small histories based largely on oral tradition and on the few written records available, for instance a colonial era Survey of India document that refers to the Siang as 'the missing link' between the Tsangpo River in Tibet and the Brahmaputra in Assam. Dai was the first woman in Arunachal to be selected for the Indian Administrative Service, a career she later abandoned for journalism. She works as a correspondent from Itanagar, Arunachal.

The Missing Link

I will remember then
the great river that turned, turning
with the fire of the first sun,
away from the old land of red robed men
and poisonous ritual,
when the seven brothers fled south
disturbing the hornbills in their summer nests.

Remember the flying dust
and the wind like a long echo
snapping the flight of the river beetle,
venomous in the caves
where men and women dwelt facing the night,
guarding the hooded poison.

There are no records.
The river was the green and white vein of our lives,
linking new terrain.
In a lust for land, brother and brother
claimed the sunrise and the sunset
in a dispute settled by the rocks,
engraved in a vanished land.

I will remember then the fading voices
of deaf women framing the root of light
in the first stories to the children of the tribe.
Remember the river's voice:
Where else could we be born,
where else could we belong
if not of memory,
divining life and form out of silence?
Water and mist,
the twin gods, water and mist,
and the cloud woman always calling
from the sanctuary of the gorge

Remember, because nothing is ended,
but it is changed,
and memory is a changing shape,
showing with these fading possessions
in lands beyond the great ocean
that all is changed but not ended.

And in the villages, the silent hill people still await
the promised letters, and the meaning of words.

Remembrance

Why did we think it was trivial
that it would rain every summer,
that nights would be still with sleep
and that the green fern would uncurl
ceaselessly by the roadside.

Why did we think survival was simple,
that river and field would stand forever
invulnerable, even to the dreams of strangers,
for we knew where the sun lay resting
in the folded silence of the hills.

This summer it rains more than ever.
The footfall of soldiers is drowned and scattered.
In the hidden exchange of news we hear
that weapons are multiplying in the forest.

The jungle is a big eater,
hiding terror in carnivorous green.

Why did we think gods would survive
deathless in memory,
in trees and stones and the sleep of babies;
now, when we close our eyes
and cease to believe, god dies.

For as long as remembrance
men stared at fire and water.
We dwell in the mountains and do not know
what the world hears about us.
Foragers for a destiny,
all the days of our lives
we stare at the outline of the hills,
lifting our eyes to the invincible sky.

No Dreams

The days are nothing.
Plant and foliage grow silently,
at night a star falls down,
a leopard leaves its footprints.

The wind blows into my eyes
sometimes, it stirs my heart
to see the land so plain and beautiful.

If I sit very still
I think I can join the big mountains
in their speechless ardour.

Where no sun is visible
the hills are washed with light.
The river sings
love floats!
love floats!
But I have no dreams.

Sky Song

The evening is
the greatest medicine maker,
testing the symptoms
of breath and demise,
without appointment
it writes prescriptions
in the changing script
of a cloud's wishbone rib,
in the expanding body of the sky.

We left the tall trees standing.
We left the children playing.
We left the women talking,
and the men were predicting
good harvests or bad,
that winged summer we left,
racing with the leopards of morning.

I do not know how we bore the years.
By ancient, arched gates
I thought I saw you waving
in greeting or farewell, I could not tell;
when summer changed hands again
only the eastern sky remained;
one morning, flowering peonies
swelled my heart with regret.

Summer's bitter pill was a portion of sky
like a bird's wing, altering design.
A race of fireflies bargaining with the night.
Attachment is a gift of time, I know,
the evening's potion provides
heaven's alchemy in chromosomes of light,
lighting cloud fires
in the thumbprints of the sky.

Small Towns and the River

Small towns always remind me of death.
My hometown lies calmly amidst the trees,
it is always the same,
in the summer or winter,
with the dust flying,
or the wind howling down the gorge.

Just the other day someone died.
In the dreadful silence we wept
looking at the sad wreath of tuberoses.
Life and death, life and death,
only the rituals are permanent.

The river has a soul.
In the summer it cuts through the land
like a torrent of grief. Sometimes,
sometimes, I think it holds its breath
seeking a land of fish and stars

The river has a soul.
It knows, stretching past the town,
from the first drop of rain to dry earth
and mist on the mountaintops,
the river knows
the immortality of water

A shrine of happy pictures
marks the days of childhood.
Small towns grow with anxiety
for the future.
The dead are placed pointing west.
When the soul rises
it will walk into the golden east,
into the house of the sun

In the cool bamboo,
restored in sunlight,
life matters, like this.

In small towns by the river
we all want to walk with the gods.

SRINIVAS RAYAPROL
(1925-98)

Born in Secunderabad, a cantonment town in Andhra Pradesh, Srinivas Rayaprol was the son of a leading modern poet in Telugu. He was educated at Benares Hindu University and Stanford, and later embarked on a career in civil engineering. But, as he liked to say, he discovered modern poetry in the United States, the country to which he owed both an education and 'my personal emancipation'. It was a debt of gratitude, but it did not make him a wide-eyed admirer of all things American. In the final issue of *East and West*, a magazine he founded – and edited from 1956 to 1961 – Rayaprol said reading contemporary American poetry with its 'beatniks and the Jazz poets and the daytime poets and the night-time poets, the poets in pony tails and the poets of the hoola-hoop school, I feel sick – of myself, of this world and this present state of writing'. His opinions endeared him to some American poets, among them William Carlos Williams, who was a contributor to *East and West* and with whom Rayaprol carried on a long correspondence.

He published three books of poems: *Bones and Distances* (1968), *Married Love and Other Poems* (1972) and *Selected Poems* (1995). In a preface to the last volume he said he was won over not by 'cleverness of artistry but by sincere and absolute lack of pretense in thought and expression'. It was a mission he shared with poets such as James Wright, but it was a mission he felt he had failed. He wrote, 'I have realised indeed rather painfully that I am no longer the genius I thought I was.' He died in Secunderabad.

Oranges on a Table

acquire
the subtle distinction
of Mahogany

No longer
a thought
on the tree
in spring

but nude
as green
its body
a summer arm

Yellow and slow
women-close

Not an ultimate order
of the orange sky
but the angular
desire

of the stone
that blocks
the river's run.

Poem

In India
women

Have a way
of growing old

My mother
for instance

Sat on the floor
a hundred years

Stirring soup
in a sauce pan

Sometimes staring
at the bitter

Neem tree
in the yard

For a hundred years
without the kitchen walls.

A Taste for Death

Shared we such a room
on Sherman Street, only
this is Washingtonova
and several years dead now.

I open the closet and find
bottles of wine, poems
on my typewriter and stories
on yours, rejection slips

and cigarette stubs on the parquette floor.
A Klee on the wall for me
and a Patchen for you, Old
Bunk Johnson shuffling by Mozart.

Such was our life, twin-bedded.
Jealous of the one and in love
with the other, a passion for apple-pie
or a taste for Death.

Shall we say Christoph,
the pact is ended
and I cannot turn a sudden tear
for the memory of your love.

Your life was so full of body,
frail but full of flesh, bursting
like an apple on the table
keenly to be killed.

Travel Poster

A Geish-
a
like a
fish
for Japan

An elephant
for India
and velvety lions
for the veldt

A cockatoo
for the Indies
And a gendarme
on Eiffel's tower
for France

Beer for Germany
on the Motor-bahns
Tulips for Holland
and a dutch treat
for the lower lands

A totem for the New-
Zealanders
An emu for Australia
for a maybe Kangaroo

Minarets and moustaches
for the Middle East
and the Albert Hall
for the English

The Good Earth
for China
And for the Russian
a smell of vodka
with a whiff of caviar

Cathedrals for Italy
and the sparkle of Lova
The gold eagle
over the Golden Gate
for the Americas

And all round this world
eternal dissatisfaction
in the eye of Man.

Married Love

Every evening
I am met at the gate by my wife
her hair in disorder and her dress a mess
from the kitchen

and the girls hang on the leaves of the gate
while my ancient car rolls in.
One carries my bag, the other
my lunch basket.
The day's work is over and I am home.
I have forgotten them all day and now
suddenly remember that I must
disappoint them again
for my evening is planned
for a meaningless excursion to the bars.
And the coffee which my wife has served
is cold in my mouth
and the tales the children have brought from school
are dull on my ears.
In spite of my love for them
I must disappoint them again tonight.

Middle Age

When the skin has stretched tighter
on the bones of the face
and the face closer shaved
with distinctive moles and warts
When lips have softened with love
and the eyes hardened with age
and the stomach achieved
a wholesome round
and the legs move with a known swagger
When a life is half over
and Death is yet to be
and beauty no longer of the body
Oh to be middle-aged
and competent
and monied and loved
among other things
Husband and father
friend and inadequate lover I

I Like the American Face

I like the American face
successful, clean shaven
closely clothed
with arrogance of chin
but soft of eye
and always ready
to break into a false-toothed smile

The kind of face
that photographs so well in *Time*
a face with the races so well mixed
Yet wholly new
and all American
as apple-pie

Individually interesting
but pointless on the whole
sexless on the surface
with a hint of pleasures
beneath the skin
carefully controlled
by the waist-band

Successful as I said
in the jut of lip
and the tooth's proclamation
of the body's supremacy
over the mind.

Life Has Been

Mostly
a matter of living the days
Simply
a subject of the senses
surrounding this body
Really
repeating the words of others
and doing the deeds
of those that have done them already

Merely
a matter of the moment
within the hand

And yet
Occasionally
Out of hand
Inexplicable
As a moment of time
A breath of splendour
A flicker of greatness
That keeps one going
For the million other hours
In a life
That has been
Mostly a matter
Of living the days

Poem for a Birthday

I have never been more
than the occasion demanded

have never been in an occasion
which demanded more than me

I have never had the mind's argument
dislodged by the horses of the heart

have never ridden horses
who did not know their riders

I have never risen above
the immediate moment

have never had a moment
which demanded my immediate answer

I have never needed a new face
to meet the faces of my friends

have never had friends without faces
that did not smile back at me.

DAVID DABYDEEN

(*b*. 1956)

Born in 1956 in Guyana, David Dabydeen went to England at the age of 12. His long poem *Turner* centres on a submerged head in the foreground of the celebrated J.M.W. Turner painting, 'The Slave Ship: Slavers Throwing Overboard the Dead and Dying, Typhoon Coming On'. This African head, 'drowned in Turner's (and other artists') sea for centuries', is the poem's speaker. He invents a past, a people and a biography that spans continents, that is Indian as much as African, but, 'stained by Turner's language and imagery', he is unable to escape the painter's depiction of him as an exotic victim of Empire. Over its voyage-like course, the poem's intention is made vigorously clear. It aims at nothing less than a refutation of the colonial enterprise. Dabydeen is the author of four novels, three collections of poetry, and several books of non-fiction and criticism. He teaches at the University of Warwick.

from Turner

XIII

Sometimes half her face grows dark, she sulks
Impatient of my arms, all my entreaties
Grappled in a storm of rain; nothing will soothe her
Then, she cries herself to sleep or curves
Like a sickle that will wake the sky's throat,
Or curls her lip in scorn of me, a mere unborn
With insufficient cowrie shells, when others,
Men, substantial, beseech her favours
With necklaces of coloured glass to loop
Around her breasts, men of presence, neither ghost
Nor portent of a past or future life
Such as I am, now. Sometimes her cheeks are puffed,
Her face lopsided, and I think I must have
Blasted her in some lover's rage, my hand,
Two centuries and more lifeless, clenched in quick
Hate, reached endlessly to bruise her face.
She disappears behind clouds for many nights.
A sudden thought writhes: she might be dead,
I might never subject her again.

XVI

I gather it to my body, this grain,
This morsel slipped from the belly of moon,
And name it Turner and will instruct it
In the knowledge of landscapes learnt as the ship
Plunged towards another world we never reached.
The grown-ups cried in the darkness of the hold
But we lay freely in his bed, gazed at

Pictures on his wall. He held a lamp
Up to his country, which I never saw.
In spite of his promises, but in images
Of hedgerows that stalked the edge of fields,
Briars, vines, gouts of wild flowers: England's
Robe unfurled, prodigal of ornament,
Victorious in spectacle, like the oaks
That stride across the land, gnarled in battle
With storms, lightning, beasts that claw and burrow
In their trunks. A rabbit starts at footsteps,
Scoots away. I walk along a path shaded
By beech; curved branches form a canopy, protect
Me from the stare of men with fat hands
Feeling my weight, prying in my mouth,
Bidding. The earth is soft here, glazed with leaves,
The path ends at a brook stippled with waterflies,
But no reflection when I gaze into it,
The water will not see me, nor the villagers
In whose midst I stray, pausing before
The butcher's shop hung with goose and pheasant,
But its window will not see me though it shines
With other faces. This old one with silver
Hair leaking from a bonnet I follow home
Through a cobbled street. In her basket
A crusty loaf wrapped in fresh white cloth:
Herself. I know her, but she stares through me,
Opens the door, disappears. I linger
At many gates, wanting to be greeted.
The elders and the young, all day I follow them
Through village green, marketplace and church
Where, my eyes accustomed to the gloom, behold
Turner nailed to a tree, naked for all to see,
His back broken and splayed like the spine
Of his own book, blood leaking like leaves
From his arms and waist, but no one among
The silent worshippers hears me cry out
In pity and surprise.

XVIII

'Nigger,' it cries, naming me from some hoard
Of superior knowledge, its tongue a viper's nest
Guarding a lore buried by priests, philosophers,
Fugitives, which I will still ransack
For pearls and coral beads to drape around
Its body, covering the sores that the sea
Bubbles on its skin, its strangulated neck
Issuing like an eel from its chest. 'Nigger,'

78

It cries, sensing its own deformity.
I look into its eyes to see my own coves,
My skin pitted and gathered like waves of sand.
I have become the sea's craft and will so shape
This creature's bone and cell and word beyond
Memory of obscene human form, but instead
It made me heed its distress at being
Human and alive, its anger at my
Coaxing it awake. For ever, it seemed,
Curled at my breast it drifted between death
And another mood, the waves slapping its face
Like my mother's hands summoning me back
To myself, at the edge of the pond. I stare
Into its face as into a daedal
Seed which Manu would hold up to the sky
For portents of flood, famine, or the crop
Of new births to supplement our tribe,
But even Manu could not prophesy
The shapes of death revolving in its eyes:
Bullwhips that play upon the backs of slaves
Hauling pillars of stone to a spot divined
By sorcerers whose throw of dice from whimsical
Hands appoints thousands to their deaths, arranges
Human bones like hieroglyphs to tell a prurient
Future age the ancient formulae of Empire.
A solitary vulture dips into one's fresh breast
As into an ink-well, wipes its beak upon
Another's parchment skin, writing its own
Version of events, whilst Pharaoh sleeps in cloths
Scented in the flow of female sacrifice.
Until a slave arose from the dead,
Cracking the seal of his mouth, waking
The buried with forbidden words. 'Revolt,'
He thundered, 'emancipation, blood', darkening
The sky with his lust, irrigating
Their stomachs, blooming courage in their skulls.
An army of sticks and sharpened flints flocked
Across the sands like ragged cacti, ripping
Down tents, encampments, cities, massacring
The men, scavenging the bellies of their wives
For scraps of joy. Wherever they settled
They made new deserts and new slaves. 'Revolt,'
He whispered, lifting aloft the Pharaoh's
Crown from a head chopped clean at the neck, hollowed
Into a drinking gourd. They cheered even as
They sipped at each other's throats in nostalgia
For death, except a child who slipped and limped

Away from the lap of men who loved him
Too much, broke him each night in frustration
Of their lives. Children appeared everywhere,
Strewn like dung at the root of palms
As if to fertilise and succour them
Against the desert, to memorialise
In the spur of leaves the veins
Once flowing with maternity. Everywhere,
Children trailing behind caravans heading
North to the auction tents of Arabia,
Sucking the air for any nipple of moisture.

XX

Shall I call to it even as the dead
Survive catastrophe to speak in one
Redemptive and prophetic voice, even
As a jackal breathing into bone
Rouses familiar song? Shall I suckle
It on tales of resurrected folk,
Invent a sister, and another, as Manu would,
Pursing his lips so all the wrinkles
On his face gathered like spokes around the hub
Of his mouth and he would stare backwards
Through his eye sockets into himself whilst
We waited at his feet in dread of the word
That would spin suddenly from his throat,
Cartwheel towards us, making us want
To scatter, but we remained rooted
At his feet in stunned obedience
To his booming voice and his quivering
Fat manitou's body pouring forth sweat
Enough to water all the animals
Herded in the savannah? The first word
Shot from his mouth, he stretched out his lizard's
Tongue after it, retrieved it instantly
On the curled tip, closed his mouth, chewed. When he
Grinded the word into bits he began his tale,
One grain at a time fed to our lips
Endlessly, the sack of his mouth bulging
With wheat, until we grew sluggish and tame
With overeating, and fell asleep, his life-
Long tale to be continued in dreams.
Each morning, the milking of the cow done,
Our father deposited us in Manu's hut
For instruction. He resumed from the previous
Day, his hands still agile as he declaimed,
His eyes frantically bright as if he was cursed

To stay awake until his story ended. Only
Then would the gods send him sleep, so peaceful
And dark a sleep: the serpent's whisper, the lover's
Melody, the prisoner wailing the hours
To his execution, the startled laughter
Of the reprieved, no such sounds of triumph or loss
Which he mimicked in his tale would awaken him.
Now restlessly he sleeps, his duty unfulfilled,
His hands still gripped to the ghost of the sword
Turner insinuated into his belly,
Withdrew, sheathed, his mouth still open as if
Wanting to continue his tale. Only flies
Perform his obsequies, gathering on his tongue
To hum eulogies to our magician,
Our childhood, our promise, our broken
Word.

XXII

The first of my sisters, stout, extravagant,
I will name Rima. Even as a child
She tempts fate, tempts the hand of my father
Blossoming at her face, but she will still deny
The sin and multiply his faith in her;
The more she doubts, the more convinced he grows
Of her purity. Afterwards she bites into
His reparation of jhal cakes with
Playful teeth. She will steal my spears, my warriors,
My fortifications. She will interrupt the most
Careful of ambushes with a stomp of her feet,
Mashing down escarpments, gouging deep holes
In the battleground with her unhewn toenail.
I report her to my mother who slaps
Me instead for playing at killing,
Nor will my father heed but turns his face
To the earth and hoes like a beaten man.
He has been vanquished by her freedom.
She is wayward and sucks her teeth,
Talks above the voices of the elders,
Will not shield her eyes before them.
When she grows up she will love women
More fiercely than men and die at childbirth
With her husband fanning her and marveling
At the deed, the village idiot whom she
Married out of jest and spite. She is all
The valour and anguish of our tribe,
My beloved, and we bury her
In a space kept only for those who have

81

Uttered peculiarity, those who have
Guarded our faith by prophecy, who have
Called out in the voices of the hunter
Or betrayer so we could recognise
Him beforehand. And the women will come
Bearing stones, each one placed on her grave
A wish for her protection against kidnapping,
Rape, pregnancy, beatings, men, all men:
Turner.

XXIV

Turner crammed our boys' mouths too with riches,
His tongue spurting strange potions upon ours
Which left us dazed, which made us forget
The very sound of our speech. Each night
Aboard ship he gave selflessly the nipple
Of his tongue until we learnt to say profitably
In his own language, we desire you, we love
You, we forgive you. He whispered eloquently
Into our ears even as we wriggled beneath him,
Breathless with pain, wanting to remove his hook
Implanted in our flesh. The more we struggled
Ungratefully, the more steadfast his resolve
To teach us words. He fished us patiently,
Obsessively, until our stubbornness gave way
To an exhaustion more complete than Manu's
Sleep after the sword bore into him
And we repeated in a trance the words
That shuddered from him: *blessed, angelic,
Sublime*; words that seemed to flow endlessly
From him, filling our mouths and bellies
Endlessly.

XXV

'Nigger,' it cries, loosening from the hook
Of my desire, drifting away from
My body of lies. I wanted to teach it
A redemption song, fashion new descriptions
Of things, new colours fountaining out of form.
I wanted to begin anew in the sea
But the child would not bear the future
Nor its inventions, and my face was rooted
In the ground of memory, a ground stampeded
By herds of foreign men who swallow all its fruit
And leave a train of dung for flies
To colonise; a tongueless earth, bereft
Of song except for the idiot witter

Of wind through a dead wood. 'Nigger'
It cries, naming itself, naming the gods,
The earth and its globe of stars. It dips
Below the surface, frantically it tries to die,
To leave me beadless, nothing and a slave
To nothingness, to the white enfolding
Wings of Turner brooding over my body,
Stopping my mouth, drowning me in the yolk
Of myself. There is no mother, family,
Savannah fattening with cows, community
Of faithful men; no elders to foretell
The conspiracy of stars; magicians to douse
Our burning temples; no moon, no seed,
No priests to appease the malice of the gods
By gifts of precious speech – rhetoric antique
And lofty, beyond the grasp and cunning
Of the heathen and conquistador –
Chants, shrieks, invocations uttered on the first
Day spontaneously, from the most obscure
Part of the self when the first of our tribe
Awoke, and was lonely, and hazarded
Foliage of thorns, earth that still smouldered,
The piercing freshness of air in his lungs
In search of another image of himself.
No savannah, moon, gods, magicians
To heal or curse, harvests, ceremonies,
No men to plough, corn to fatten their herds,
No stars, no land, no words, no community,
No mother.

K. SRILATA

(*b*. 1968)

K. Srilata was born in 1968 in Ranchi, then in Bihar and now part of the new state of Jharkhand. She 'speaks three languages and writes in one', and she teaches at the Indian Institute of Technology in Madras.

Two Stories

A thousand waves. How many? asks my son.
So how are we? the man asks, lips curling.
Let's say two thousand for fun
It is dark in the room and cold.

break every morning on these shores,
And whom did you sleep with today?
my beach with sands so happy they
And you, little fellow, have you failed me again?
slip through my fingers and dance on
The belt again, a fledgling dies,
my toes, he says.
blood fills the evening tea cup.
My beach I share with a thousand
I dream of lost skipping ropes,
let's say two thousand for fun
of my daughter who hasn't found them yet.
gay strangers,
Clouds unhappy like smoke rings near a grave
shovels, glow in the dark green bucket lost and found, a
float outside the house
handful of seashells clinging to the last of the sands,
where no cakes are baked,
a balloon,
lampshades that sit heavily in the darkness
a fisherman sitting on a giddy catamaran
quite forgetting to fish.

TABISH KHAIR

(*b*. 1966)

Tabish Khair was born in 1966 in Ranchi into a family of middle-class, professional Indian Muslims, 'a minority within a minority'. His father, grandfather and great grandfather were doctors. His mother was the daughter of a police officer and had run her own business. His first collection of poems appeared when he was still living in Gaya, the small town in Bihar where he was raised. The poems selected here are from his second volume, *Where Parallel Lines Meet* (Penguin Books, 2000) and from more recent work. He writes of India in stories and poems that recall 'a warm smell like that of shawls worn by young women', and he writes of freefall in a colder, northern climate. He lives in Denmark and teaches at Aarhus University.

Nurse's Tales, Retold

Because the east wind bears the semen smell of rain,
A warm smell like that of shawls worn by young women
Over a long journey of sea, plain and mountains,
The peacock spreads the Japanese fan of its tail and dances,
And dances until it catches sight of its scaled and ugly feet.

Because the *koel* cannot raise its own chicks –
Nature's fickle mother who leaves her children on doorsteps
In the thick of night, wrapped in controversy and storm –
Because the *koel* will remain eternally young, untied,
It fills the long and empty afternoons with sad and sweet songs.

Because the rare *Surkhaab* loves but once, marries for life,
The survivor circles the spot of its partner's death uttering cries,
Until, shot by kind hunters or emaciated by hunger and loss,
It falls to the ground, moulting feathers, searching for death.
O child, my nurse had said, may you never see a *Surkhaab* die.

The Birds of North Europe

Twenty-four years in different European cities and he had not lost
His surprise at how birds stopped at the threshold
Of their houses. Never

Flying into rooms, to be decapitated by fan-blades or carefully
Herded through open windows to another life, never
Building on the lampshade

Or on some forgotten, cool corner-beam where droppings and straw
Would be tolerated until the fateful day hatched
And the world was fragile

Shell, feathers, a conspiratorial rustle of wings above and of
An intrigued girl below. Even the birds in their neat towns
Knew their place. They

Did not intrude into private spheres, demanding to be overlooked
Or worshipped. They did not consider houses simply
Exotic trees or hollowed

Hills. Not being particularly learned he did not know the thread
Of fear that knots the wild to the willed; not
Being well-read he

Did not remember the history behind their old and geometrical
Gardens, could not recall a time when the English
Parliament had killed a bill,

Shocked by a jackdaw's flight across the room. He simply marked
The absence of uncaged birds in their homes. He thought
It was strange.

Lorca in New York

Federico García Lorca lonely in New York
With his list of English words to get by barely
(Shishpil: sex appeal), on the edge of hecho poetico
Where an image falls together not like clouds in the sky
But a hurt's shadow on the great cold wall of show,

Writes about a hurricane of black pigeons splashing,
Writes about the furious swarming coins that devour children,
Writes about the poisonous mushroom (this is pre-Hiroshima),
Writes about wiping moonlight from the temples of the dead,
Writes about the fire that sleeps in dark flints, sleeps,

Awakes to his own private memories of sorrow and loss,
That blue horse of his insanity that makes him see
The three who were frozen, the three burned, the buried three.
Spanish Siddhartha, Buddha of the beautiful body, poet
Of crystallised fish dying inside tinfoil tree trunks,

Hear the pain in her smile here where only teeth exist
And flints have long been caped in satin, dogs stay dogs,
Watch the voice outside that ethnic shop – *Fucking Paki*
Place is like always open – put a stainless steel lock
On Earth and its timeless doors which lead to the blush of fruits.

Monsters

Theirs the city of the sayable. Hers its suburbs,
Filling with the screamed obscenities of graffiti, gestures
At coherent articulation, the word within that world
Of splashed red, aerosoled blue, skulls and crossbones,
Crashing cars, rose out of a gun barrel, space monsters, all
Unable to utter a sound that will count as speech.

It is in such a moment of sheer scream, unsayable,
That Shakuntala looks in the mirror and is surprised
To see fangs and fire, a gaping mouth like Kali's,
Goddess culled from the anger of colonisation:
It is a vision that lasts only a second, but in it
Are contained the silent stories of her history.

Her lineage is monstrous. Scylax said so:
Daughter of the dog-faced and blanket-eared.
Such many-armed, hydra-headed ancestors
Shocked the evangelising white man, puzzled
The aesthetes of Europe in later centuries:
Truth and beauty have long been denied her.

Did her mothers know what she has forgotten:
The choice was between mirror and monster?
How to keep their devdasis from turning nuns
In *Danse des servantes ou esclaves des dieux*,
They loosened their limbs in the cosmic dance
Of the oppressed – fingers, arms, heads flew off

Leonardo da Vinci's symmetrical bodies
And the mirror of that white gaze shattered
On *develish formes and uglie shapes*. Adam
Stood speechless before monstrous Ada,
Which hath foure hands with clawes...
The better to rip you with, coloniser?

Faced with humanity, they could not look
Into those eyes and fail to be struck blind
By the injustice of it all, their own greed:
Monsters filled their mirrors. It was safer
To lose in that adytum of demons the truth
Of bodies with blackened teeth, minds on fire.

Falling

1

What she felt most of all was a sensation of weightlessness
And something building up in her head like wet sponge:
The difference between mass and weight, a technical matter
Future generations would discover, forget, insist on, knowing
Well that in their world they differed only in the word.

In the beginning had been the word, sharp, mocking, male,
And then things really started happening. First Adam's smile
Cracked, then pieces of heaven floated by like memories of cloud.
It was then she discovered the difference between weight and mass
And sank into the couch of weightlessness. The blue ball
Of Earth whistled close, tattooed with white lines of water and spots.

When she saw the first trees stretching forth their arms in yearning
Like small lip-sticked girls outside the concert hall of a pop star,
When she saw how closely this had been made to remind her of that,
The heavenly sameness that was touched by differences of definition,
She felt the full sucking force of God's jealousy in this weightlessness
And continued to fall, for the first time thinking furiously.

2

It is precision bombing of sorts, this falling on the spot,
Just inside the railings of Homebase carpark, just outside
A DIY superstore in Richmond, London. BVRs
And smart bombs couldn't have been smarter.
At three angles when the 777 unfurled the claws
Of its 12 wheels what fell out was not met with shouts
(Though it could have been) of bogey, bandit, body.
It had crossed like the shadow of a swooping bird
In the back-view mirror of a busily backing Mercedes,
A workman at nearby Heathrow airport had looked up,
And seen something amazing, a boy falling out of the sky.

How he had homed in finally like an Air-Launched
Anti-Radiation Missile on the target of his heated
Imagination (they used to call it dreams): billboards,
Cars, trolleys, broad avenues, a supermarket;
To sit tucked under a tree like a morning drunk,
The weight of his fallen hopes a lumpy mass,
His brains spreading around him like vomit.
Peasant whose parents packed him no sage advice
(Like: at 14,000 feet even blood turns to ice),
Mohammad Ayaz, wheelbay contortionist,
Flying by wire, freezing to death a few feet
From gin and tonic being served to passengers
Settling down to watch the in-flight movie.
When he began to hallucinate for lack of O_2
Did he see cars, avenues, green dollars? Could
He distinguish between those dreams and these?
Or did he see in the cramped space allowed him
The ghosts of those who had crouched before him,
Chafing their hands against strips of metal –
Vijay Saini, or the unknown body that fell
And disappeared into a building reservoir,
Something taking them up worlds apart,
Something dragging them down the same place.
It is raining frozen bodies all over Europe.

VINAY DHARWADKER

(*b*. 1954)

Born in Pune, Maharashtra, in 1954, Vinay Dharwadker edited or co-edited *The Oxford Anthology of Modern Indian Poetry* (1994), *The Collected Poems of A.K. Ramanujan* (1995) and *The Collected Essays of A.K. Ramanujan* (1999). He also makes translations of modern poetry from the Hindi, Punjabi, Urdu and Marathi, including selections from the work of Kabir and Arun Kolatkar. His own poems rarely use the first person, though biographical information is available if the reader is looking for it. He teaches South Asian literature at the University of Wisconsin-Madison.

Houseflies

Like a pair
trapped indoors
by the summer screens on the windows,
we flit about in zigzag flight:

in a corner of the ceiling's
inverted floor,
from where the giant room
seems to loom upside down above us,

we nuzzle up to each other,
twelve hairy legs
intertwined at once,
giddy with the vertigo

of watching our mirror selves
multiplied a thousand times,
as we mate in every facet
of our big domed eyes.

Words and Things

Words evaporate like water in a dish,
leaving you with a sense of something meant,
but not the memory of what was said,
or how, or when.
Things stay as they are (call them facts)
even with the names you learn to give them;
poems (you tell yourself) are so many ways

of naming things you've seen
once and may not see again,
except for tricks of remembering;
for words forget themselves
and move among the things you cannot name,
and what you know by touch and tact
seems merely a vanishing thing.

Walking toward the Horizon

Maybe it will be like this: a notebook
left open the previous night on the desk,
his glasses set down on a half-finished page;
in the early morning light, blue lines
crossed by a thin red vertical on the left,
the hand sloping neatly, in the black ink he liked;
close to the edge of the desk, a box of clips,
pens and pencils in a silver cup he meant
to polish for months, but never did; a cheap
stiletto for letters, five envelopes slit open;
an ashtray; a checkbook in a brown plastic jacket.

In the other room, toys scattered on the rug,
his wife's coat flung on the arm of the couch,
a bunch of keys and magazines on the coffee table;
pots and pans in the kitchen sink, three dinner plates
and forks, waiting to be scrubbed in the morning;
outside the window, a parking lot shared by a school
and a hospital, half empty; a few leaves fallen
between the sidewalk and the street, brown lumps
of dog-shit under the maple tree turning red; a van,
newspapers in vending machines, a woman walking;
a patch of blue; and a horizon, out of sight, somewhere.

Life Cycles

In Chattisgarh, near Bilaspur
clouds drift low above the monsoon town:
loose wads of wool, not yet spun to yarn,
swirling slowly in the wind. The sky drips
all day, all night, bringing down a foot of rain:

red mud in puddles; pools of saffron water;
sludge squelching underfoot: a foot of rain.

A liquid sheet, mirroring the sky,
is stretched across the paddy fields squared off
by banks of matted clay: blue, green, ocher
smeared with gray. Uneven squares, trapeziums,
sewn like patches on a checkered cloth:
the paddy, standing in a foot of water, velvet green.

So many butterflies swarming in the brush:
orange, purple, white, electric-blue,
their yellows bright as ripened mustard fields.
Brown, furry caterpillars; fat centipedes,
black and amber. A newborn calf, wobbling in the grass:
coat white as wool, eyes like glistening marbles.

Young rice plants, emerald filaments,
calf-deep in ruddy water. Rows of men and women,
bent over, moving through the fields in rhythm,
like combs through hair. Fingers grasp
the saplings, scoop them out, tie them up
in bundles, in tandem. Far in the distance,

a single tractor, plumed with diesel fumes,
turns up the soil in mechanical clods. But here
all the work is done by hand: bare bodies,
bare heads, bare hands. Trees blur into the sky,
their hues washed like watercolors: the earth,
fresh, full of life, swells and sways beneath them.

MANI RAO

(*b*. 1965)

Mani Rao was born in Bombay in 1965. In two books published with Writers Workshop, Calcutta, she introduced the odd, jagged, vaguely menacing stance that she developed in later collections: 'But this is a deathfuck, different, the more I dismember, the more I want.' The 'you' in her poems is a woman, but it is a mistake to put the work into a sexuality box marked 'Straight' or 'Queer' or 'Other'. The poems deserve closer, less clichéd attention. They are reflections of sex, blood, bile, and god, and while they look like prose on the page, in the mouth they feel like poetry. She lives in India, Hongkong, and the United States.

Untitled

1

If you smile when you wake up, if you don't smile when you wake up.
When we woke up dreaming of each other. When I slept right through your dream.
She wakes up slowly, still talking to her dreams. He is spat out by the night, turns to the tide of the radio.

2

I leave myself in the terrace and go downstairs. I leave myself in the living room and go to the kitchen.
I get together sometimes, a hall of mirrors, swearing different stories, playing you-know-that-I-know-that-you-know-that-I-know.
They are all true, some truths you know, some you don't.
You look for too much explanation.
I can go back to fetch a better memory. And I can recur if you wish.

3

Bury me in a frozen lake, saltless and safe, some day lifted to the eyes of a new person, telling her what to call me as she probes me.
Drop me on coral entangled, hair streaming in the current, rocking on a seabed of pistons.
Leave me in the garden slope, a dial tilted to the stars, on the orange trail as they roll to rot.
Bury me bare as a bird obvious on a tree in autumn.
Was desire meant to be saved, kept alive, unanswered? But this is a deathfuck, different, the more I dismember, the more I want,
And you my queen of honeylips, the only one who ever knew how to make a ghost of me, play me a new song, recall me.
The nagman brings a daily death, squeezes my breasts, a clay clasp cooler than your hand, gives me fingers and teeth.
The gardener of dust is using my frame as a mould for the shape of future dust.
This is how the dust will grow and the pencilling will fall to bits.

4

Two can play silence. Silence for two players. The time it takes to play silence.
We seize the silence together, own it separately.
You plant a silent minefield, I walk on it, flashes of meaning
exploding in my head.

5

I always ask for her name. Yellow-Shower. Purple-Me-Not. Hibis-Cus. Lily the adverb comes home with me. The florist says she will last, I dare not imagine how many days.
My fading beauties of dryness and rind. Their bones get sucked at night, their sweat splatters fragrant fear white at the root of my hair.
Generation, separation.
Love in-toxicated, lust retch-ed.

6

I wait
for a big
soft whale

I know
he is
in the water

His voice
is like a vowel gliding
between m and n

. . .

Owlside she sits
burning her feathers
beakshut
bulleteyed
She

dials his number
when he's away
Black
block
bleak
Empty ringing
burgles his space
Curls
on his walls
Lies
on the floor
Speaks
to his plants
Sows
her longing in their soil
Release, release,
she cries
but each act belies

this. It seems
she will not rest
until she is furthest
from release

. . .

I do
I do
I do
I deny
I deny
I stand so close to the mirror
my breasts go cold kissing themselves
My song
is written
for you
Distributed
to others

. . .

Ishmael knows
Approach
Restraint
Pace
Bait
Ishmael is not foolish
But he wears his obsession
on his teeth
He sings aloud
He announces himself
He begs
He cloys
He does not call you for dinner
He says come,
let me eat
your delicious
breasts, roe eyes
and tender heart
What is his game?
Desperate, self defeating,
malicious to himself
Why does he seek suffering?
Then why does he reveal this
to his friend, hoping
understanding

War is a place all thoughts have left. Birds crash when wind caves in. Green salad fields sprinkled with blood and bone. The cigarette drops from your hands as you water plants with gasoline.

Mountains wait on the bodies of reptiles. Snakes run from burning skin.

Mountains fall into lakes. The ground hangs on to trees as boats to sails.

Nipples get hot as craters, beards are stroked, eyebrows pinched, faces taken off, eyes recruited by cameras, decades of time stolen from bee pollen and clover harvests returned to the apiaries.

You know a language well if it does things you don't have control over. Bring me the words without meanings, words all meanings have abandoned, sentenced to meaninglessness.

Fortunetellers smile in magazine columns. A mystery hero steals the fantasies of people he likes the look of.

R. PARTHASARATHY
(*b.* 1934)

R. Parthasarathy was born in Tirupparaitturai, Tamil Nadu, in 1934. 'My tongue in English chains,' he wrote in *Rough Passage* (OUP, 1977) – a long poem in tight, three-line stanzas – and the phrase became a motif in Indian literary criticism. *Rough Passage* takes for its subject the life of an exile, a word that was to lose much of its resonance by the end of the 20th century when it was replaced by words such as 'immigrant' and 'alien'. While he continues to mine the condition of living in one place and imagining another, he also writes love poems that contemporise an Indian tradition of erotic poetry. He is the editor of an influential anthology, *Ten Twentieth-Century Indian Poets* (OUP, 1976), and translator of the Old Tamil epic *The Tale of an Anklet* (Columbia UP, 1993). He is a professor of English and Asian Studies at Skidmore College, Saratoga Springs, New York.

Remembered Village

If you love your country, he said, *why are you here?*
Say, you are tired of hearing about
all that wonder-that-was-India crap.
It is tea that's gone cold: time to brew a fresh pot.

But what wouldn't you give for one or two places in it?
Aunt's house near Kulittalai, for instance.
It often gets its feet wet in the river,
and coils of rain hiss and slither on the roof.
Even the well boils over.
Her twelve-house lane is bloated with the full moon,
and bamboos tie up the eerie riverfront
with a knot of toads.

A Black Pillaiyar temple squats at one end of the village –
stone drum that is beaten thin on festivals by the devout.
Bells curl their lips at the priest's rustic Sanskrit.
Outside, pariah dogs kick up an incense of howls.

And beyond the paddy fields,
dead on time, the Erode Mail rumbles past,
a light needle of smoke threading remote villages
such as yours that are routinely dropped by schedules,
and no trains are ever missed.

from The Concise Kamasutra

1

Under the warm coverlet my woman sleeps on;
I am drenched in the intractable scent of her hair.
The notion has often crossed my mind:
I should crumple it up like a handkerchief
that I could press to my face from time to time.

Meanwhile wakeful hands peel the skin off the night;
I drink from her tongue in the dark.
Our breath tips the room over to one side:
the tight hardwood floor groans
under the slew of discarded clothes.

We shut the whole untidy threadbare world out –
dogs, telephones, even the small indifferent rain.

2

As you untie your long flowing hair in bed,
it spreads over slowly and colors the sheets,
leaving behind a pool of black
caught in the red glare of the lamplight.
You turn towards me, disturbing the pool:
hands and tongues lose no time in spinning their moist web,
and we fall into their delicate net.

Day breaks: the window empties its pail
of light over us, waking us up.
It is our sweat now that colors the sheets;
it is the clean scent of your hair in the morning
that keeps me awake, and I am unable to rise.

East Window

1

It is noon: oak and maple fight
over the sun in our backyard.
A flowering crab scuttles past the east window.
We burn each other with the stubs of profanities,
drop the ash all over the bed.
The unspent days we fold and put away
like a leaf pressed in a book.

Few are the body's needs:
it is the mind's that are insatiable.
May our hands and eyes open this spring afternoon
as the blue phlox open on a calm Salem Drive
to the truth of each ordinary day:
the miracle is all in the unevent.

What home have I, an exile,
other than the threshold of your hand?
Love is the only word there is:
a fool wears out his tongue learning to say it,
as I have, every day of his life.

2

The fragrant breath of crab apple
wipes the sweat off our foreheads.
We lie in bed, you and I,
our hands on pasture
on the rolling crumpled bedspread.
We have drunk the bitter tea
of exile to the last drop.
And this is our penance:
not to be at home anywhere.

No, it won't help to drag our feet
through one intimate neighborhood
after another, to entertain fond hopes
of leaning against the door
of this or that out-of-touch friend;
it is a real slap in the face.
All the streets are changed;
not one sound has a familiar ring to it.
Every step we take is cursed: it leads nowhere.

3 *Taj Mahal*

Children on their way to school
barely notice it squatting
on the river like a humped bull,

swishing its tail occasionally
at the swarms of barefoot
tourists. They have been gone now,

the emperor and his favorite queen,
for some three-hundred-odd
years. But this marble flame,

Earth's other moon, how
it rubs expensive delicate salt
in the wound of unrequited love!

from A House Divided
(for Attia Hosain, 1913–98)

1 *At Ghalib's Tomb*

Wandering through dark tangled lanes, notice
how everything round here, not to mention
the dust under your feet, is touched by his breath.
Their faces scarred by graffiti, one by one

the havelis open their shuddering arms
only to be brushed aside by the passerby.
Will Time, that had once tightened its noose
around the poet's neck, keep its vaunted promise

not to disturb his peace? For how long
must Lal Qila, its florid pelt ruffled by the wind,
pace about the river before night

swoops down on it? 'Today our verses,
Asad, are only an idle pastime.
What's the use of flaunting our talent, then?'

Here lane after crumpled lane unfurls out of time
to shroud the poet's marble tomb in flowers:
marigolds fester in pools of incense;
Persian names crowd the enclosure walls.

As orange banners tear into the heart
of your beloved city, your tongue grovels in the dirt;
and behind closed doors, a frightened people
speak in whispers, uncertain and afraid

of the future paved with stones of blood.
What are mosque and temple but a pair of dice
that the emperor of dust rolls in the mud?

How long will it be, Khusrau, before
the indignant crows start pecking out
Delhi's shimmering eyes, leaving us all blind?

VIJAY NAMBISAN
(*b*. 1963)

Vijay Nambisan was born in 1963 in Neyveli, Tamil Nadu, and educated at the Indian Institute of Technology, Madras (not Chennai). In his non-fiction he has said he is happiest away from cities, in rural Bihar, Kerala, Tamil Nadu and Karnataka. He wrote an unhappy book about Bihar, *Bihar is in the Eye of the Beholder* (Penguin India, 2000), in which he described the 18 months he spent there with his wife, the novelist and surgeon Kavery Nambisan. He uses a wide range of source material. His poems are as likely to refer to the Old Testament as Old English or Sanskrit, and they employ a beguiling lightness of touch. He lives in Lonavala, Maharashtra.

Millennium

There was not much light in the world when we left.
The stairs were dank and smelled of anger.
At their foot was a heap of straw, soaked in blood:
We did not ask whose, for all was conjecture, and this
Fresh sign would have yielded us little more.

They say there are signs in all things; well, there were
Some we could have done without that day. For the sun set
The instant we had emerged from the passage-way
And we had to grope our road to the little shed where,
Little and unannounced, our mission lay.

Frost steamed the air. Our blood pulsed thin and shrill.
My brother pushed open the door. In the wild light
Of a torch, we saw the mother's breast was white and plump,
And the child's lips were red as any rose. None of us
Dared hesitate, or be afraid; we drew our swords.

It is long after that I tell this, and it may differ
From the tales you must have heard. What matters?
There was no light in the world when we did our deed.
There is no light now. Is it at all possible
That I should say more or less than that I know?

Yes, I have heard the stories. Yes, there was some talk
Of a brave man whose bravery passed all foolishness.
Yes, we are a weak people now but we were not so
When lured by gold but hardly less by strength,
We let our faith die and put away our books
And enrolled ourselves under the Idumean.

He was a false king, at last, but what would you have?
There have been falser. One rules now, in Rome.
But this one thing I can say, because upon my steel
There sang the blood, and almost on my lips: with
That blade which now rotten hangs upon the wall,
With that blade and no other, I slew David's heir.

Holy, Holy

The rain threatens this ordinary day
With magic. Things that grow manifest,
Plainly, the unnatural: more sure
And permanent is the unwalked way,
Lifeless air, stone unencumbered
With feelings: not obsessed, therefore pure.

Yet even metal has a life that cries
For use, even crystals ask to be touched –
How much weaker are these green and clinging loves,
These hollow souls which populate the skies
With what they aspire to. Reality
In itself is content, and needs no proofs.

When I was young enough to treat these things
Without consciousness, I could cast my mind
Into that emptiness whereof all is made
And ask, Without my imaginings,
What is?
    Nothing answered nothing, and in that space
I knew myself unliving, unafraid.

First Infinities

1 *Need*

Desperate with knowledge, opened wide by drink,
How I've thrown my need about the houses
I've partied in; how tainting the responses.
How crudely eager to be loved, and how
Vile next day, with J flinging in my face

My sottishness, not allowing me to think,
His poisoned tongue flickering, my vulgar vows
To be good again. I took my chances
And paraded them; and now,
Put out to grass in an accustomed place

I count them one by one. To find a city
Where I have not been foolish: Difficult lies
And truths despicable in their fragility,
Both lack the charm of inadequacy.

2 *Hospital*

The doctor's hand was asking what my liver
Meant to do. I thought behind the curtains of
This purpose of my birth, to lie and act
Like one soon to be a corpse. Wayside station
Blues, city living blues, writer's cramp blues.

I had of countless bottles made a river
And discovered its source. Yet one more dropped its love
Into my slow veins. The tiled walls did not in fact
Confine; they wrung from me definition
And made me what I am. Tell me now what use

The pills, the fruit, nurse's disgusted eye
Or glucose, or molasses. No life is short
That at its centre has this clarity.

3 *Drying Out*

For I asked my spirit, What is worth this pain?
And my spirit said: Do not think of Hell
Or hope of Hereafter. Breathing this filth
In a stale room, aching for the fire
To flow in you again – only believe this.

Only ashes clog and clot my veins.
It is in another life that I was well
And time moves like the sea. I spew and spit
The yellow bile. My bones are torn entire.
They look at me and laugh. I am what is.
And what is this I am, in a rude day
Bright with the flame of fever? Spirit replied,
I am the Truth, and the Life, and the Way.

Madras Central

The black train pulls in at the platform,
Hissing into silence like hot steel in water.
Tell the porters not to be so precipitate:
It is good, after a desperate journey,
To rest a moment with your perils upon you.

The long rails decline into a distance
Where tomorrow will come before I know it.
I cannot be in two places at once:
That is axiomatic. Come, we will go and drink
A filthy cup of tea in a filthy restaurant.

It is difficult to relax. But my head spins
Slower and slower as the journey recedes.
I do not think I shall smoke a cigarette now:
Time enough for that. Let me make sure first
For the hundredth time, that everything's complete.

My wallet's in my pocket; the white nylon bag
With the papers safe in its lining – fine;
The book and my notes are in the outside pocket;
The brown case is here with all its straps secure.
I have everything I began the journey with

And also a memory of my setting out
When I was confused, so confused. Terrifying
To think we have such power to alter our states,
Order comings and goings; know where we're not wanted
And carry our unwantedness somewhere else.

Cats Have No Language

Cats have no language to tell their world.
The moon is a midsummer madness
Which satisfies foolish chroniclers;
But their paws gloat on the captured mouse
– The slither beneath the stair – the silent bat
That drifted on a moonbeam into the house
Slashed a slitted eye into a flicker
And was gone. The moon is too much for the cat.

The light is too much for cats: that is why
At the human snarl behind the torch
The keen eyes turn slate, and a careless slouch
Replaces the studied artistry, frozen flash
Before the kill. They do not like the light
But have no language save the curving slash
And the sideways sculpture at a whisker's touch.
Cats are dumb when they walk in the night.

Cats are clever at night; but the sun
Melts the moon's glitter from their eyes,
Leaves them children's toys and the green trees.
Now how can fingers soothe the shoulder-knots,

Trust the silken purr, the trusting eyes? Cat,
I know, I have seen her sleeping thoughts
Tense and stalk savagely in the night's peace.
But cats need no language to do all that.

Dirge

The poets die like flies but I am lying slightly to one side,
Contented in my Spain or Siam, content too to keep my hide.
How well they wrote, those friends now fettered, how the Indo-Anglian tongue
Allowed them to be lovely-lettered, their lives lived when the world was young.
I'll live and hold my words in, for I am wearied of hypothesis;
And, in place of getting glory, kisses take from my missis.

Then the world shone, by their showing; then publishers seemed to care;
Then calls for cheques of last year's owing did not fall on empty air.
Then newspapers asked them for pieces; and printed them unchanged; and paid;
But now there are so many wheezes which make the craft a thrifty trade.
In a wilder whirl of weeklies, tabloids titting on page threes,
I will shirk my duty meekly and kisses take from my missis.

They did not care much what the world said: they taught it instead how to speak.
They did not, when a poem pleaded, to meetings go in Mozambique.
But I will stay my poems, spending strength now with a shriller pen,
My theme and language both defending, to live fourscore years and ten.
And if it prove my prime is over, if I've no chance at wordly bliss,
Why I will spurn so false a lover and kisses take from my missis.

This hand once penned those poems; never shall I find as true a friend.
I've a thirst for all forever, but the lines come to an end.
So Arun and Dom and Nissim – I will shun their hard-earned grief
And much though I will always miss 'em, in softer shadows find relief.
And when I'm ninety and young writers ask why I wrote no more than this
I will answer, 'But, you blighters! I kisses took from my missis.'

MONICA FERRELL

(*b*. 1975)

Born in 1975 in New Delhi, Monica Ferrell was raised in the United States by a Punjabi
mother and a father who hailed from a small town in Arkansas. In her myth-soaked poems,
a Biblical menagerie proliferates – the wolf and the hamster, the lamb and the lion, the water-
snake, the beetle, the fly. Beasts are mute embodiments of lust and forgiveness, ambiguous,
impetuous, noble and ignoble. Like Ovid's metahumans, they know that 'A thing we do
can change us forever / Imprisoning us in a shape'. The narrator of these tales – and they
are all tales – parses meaning out of a diverse set of legends, both personal and oracular,
but her real quest is for wholeness of expression. She teaches at the State University of
New York.

Nighttalking

As I lay down in the echo of the day
The moon became a brazen mirror.
The sun became a lion grazing under earth,
Memories grew wings like flies and clouded here.

No one but the dead understands me tonight,
They've put their blue hands to my marble mouth.
They murmured among themselves and checked their notes
Then at last decided to leave without speaking to me.

Darkness, when you place your hand on my forehead
What do you feel, sickness or that fever
Lifting from me as the lake clears of fog?
I would like to be useful as these springing streetlights

And unbreakable as my kitchen knives.
I would like to be wound very tightly, like
A mummy made of gold thread coiled around
Some wax statue, which inside is let to rest and heal.

Queen of the future, I will wake with amethyst eyes
When the moon has finished with her witching.
Then all the gold lights of heaven will fall in me like seeds
And sprout marvelous trees, drooping with heavy love.

In the Gabinetti Segretti

*(after the room of sexually explicit frescoes from Pompeii
in the Museo Archaelogico, Naples)*

What is simplest is before you
all the time, in any room, the intimacy
passed between two people like breath,
like the golden mirroring between
a lake and tree and lake:
none of which is original, but reflection
folded in many pleats as water,
as a smile floating up willless
from happiness when laughter is startled
out the way a bird takes sudden,
spotless wing.

On all these walls, still living, peach
and yellow and burnt red: all to describe
the intensity of his gaze as he draws
her toward him, as if actually saying
I mean this all the time. And she cannot
be frightened: everything is pulled
so clear, the time for fear is over,
it belongs to that whole other world
now reduced to a droplet dimly
there stirring then vanished,
a dream in a deer's eye.

Now all the sky shivers with storm
clouds and as if someone is taking
her, very carefully, into a barn; ducking under
the low door's lip, she trembling at the hand
and along the skin – it is almost
like an Annunciation, light lasering through
the body to that hidden eye in the chest
and opening it. How can it ever now close?
Leaving the blue shadows of the barn,
the world will be new with rain:
white, wet black branches, irretrievably

alive. Someone has touched that sole silver string
in her and plucked it – it startled them both
with a sound that had never before been heard
only *heard of*, like a bedtime story told then forgotten.
And this other one, here on the opposite wall,
he is nothing if not unpeeling, and so rapidly,

with such brilliance and no stoppable
momentum – and *she* taking it all in, making
sure there is nothing of him left outside,
nothing left like a dog

in rain at the back door, no particle
of his inness – as when a candle burns straight
through its good wick, not a speck unlicked
by the pure tongue of flame. And I, to think,
I wandering all this time, practically on my knees,
through disbelief and the more terrible
belief, raying ever straight like a targetless
arrow over land and sea and toxic, salt-cursed
vaporous nights after what can be found in a place
as four-walled and small as a heart:
contained in one plain room.

Geburt des Monicakinds

I woke. A tiny knot of skin on a silver table
Set in the birth-theater, blinking in the glare
Of electric lights and a strange arranged

Passel of faces: huge as gods in their council.
I was the actor who forgets his lines and enters
On stage suddenly wanting to say, *I am.*

I was almost all eye: they weighed me down,
Two lump-big brown-sugar bags in a face
Which did not yet know struggle, burden;

How the look of newborns unnerves. Then
They wrapped me in pale yellow like a new sun
Still too small to throw up into the sky.

It was midnight when they injected me
With a plague; tamed, faded as imperialism, pox
Had once put its palm-leaf hand over a quarter of Earth

Saying, *these.* Now it was contracted to a drop:
And in the morning I knew both death and life.
Lapped in my nimbus of old gold light, my

Huge lashes drooped over my deepened eyes, like
Ostrich-feather shades over twin crown princes: wet heads
Sleek and doomed as the black soul of an open poppy.

Walking Home

A cold yellow light on the cobblestones, you
Stumble from the bar, a wayward star
Falling off its chart. October's darkness
Takes your temperature, presses a cool moon
Sliver to your fevering brow. You speak the moon,
Hieroglyphs of jade drop from your stone lips.

Night rises out of the river like a bad Aphrodite:
Jet, burnished as a rococo tomb.
She walks you home, coyly taking an arm,
Dripping her curled locks over your shoulders
As if tonight all your kisses were hers. She whispers
A name into your auricle that turns its cartilage

To bone; she nudges your ball of yarn down still another
Tangle of lit alleys. You pass by the deluging world
Greying in its watery obsolescence, light-strafed,
Where cars sleep the dreamless sleep of steel
And fountains purl like minxing cats, a stirring
Avalanche: the sound fills up the silence like a bowl.

Blue-grey pigeons shatter the air – ungainly,
Deprecating, fatly hurrying to their sick moults.
A thousand minuets lie coiled in a pomander ball
Raised in the pale yellow hall of an Austrian queen;
A thousands minuets lie under the sea
And you too will be one of these, you have only

To find the house in this long row of painted doors
With your number. But the hours spin you on their fortune-wheel
And you walk on, as if one thin bone finger were
Pressing you, a chess-piece through the white and black
Squares of these vacant streets; you walk as the genius
Of yourself – as a shooting star: instant, irresponsibly beautiful,

Without issue. And yet if the good monk should find you,
Guide you up the stair to his tower room, holding a taper
To show you the star chart of all your fatal incidents,

Your sketched-out combinations and imprecations,
Your storied path like ice-skates on the frozen lake,
By morning it would all, all, as always, be forgotten.

In the Binary Alleys of the Lion's Virus

Sorrento, your sun is light yellow lemonskin, your sky
Purling out like a farther surf on which I ride away
From that secret in a German town. I left behind
A dragon of enigma to fester there without me, I left
A small god ticking like a time bomb: a tiny jade statue suspended
By magnets in the vulva of a prehistoric temple. Here
In the oyster of your mornings I wake as lead.
                                        Once I was a knight
Who rode out in search of grail, now I am just a husk
Of armor with the grey squid of memory inside – I have forgotten
Land and tongue, I have forgotten everyone. Only I see
An emblem, some kind of lion arrant on ash-argent ground,
A creature I greeted once in a dream: yes, at the crossroads of the hallowed grove
He kissed me – and must have slipped this curse between my lips.

Mohn des Gedächtnis

Picture it: a girl in a strange city
Unpacking her suitcase, setting things on shelves
In the middle of the folds rises the berry
Of her determination, a black pearl on white cloth
As fine-wrapped as a baby Jesus
Or new star – she the one who will set it in the sky
Tomorrow, it's only the night before still. Picture it,

This stranger: doer of an incomprehensible,
Resonant past thing, which echoes in the oyster miles beneath.
Who was she? Some figment, miniature self,
A toy soldier set in motion by
An accidental kick of the dreaming real girl,
Far away untouched and unblemished in sleep.
Yet I was she: I was the eunuch who, smiling, salaaming,

Lets in the ghostly sahib to the huge jewel room
While his hukkaed shah lies fallen. That night,
A little doll stuffed tight with my fell purpose,
How I wandered the city, outdated treasure map to hand,
Searching my buried gold. Where my fear went
Skipping a few paces ahead, a paper butterfly, later
I hung my tears like earrings from the lampposts.

                              – No!

I could make a thousand poems from this
There came in one day enough pain for ten
Natural lives laid end to end,
I could make a whole galaxy of glowing suns
Heating their decades of planets and trash –
But how can I let this live through me any more? Or
I should be the girl of the music box

Open her red coffer, out
Pops the same old song,
Only magical for never changing,
Crystalline, distilling
Its own liquor of eternity
From the sole inexhaustible god-grape – directing,
Suspending me as the magnet-chip in the old jade statue.

Now I may lie tossed up by this ocean, like an old
Jellyfish losing its clarity, hexed
By a curse ancient as a blue faïence
Scarab carved with hieratic marks,
But even if it means a change as came
To Anthony, after the god abandoned him –
Human, no longer tragically, singularly destinied –

I will live through *it*: burn it up
With my breath. For after all I am alive
While what is past has lost that art.

Alexander Leaves Babylon

Alexander wept in Babylon, not because
his father had died or his old tutor
had looked at him finally with those eyes of stone

but because the drink of Babylon
was so good. It tasted of dandelion milk
squeezed from a stalk still in its greenness.

Here in his hand – the world: but first this glass of clarity
swelling like sunlight and as sharp. Yes, winter
had aged him suddenly as a straw statue left outdoors

in the everness of the terrible Gedrosian:
that skin-colored bowl soft as the palm of God
where the urge to understand met the urge to disappear

and the two lay down to couple in the dust.
Sand scrubbed him clean as a glass there; he came out
empty as the strange room that widens between

two heart-beats: vacant as this circle of faces gathered at table –
flames staring quietly from a white fire
visionlessly patient in its dinner of elimination.

I need no one else I am a star
                              Then the gemmed
cats ranged under the table, and a rainbow-
colored snail kissed the marbling foot.

The Lace World
(after a piece of 16th-century Breton lace)

How eerie it all is, as if linked by synapses;
a face stutters out of the cloud of lace,
a tiny decorative lion dances in a frieze,
a woman, needy arms outstretched, holds on

to thread bulwarks against some unseen flood
while her body dissolves into netting, the knots
widen and widen until the limn of her
is finished, she melted to loops of distance...and isn't

that how *you've* transformed, once-love, while
this strait sleeping-car, this *time*
spirits me away from you and that night we lay
two palms folded to each other in prayer:

how the cat yowled to be let in! and the moths,
darting abortively forward, all ended up
by clinging to the screen in the sleep-sacs
of their wings, while I rolled to the top of my tongue

that word which would end everything and
like Sisyphus, let it fall.
                                        Nothing
brings that second back, yet nothing gets lost;

hours that separate me from you only
tighten the memory-chain, where my thoughts
like these light acrobats trapeze:
in the white spiderwebbing, in the network

here's a sea serpent, a helmeted soldier,
a boy pausing to sing, two dogs leaving a fountain,
someone pushing aside a harp.
The tiny o of her mouth. Those gouged-out holes, her eyes.

Des Esseintes's Last Book
(after Huysmans's À Rebours*)*

It was red, which pleased him. Small
and hard, it fit in his palm
as if it loved him and was listening
to the strange, murmurous thumps
of his ambivalent heart. How sleekly
the pages brushed his skin, like sunlight
after a late afternoon bathe, when
suddenly the world is believable
and for an instant he does not want to die.
Yet the empty shelves still sing to him, those slim
alabaster brides, calling him in
from the garden, raising a glass of light.
Through the brambles, one breaks out onto
a rock-cut stair down to the sea.

VIVEK NARAYANAN

(*b.* 1972)

Vivek Narayanan was born in 1972 in Ranchi into a family of Tamil Brahmins. His mother Padma Narayanan is a translator and short story writer, and his father is a retired accountant. Educated in Africa and the United States, he writes poems located in several places at once. A man can fall through the ice in 'forgotten America' and land in a river in South India; the prince of Botswana may make an appearance, or the Powerpuff Girls, or Auden, or Bob Marley. He likes to tell tall extemporised tales – no less believable because they use elements of fiction and rap – in a language that resembles prose but aims 'for the vertical reach of verse'. He lives and works in New Delhi.

Learning to Drown
(for Jan Wojcik)

Before

His older sister let my father sneak out of the house
so he learned to swim in the Kaveri, splashing wild, staying afloat:

Imagine the strokes into survival, he teaches his son unwittingly,
not technique, but an instinct for what more there is to water than physics:

The stone they used to build the square is water,
which is water before the stone.
Standing after land had already spoken this way to telegraphic water,

I heard his voice. The ice cracked into a hand-drawn map
of the first, the final continent. A fissure, which is genealogy,
and this was no different that night on the banks of the Racquette nearly
unknown to man, footnote to the St Lawrence, fugue
of forgotten America – but writ was my name and the names of
others who had dropped, writ was the name *Racquette,*
a truce between tongues after slaughter.

Beneath the bridge bending to join the shores,
taking a looming, unpossessed church for totem,
I begged a promise, offered myself in heavy boots

and for a moment misunderstood gravity. I made a drama,
doubled as witness and mistress. I kindly stopped for time
because by then he could not stop for me.
Thus with the darkly dreaming town colluding
I iced my post-adolescent angst in a heartbeat.

And

A simple plunge will plummet you through the black sky.
Once, Pamela's palm kept me floating –

in the moment before   of the moment after
crystallised in between,   Florentine, who can't swim
stands and watches.   And the houses
and the bars and   Mary and Jimmy's remorse

and Scooby's and Thatha's willing commingling,
and the twenty-year-old who wrote this,
and the thirty-two years he revised,
and Jan whose book *The River Why* made him live it,
and the fifteen-year-old who told himself the tale,

and of the now in which it is alien,
in the now which was the moment of,
what can be said, except that the universe stayed mostly empty
despite the lively plots we farmed. And this
another fraction of that irrelevance
a hole in a second of the infinite sentence
made homely by microscopy.

It was night, but no one heard me.

After

I'm gonna be fished out and slid ashore by three large amphibian policemen
into an ambulance full of quite-serious nurses. To them
I'll say I love you I love you and mean it
and though behind the Lynchian curtains of that charming town
gruesomer tales did exist, for a week I was
the prince of Botswana
who'd not known ice. The river, perpetual, drawled ferocious
through property. Dogs barked. I'd bloated my feet
in these damp very woods. My future flashed past me
not my past.

'What happened here?' they asked.

'Looking for bodies,' joked Hugh.

Cut to the camera on the graphic of the rescue van,
cut to the bearded radio man. My newly-fashioned self
reproduced so – in mouths intent on parable
or in short-lived digital slivers,

in the cops who saved my life
or the frat boys who saved my life by calling them,

and in my help-cries that echo still and expand
to burst against the clapboard facades of the shore,
in my legs and torso drawn
into the maw below
the dissembling ice floes, air viscous
as water, the senses slowed and cancelled,
the image persisting, ravelled

in the moment after the half-conscious photo-still,
in a swarming space, dispossessed of objects.

Three Elegies for Silk Smitha

She's the slut
among white hippies on the beach,
behind the campfire, hot pants
and an upright pony tail
for style; she's the dancer
in metallic feathers
and red plastic shoes. Foil
to the gangster's drink,
blackmailer's bait, the woman
you never brought home
to mother, she is
and is not
the salt of what she is.

*

At eleven I didn't know a woman's body
could be different. I didn't know
what my body could do. I watched
terrified, tranquillised. It was early
for irony. Later without yet a jot
of post-colonial theory I knew
that this was kitsch. I was leery of her
and of the Dancing Queens on TVZ
who wore tennis shoes below their skirts,
but I remembered enough to know she had it,
a shimmer, a handclap, a match's flame.

*

My last of her is borrowed too. She hangs
from the fan of a bright North Madras apartment,
a thin white cotton sari wrapped
around a blouse equally white; invisible
by implication, as always was
her way. A note in Telugu says, 'I
was an uneducated woman. No one
loves me.' Woman
of the famous breasts and thighs,
of the only eyes, you were
the secret darling of Censor Board
auditoriums, capacious
and full of faces turned
from the projection's
breaching beamlight.

Ode to Prose
(for Ratika)

For we long for the vertical reach of verse,
its first-dipping rise into the blue,
its way of fixing the stars in their firmament –

for we are at home in the world sometimes –

...but on other days the dark pebbly-smooth noun-stones in a well of prose
        will do;
prose straining towards the spirit of prose,
prose that rarely walks unplanted, scythe among the stalks,
prose that in the rainbow-arching reach of the line rolls into plain view,
        like a hippo, like a tank, like a combine-harvester drawing
        steadily across;
that prose is the mat we slept on,
the only heart we can trust if only because it beat so firmly,
that prose is black bread, the grain we power our machines with,
that prose is not averse to philosophy,
that it pulls back from sophistry

...that one day among the robotic contractors and their forklifts,
the elephants devoted to their granite blocks and their mahout,
the tracts of arable land as seen from the sentinel's smug cabin,
or at the marketplace, bursting with spoiled tomatoes, tasty slabs of meat –

among all this, or in the stable near the screeching pigs,
in the hour of the blood sacrifice,
at the moment of that offering,
humble, hewn from a human hand –

that quadrangular prose, at that very moment, be born.

No More Indian Women

'There are no more Indian women,'
mourned big-eyed Bal Thackeray
gazing down at his cute

little white rubber pumps.
Truth is, there never were.
A hundred years earlier, for instance,

my grandfather clipped his toenails and
while his supposedly incompetent
assistant tried to tot up the grain

bought or sold, he yelled, 'Work
harder, you lazy kamnati!' i.e., you
lazy widow. But the assistant

was not at all a widow, and the real widows
were dead. Not on the pyre, you understand,
but in the dimmed light of private rooms.

Not Far from the Mutiny Memorial

A banned dog visited
us on the lawn. His red collar
carried tiny serrations and
a bell. There was a brick
lamphouse, small but high, built
with a gazebo roof where
like a sentry a weak
bulb burned. Crows cawed, a bird
made three identical notes
in a sharp three-note plaint.

Manohar Shetty, Miramar, Goa, 2001

'This place was built in 1941,'
she said. The sun dimmed,
a far conversation was
turning violet, riverish,
a pliant, frangible noise. It could never
have stated itself as the case.
The crows call and response.

MANOHAR SHETTY

(*b.* 1953)

Manohar Shetty was born in 1953 in Bombay. He was educated there and at a boarding
school in Panchgani. His family was in the restaurant business, and for two years he managed
a vegetarian eatery in South Bombay. He left the city and the business when he married and
moved to Goa. The move from India's financial capital to 'an eyrie of a house overlooking
the Arabian Sea' had little discernible effect on his writing. The Goa of the tourist brochures
does not occur in his poems, or it does not occur other than as an instrument of irony. In-
stead, the reader visits a place of unchecked development, enduring ambivalence, corruption,
and fatigue: a place much like the Bombay of his earlier work.

May

The gardens are agog
With bougainvillaea and buttercup.
Wild berries carpet the backyard.
Pepper vines blister round
Tree trunks, and pumpkins,
Fecund as eggs, fatten in the shade.
Incense in the frangipani.
Succulence in the cactus.
Dreadlocks of dates
Garland the wild palm.

This, then, is your plot of heaven.
Or heaven's plot, his wry response.

Screenings from the quarry
Film the air; gas spirals
From refinery chimneys
Silvery as guided missiles.
The river is a shallow pond
Of foam-lipped buffaloes and belly-up fish.

Sugarcane, that tall grass,
Keels dryly over the paddy fields'
Brittle rectangles; starved millet
Is scarred by congress weed.
The cloudless sky is a taut mask.
Sweat drops from his eyelids.

In the far horizon, the highway
Glitters like tin.

The Hyenas

My asthmatic child coughs – her throat
Is emery paper. Her tiny
Hands are wet
Petals in my hand. Hyenas cackle
From the Governor's banquet grounds.

Eyes glint as a fencer's
Mask, I stare them down. I whisper,
They've gone, dearest child, sleep;
They laugh with the Governor's gang
Of kingmakers, fatcats, gold-toting ogres.

She sleeps, her temples damp.
To the carrion call the drooling
Packs converge: amidst red

Laughter, claws tear
At gizzard, sweating pigling,
Roe, soft brain, and lamb.

Stills from Baga Beach

Vast freckled Englishwomen
Pylon-limbed
Thaw in the sun. Their breasts
Loll out like baby
Sealions.

* * *

Flabby leftovers of Valhalla
Diet on bread and bananas.
Their dozing blue eyes stroke
Small boys in torn
Pyjamas.

* * *

The German studies the Vedanta
In translation through chromax
Dark glasses, her oozing
Tattoo mobbed by
Bluebottles.

* * *

The temple elephant, vermilion
Swastika on its domed
Forehead, lumbers
Unblinking over the buff
Sands.

Moving Out

After the packing the leavetaking.
The rooms were hollow cartons.
The gecko listened stilly –
An old custom – for the heartbeat
Of the family clock.

After the springcleanings
Now the drawing of curtains.
I thought of the years between
These grey walls, these walls
Which are more than tympanic.

There remained much, dead and living,
Uncleared, unchecked: dust mottled
Into shreds under loaded bookshelves;
The fine twine of a cobweb
Shone in the veranda sunlight.

All this I brushed aside along
With the silverfish in flaking tomes,

The stains on marble and tile
Scoured with acid; but the ghosts
Loomed like windstruck drapes;

Like the rectangle left by
A picture frame: below a nail
Hooked into a questionmark,
A faint corona,
A contrasting shade.

The Old Printer

I long for the hot slug in my hand,
The lines in metal I set
Like books in a library shelf.

And I long for the clanking rhythm,
The fingerprints of honest grief, and fresh
As paint the proof rolling out.

Now I sit in a cool cabin, the size
Of my size, my hand wrapped
Round a smooth, noiseless mouse.
But to me this is neither home nor house.

Torpor

Fatigue, the sun's dutiful heat,
Time and Motion drudgery,
Chimerical boredom, anxiety –
These my lackeys, my henchmen.

You may unwind from the plump
Cushion, browse through wise
Classics saved for your anecdotage,
Or potter about in your garden,

And I'll decline like a shadow
At nightfall, only to edge back
(With profound regret), a laden,
Cloudlike fixture in your head.

I do not send the quotidian
Reminders: the young man playing
Leapfrog over burning
Children, his eyes

Saffron as embers, and the wraith-
Like waif who
Disintegrates into the air
You inhale.

This unmarked map of death
Surfaces like a skull
From the ocean bed.
But I'm here to help,

To offer you the warm
Blanket of forgetfulness,
A bandage of silence
And absentness. Through me

You're half-asleep, but still alive.
Sleep deeply, my friend,
There's little you can do
To unwrap me from you.

Pin the blame on ill-health and drink
For the melting of an iron will.
Soon I'll be ready for the kill,
And you to welcome me like a gift.

Gifts

You unfold, like starfish
On a beach, your touch
Stills the rumpled sea,
Hair plastered seaweed.

I come from the labyrinths:
Traffic lights park in my eyes
Before I cross, highways fork
And stream like veins in my hand.

You hunger for a blade of grass
In the welter of concrete,
I step on softening sand
Suspiciously. Together

We trace a bridge: you pick
A shell translucent as neon,
And I a tribal earring
Reflected in plate-glass.

H. MASUD TAJ

(b. 1956)

H. Masud Taj was born in 1956 in Moradabad, Uttar Pradesh. He was educated in Bombay, in Ooty, and in Panchgani (at the same school as Manohar Shetty). He recites poems by heart, in sequence, the recitation a return to an early Urdu tradition. No such tradition is evident in the poems, which belong at a sideways angle to reality, as if spoken by a newly arrived visitor to the planet. He lives in Ottawa and works as an architect and calligrapher.

The Travelling Nonvegetarian

The man who spoke with suitcases
Said wisdom was hydrogen peroxide,
Wore a white wig of fibre optic cables,
And dentures that were pure African ivory.
When he smiled, elephants burst into tears.

The man who spoke with suitcases
Said homing pigeons were edible pagers
And grey parrots that spoke too many languages
Tasted no better than those that were dumb,
And all birds on TV were cyber-tandooris.

The man who spoke with suitcases
Said the onion was the final package
That packed the process of packing itself,
Which explained the missing mass of the universe
And the tears onion-peelers and stargazers shed.

The man who spoke with suitcases
Said the banana skin was a continuum of zippers,
And all coconuts were neo-colonials
Smashed on occasions of celebration;
All brown outside, all white within.

The man who spoke with suitcases
Said neckties were nooses, wristwatches handcuffs,
And honest heroes who wore underpants outside
Were neurotics packaged in designer masks
Which they removed only to eat.

The man who spoke with suitcases
Said brinjals were boiled with equine eyeballs,
Applied gold glitter-dust to horses' eyebrows,
And powder-coated his finger and toe nails.
He ate candle-lit dinners in fireproof stables.

The man who spoke with suitcases
Said hunchbacks were born-again backpackers,
And slim briefcases made of crocodile skins
Were chromium-plated mouths to snap off space
To declare at the last border crossing.

Cockroach

I wait on the hard edge of his bed,
Watching the blur of newspaper
Rolled into a taut cylinder
Arcing towards me.

Species are forever, I shall not flee.
Survival, after a while, is tiresome.
Individuals must, once in a while,
Learn to let go.

The cylinder is approaching
At an unnecessary speed, driven
Less by the need of the moment,
More by his fear of machines.

My glinting bronze exterior
Belies an inner yielding;
He is soft outside, hard within,
But bones only wrap around voids.

I am supremely articulated,
My structure is my ornament.
He is a blob with a brain and four limbs,
One of which he is swinging in.

The aim of all his existence
At this instance is to snuff out mine.
He does not know, even as he does so,
He is bending to my will.

Close up and the greyness of the cylinder
Separates into patterns black and white.
Zooming in, black explodes into planets
In panic fleeing white space.

And then I am touched by the cylinder,
Knighted I shall arise in a new age of bronze,
Oh the sweetness of surrender that ignores
The crushing weight of a mind once set.

My sides burst symmetrically –
Is there life after death?
Is there death after life after death?
Is there life after death after life after death?

Turn to the back page
Of yesterday's newspaper:
I am a Rorschach smear in relief.
Read me.

Approaching Manhattan

Charred threads of calligraphy
Lamenting as they lose themselves

To thoughts that turn from north to south.
Return via yellow earth, green hills, blue sky:

White clouds inhale and drift away,
Winds die, we escape the frame; exhale.

Return to slip slide on red and yellow
Synapses of a scorching Internet

Electronic diagram wiring together
While keeping apart three floating squares:

Blood in one, with a green horizon
Displaced in a sky unbelievably blue.

Airplane leaving another,
Leaving borders as yet intact.

Water, in the final frame,
Approaching Manhattan.

Nothing can stall what happens next
But that is not what I meant, I swear,

That is not what I meant at all.

VIKRAM SETH

(*b*. 1952)

Vikram Seth was born in Calcutta in 1952. His father came to newly partitioned India from West Punjab, now in Pakistan, and settled in Delhi where he worked as an executive with the Bata shoe company. His mother was the first woman judge on the Delhi High Court, and the first woman Chief Justice at a State court. Seth was educated at a succession of far-flung locales, among them, Doon School, Corpus Christi College, Stanford University and Nanjing University. He is the author of a number of books in various genres, including the novels *A Suitable Boy* and *An Equal Music*, a novel-in-verse *The Golden Gate*, and a memoir *Two Lives*. Despite his many books of prose, he is essentially a poet whose use of fixed forms is belied by a tone that is conversational and seemingly casual. There is playfulness and gravitas, frequent use of the first person, skilful handling of mood and narrative, and a profound weariness with the self ('The fact is this work is as dreary as shit. / I do not like it a bit.'). And there is an ambivalence too: the poems are both intimate and distancing, as if they would keep the reader at arm's length and draw him in at the same time. Seth lives in New Delhi and London.

Unclaimed

To make love with a stranger is the best.
There is no riddle and there is no test –

To lie and love, not aching to make sense
Of this night in the mesh of reference.

To touch, unclaimed by fear of imminent day,
And understand, as only strangers may.

To feel the beat of foreign heart to heart
Preferring neither to prolong nor part.

To rest within the unknown arms and know
That this is all there is; that this is so.

Love and Work

The fact is, this work is as dreary as shit.
I do not like it a bit.
While at it I wander off into a dream.
When I return, I scream.

If I had a lover
I'd bear it all, because when day is over
I could go home and find peace in bed.
Instead

The boredom pulps my brain
And there is nothing at day's end to help assuage the pain.
I am alone, as I have always been.
The lawn is green.

The robin hops into the sprinkler's spray.
Day after day
I fill the feeder with bird-seed,
My one good deed.

Night after night
I turn off the porch light, the kitchen light.
The weight lodged in my spirit will not go
For years, I know.

There is so much to do
There isn't any time for feeling blue.
There isn't any point in feeling sad.
Things could be worse. Right now they're only bad.

Ceasing upon the Midnight

He stacks the dishes on the table.
He wants to die, but is unable
   To decide when and how.
   Why not, he wonders, now?

A piece of gristle catches his eye.
The phone rings; he turns to reply.
   A smell of burning comes
   From somewhere. Something hums.

The fridge. He looks at it. This room
Would make an unpacific tomb.
　　He walks outside. The breeze
　　Blows warmly, and he sees

A sky brushed clean of dust and haze.
He wanders in a lucid daze
　　Beneath the live-oak tree
　　Whose creaks accompany

The drifting hub of yellow light
Low on the hillcrest. Ah, tonight,
　　How rich it seems to be
　　Alive unhappily.

'O sähst du, voller Mondenschein,
Zum letztenmal auf meine Pein,'
　　He murmurs to convince
　　Himself its force will rinse

The pus of memory from his mind,
Dispel the dust he's swept behind
　　The furniture of days,
　　And with beneficent rays

Kindle the taut and tearless eyes
With the quick current of surprise,
　　Joy, frenzy, anything
　　But this meandering

Down a dead river on a plain,
Null, unhorizoned, whose terrain,
　　Devoid of entity,
　　Leads to no open sea.

The moon, himself, his shadow, wine
And Li Bai's poem may define
　　A breath, an appetite,
　　His link to earth tonight.

He gets a bottle, pours a glass,
A few red droplets on the grass,
　　Libation to the god
　　Of oak-trees and of mud,

Holds up its colour to the moon,
Drinks slowly, listens to the tune
　　The branches improvise,
　　Drinks, pours, drinks, pours, and lies

Face down on the moist grass and drinks
The dewdrops off its leaves. He thinks
      Of other moons he's seen
      And creatures he has been.

The breeze comforts him where he sprawls.
Raccoon's eyes shine. A grey owl calls.
      He imitates its cries,
      Chants shreds, invents replies.

The alcohol, his molecules,
The clear and intimate air, the rules
      Of metre, shield him from
      Himself. To cease upon

The midnight under the live-oak
Seems too derisory a joke.
      The bottle lies on the ground.
      He sleeps. His sleep is sound.

On the Fiftieth Anniversary of the Golden Gate Bridge

The gray Pacific, curved and old,
      Indented, bare,
Flings out, day after day, its cold
      Breakers to where

Marin and San Francisco shore
      The rapid strait
Christened a century before,
      The Golden Gate.

Both counties know this still might be
      A wistful view
If Strauss had not resolved to see
      The matter through.

Though courts twice threatened it, though storms
      Once washed away
The trestles of his bridge, two forms
      Inched day by day

Closer so that the ocean's rift
      Might disappear.
Two stubborn decades were his gift;
      He died next year.

How fortunate such greatness stirred
    In his small frame
That even obstacles deferred
    To set his fame.

How sad that he should be so small
    In his great mind
To disacknowledge after all
    Him who designed

This shape of use and loveliness
    And to subject
Ellis, his partner in success,
    To long neglect.

Two towers hold the cable; ton
    On ton of it
Hangs chainlike from their peaks, yet one
    Alone is lit.

But let us leave blurred facts behind
    In the plain hope
That each will be at last assigned
    His equal scope

– A claim that justice can in no
    Clear light refuse –
And glimpse the fifty years that flow
    Down from those views.

How much of life has passed above,
    Below, upon.
How much of hatred and of love
    Has come and gone!

What portion of the soldiers who
    Sailed out to war
Sailed back beneath the bridge they knew
    Four years before?

How many lovers who have found
    A world of mist
To cloak them from the world around
    Have stood and kissed

Where others, who have walked alone
    On a bright day,
In unsupported grief have thrown
    Their lives away.

How many more have been impelled
   From death they craved,
By force or by persuasion held,
   And somehow saved.

'I would have been happy and dead,
   I'm sure, by now,
If it weren't for those heroes,' said
   One saved somehow.

And surely, if one had to die,
   What happier place
To quit that over-salted pie,
   The human race?

Indeed this morning's pilgrimage
   Just after light
Saw us frail lemmings on the bridge
   Jammed in so tight,

Breathing against a neighbour's face,
   Gasping for air,
We almost quit the human race
   Right then and there.

But panic could not scuttle love,
   A love half-blind,
An amiable affection of
   A civic kind

For what we've known for years, for all
   Who feel the same,
As when in darkness we recall
   A common name.

It is as if the bridge's core,
   Its grace, its strength
Could not have not been on this shore,
   And that at length

The green and empty hills agreed
   That humankind
Might be allowed this binding deed –
   Which brings to mind

The engineering dean's reply
   To her who said,
'If such a manmade thing should lie,
   Metalled and dead

Across God's natural world, why should
    We think it best?' –
'That's a fine pendant on your God-
    Created breast.'

Cool repartee; but would it still
    Suffice to douse
The later, enigmatic will
    Of Mrs Strauss?

The plaque upon his tomb displays
    The bridge; on hers
The bridgeless strait, as if she says
    That she demurs.

The Stray Cat

The gray cat stirs upon the ledge
Outside the glass doors just at dawn.
I open it; he tries to wedge
His nose indoors. It is withdrawn.
He sits back to assess my mood.
He sees me frown; he thinks of food.

I am familiar with his stunts.
His Grace, unfed, will not expire.
He may be hungry, but he hunts
When need compels him, or desire.
Just yesterday he caught a mouse
And yoyo'd it outside the house.

But now he turns his topaz eyes
Upon my eyes, which must reveal
The private pressures of these days,
The numb anxieties I feel.
But no, his grayness settles back
And yawns, and lets his limbs go slack.

He ventures forth an easy paw
As if in bargain. Thus addressed,
I fetch a bowl, and watch him gnaw
The star-shaped nuggets he likes best.
He is permitted food, and I
The furred indulgence of a sigh.

Things

Put back the letter, half conceived
From error, half to see you grieved.
Some things are seen and disbelieved.

Some talk of failings, some of love –
That terms are reckoned from above –
What could she have been thinking of?

As if aloneness were a sign
Of greater wisdom in design
To bear the torque of me and mine.

As if the years were lists of goods,
A helve of dares, a head of shoulds
To hack a route through rotten woods.

As if creation wrapped the heart
Impenetrably in its art,
As if the land upon the chart

Were prior to the acred land
And that a mark could countermand
The houses and the trees that stand.

Though she would fell them if she could,
They will stand, and they will have stood
For all the will of dare and should.

Put it away. You cannot find
In a far reading of this kind
One character for heart or mind.

Read into things; they will remain.
Things fall apart and feel no pain.
And things, if not the world, are sane.

The Gift

Awake, he recalls
The district of his sleep.
It was desert land,
The dunes gold, steep,

134

Warm to the bare foot, walls
Of pliant sand.

Someone, was he a friend?
Placed a stone of jade
In his hand
And, laughing, said
'When this comes to an end
You will not understand.'

He is awake, yet through
The ache of light
He longs to dream again.
He longs for night,
The contour of the sand, the rendezvous,
The gift of jade, of sight.

A Little Night Music

White walls. Moonlight. I wander through
The alleys skein-drawn by the sound
Of someone playing the erhu.
A courtyard; two chairs on the ground.

As if he knew I'd come tonight
He gestures, only half-surprised.
The old hands poise. The bow takes flight
And unwished tears come to my eyes.

He pauses, tunes, and plays again
An hour beneath the wutong trees
For self and stranger, as if all men
Were brothers within the enclosing seas.

Souzhou Park

Magnolia trees float out their flowers,
Vast, soft, upon a rubbish heap.
The grandfather sits still for hours:
His lap-held grandson is asleep.

Above him plane trees fan the sky.
Nearby, a man in muted dance
Does tai-qi-quan. A butterfly
Flies whitely past his easy trance.
A magpie flaps back to its pine.
A sparrow dust-rolls, fluffs, and cheeps.
The humans rest in a design:
One writes, one thinks, one moves, one sleeps.
The leaves trace out the stencilled stone,
And each is in his dream alone.

Qingdao: December

Here by the sea this quiet night
I see the moon through misted light.
The water laps the rocks below.
I hear it lap and swash and go.
The pine trees, dense and earthward-bent,
Suffuse the air with resin-scent.
A landmark breeze combs through my hair
And cools the earth with salted air.

Here all attempt in life appears
Irrelevant. The erosive years
That built the moon and rock and tree
Speak of a sweet futility
And say that we who are from birth
Caressed by unimpulsive earth
Should yield our fever to the trees,
The seaward light and resined breeze.

Here by the sea this quiet night
Where my still spirit could take flight
And nullify the heart's distress
Into the peace of wordlessness,
I see the light, I breathe the scent,
I touch the insight, but a bent
Of heart exacts its old designs
And draws my hands to write these lines.

The Crocodile and the Monkey

On the Ganga's greenest isle
Lived Kuroop the crocodile:
Greeny-brown with gentle grin,
Stubby legs and scaly skin,
He would view with tepid eyes
Prey below a certain size –
But when a substantial dish
– Dolphin, turtle, fatter fish –
Swam across his field of view,
He would test the water too.
Out he'd glide, a floating log,
Silent as a polliwog –
Nearer, nearer, till his prey
Swam a single length away;
Then he'd lunge with smiling head,
Grab, and snap, and rip it dead –
Then (prime pleasure of his life)
Drag the carcass to his wife,
Lay it humbly at her feet,
Eat a bit, and watch her eat.

All along the river-bank
Mango trees stood rank on rank,
And his monkey friend would throw
To him as he swam below
Mangoes gold and ripe and sweet
As a special summer treat.
Crocodile, your wife, I know
Hungers after mangoes so
That she'd pine and weep and swoon,
Mango-less in burning June.'
Then Kuroop the crocodile,
Gazing upwards with a smile,
Thus addressed his monkey friend:
'Dearest monkey, in the end,
Not the fruit, but your sweet love,
Showered on us from above,
Constant through the changing years,
Slakes her griefs and dries her tears.'
(This was only partly true.
She liked love, and mangoes too.)

One day, Mrs Crocodile,
Gorged on mangoes, with a smile

– Sad, yet tender – turned and said:
'Scalykins, since we've been wed,
You've fulfilled my every wish
– Dolphins, turtles, mangoes, fish –
But I now desire to eat,
As an anniversary treat,
Something sweeter still than fruit,
Sugar-cane or sugar-root:
I must eat that monkey's heart.'
'What?' 'Well, darling, for a start,
He has been so kind to me;
Think how sweet his heart must be.
Then, the mango pulp he's eaten
Year on year must serve to sweeten
Further yet each pore and part,
Concentrating in his heart.'
'Darling, he's my friend.' 'I know;
And he trusts you. Therefore go –
Go at once and fetch him here.
Oh, my breath grows faint, I fear…'
'Let me fan you – it's the heat – '
'No – I long for something sweet.
Every fruit tastes bitter now.
I must eat his heart somehow.
Get him here, my love, or I,
Filled with bitterness, will die.'

When the monkey saw Kuroop
He let out a joyful whoop,
Jumped from branch to branch with pleasure,
Flinging down the golden treasure:
'Eat, my friend, and take your wife
Nectar from the tree of life –
Mangoes ripe and mangoes rare,
Mangoes, mangoes everywhere.'
Then Kuroop the crocodile
Gazed up with a gentle smile:
'Monkey, you are far too kind,
But today, if you don't mind,
Dine with both of us, and meet
Her whose life you've made so sweet.
When you meet her you will see
Why she means so much to me.
When she takes you by the paw
Something at your heart will gnaw.
When you gaze into her eyes
You will enter Paradise.

Let us show our gratitude:
Share our friendship and our food.'

'Dear Kuroop, dear crocodile,
You can swim from isle to isle.
I can leap from limb to limb,
But, my friend, I cannot swim.
And your island's far away.
If I get a boat some day...'
'Nonsense; jump upon my back.
You're no heavier than my sack
Filled with mangoes to the crown.'
So the monkey clambered down,
Bearing mangoes, and delighted
With such warmth to be invited.

They were just halfway across
When the crocodile said: 'Toss
All those mangoes in the water.'
'But these fruits are all I've brought her.'
'You yourself are gift enough,'
Said Kuroop in accents gruff.
'Ah, my friend, that's very gracious.'
'Well, my wife's not so voracious –
And I'm certain that today
She won't eat fruit. By the way,
Tell me what your breast contains.
Mango nectar fills your veins.
Does it also fill your heart?'
Said the monkey with a start:
'What a very curious question.'
'Well, she might get indigestion
If it's too rich, I suspect.'
'What?' 'Your heart.' 'My heart?' 'Correct.'
'Now,' Kuroop said with a frown,
Which would you prefer – to drown
In the Ganga or to be
Gutted by my wife and me?
I will let you choose your end
After all, you are my friend.'
Then he slowly started sinking.
'Wait – ' the monkey said, 'I'm thinking.
Death by drowning, death by slaughter
– Death by land or death by water –
I'd face either with a smile
For your sake, O crocodile!
But your wife's felicity –

That's what means the most to me.
Noble Lady! How she'll freeze,
Dumb with sorrow, when she sees,
Having prised my ribs apart,
That my breast contains no heart.
If you had not rushed me so,
I'd have found the time to go
To the hollow where I keep
Heart and liver when I sleep,
Half my brain, a fingernail,
Cufflinks, chutney, and spare tail.
I had scarcely woken up
When you asked me here to sup.
Why did you not speak before?
I'd have fetched them from the shore.'

Now Kuroop the crocodile
Lost, then quickly found, his smile.
'How my sweetheart will upbraid me!
Monkey, monkey – you must aid me.'
'Well...' – the monkey placed his paw
Thoughtfully upon his jaw –
'Well, although the day is hot
And I'd really rather not –
We could go back, fetch my heart,
Check its sweetness, and depart.'

So the crocodile once more
Swam the monkey back to shore,
And, with tears of thankfulness
Mingled with concern and stress,
Worried what his wife would say
With regard to his delay,
Begged his friend: 'Come back at once.'
'I'm not such a double-dunce,'
Yelled the monkey from on high;
'Tell your scaly wife to try
Eating her own wicked heart
– If she has one – for a start.
Mine's been beating in my breast
Night and day without a rest.
Tell her that – and as for you,
Here's my parting gift – ' He threw
Mangoes – squishy, rotten, dead –
Down upon the reptile's head,
Who, with a regretful smile,
Sat and eyed him for a while.

RAVI SHANKAR

(*b*. 1975)

Ravi Shankar's mother and father moved to the US from Coimbatore and Madras respectively. He was born in 1975 in Washington, DC, and is poet in residence at Central Connecticut State University. His first collection *Instrumentality* introduced a tone that seems striking because it is used so sparingly in contemporary American poetry. It is a tone without irony, inclined toward long meditative moments and unembarrassed philosophising, and it does not depend for its effect solely on the image. His poems make a formal shape on the page; they assume, and demand from the reader, a facility 'akin / To dance, not cartography'.

Plumbing the Deepening Groove

That survival is impossible without repetition
of patterns is platitude – see moon rise or whorls in wolf fur –

but how explain the human need to reenact primal dramas,
even when the act perpetuates a cycle of abuse?

The boy who hides in the tool shed with buckle-shaped welts
rising like figs from his arms will curse his father,

and in turn beat his son. Like a wave anguish rises,
never understands itself before emptying in a fist.

The spurned daughter will seek out lovers who abandon her,
self-will degenerating in the face of what feels familiar.

Childhood, seen in light of recurrence, takes on the heft
of conspiracy, casts a shadow across an entire life,

making it appear that nothing could have happened
differently, that free and easy is the stuff of semblance.

Then of the prerogatives, reclamation is principal,
to appraise the past the way a painter subsumes old canvas

with new layers of paint, each brushstroke unconcerned,
sure, dismantling the contour of what once was realised

so that new forms can emerge to contradict the suggestion
that survival is impossible without repetition.

A Square of Blue Infinity

In it was an iron cot, a washstand and a chair. A shelf was the dresser. Its four bare walls seemed to close in upon you like the sides of a coffin. Your hand crept to your throat, you gasped, you looked up as from a well – and breathed once more. Through the glass of the little skylight you saw a square of blue infinity.
O. HENRY, 'The Skylight Room'

Snookered by traffic lights that turn
The swim up 9 into a knot,
Middletown's fringe tediously damp
With the same almost-wet that streaks

The windshields in such a way
That wipers twitch ineffectively
Against the hard light, clear edges,
What Pound claimed no democratised

Campaign could maintain stages
Its revival upon the smudged glass.
Morning. Red stutter of brakelights.
Wide world winnowed to a stretch

Of road from the coast to Hartford,
My passage sealed from traffic
And saturated with felicitous diction,
The glories of books on tape,

Dear sir, your stories spoken by
A second-rate thespian for whom
Even commercials have dried up.
Nearly a century since you hopped

A freighter into the banana boom,
Wanted by the feds for bank fraud,
Just another *gringo* in Honduras
With a scar the source of which

He'd rather not reveal over mojitos.
Did prison teach you the difference
Between prosaic and prosodic
Prose or was it being feted

In the streets of the city you died in as
'Caliph of Baghdad-by-the-Subway',
Most colorful newspaperman in the five
Boroughs? You'd work all winter

On fifths of scotch while editors
Screamed for copy, putting down
The occasional yarn on a typewriter
Missing a few keys. You outwitted it

By using a period for an apostrophe.
Somewhere pent in your small flat,
Hunched over an overflowing ashtray,
Memories of endless, rolling Prairie

Must have uncharted the city's grid,
Leaving you a brief glimpse
Into something so large that no one
Could ever belong to or even trace

Its terrible shape, though you tried
With sinuously wound sentences
Laden with polysyllables, brogue,
And what became a characteristic

Plot twist. I've heard your critics
Complain that you're too mannered,
Your phraseology ostentatious,
Your enduring reputation as a hack,

But what art rebuffs contrivance?
Even the trees flaming into autumn
North of Middletown *look* different
To each of the passing drivers

And *are* something altogether other,
Like your stately delineations
That run from the 'hectic, haggard
Perfunctory welcome like the specious

Smile of a demirep' to 'a polychromatic
Rug like some brilliant-flowered,
Rectangular, tropical islet surrounded
By a billowy sea of soiled matting',

All in the course of the same story,
One that is not believable, true,
But not meant to be, any more
Than Sophocles intended Oedipus

Rex to be a literal transcription
Of a typical Athenian nobleman's
Quirky yet predestined misfortune.
No, you are like the conductor

Of a Viennese waltz, peering
Past your gloves as the orchestra
Swells, as a gentleman in tails
Bows low above his lady's hand,

Lips poised above but never making
Contact with her niveous flesh,
Proving that between a thought
And its realisation, space is infinite.

In your world, the wrong man
Gets the right job, bums who want
To be arrested can't, while rich
Misers receive sudden comeuppance.

You and I both know it's akin
To dance, not cartography,
Analogy, not mimetic affirmation,
That the trajectory of no life

Could so gracefully arc towards
A spindle of fate, abruptly changing
Direction. Unless of course we take
Yours: frail North Carolina

Ex-con who rose to international
Literary renown in less than nine years,
Then died in a New York hospital,
Penniless, drunk, and alone, uttering

Last words that one of his own
Characters might have spoken:
'Turn up the lights, I don't want
To go home in the dark.'

From where I'm sitting,
There is no dark, the whole sky
Is lit up like a stadium, a thick braid
Of traffic forms then unravels,

The Cisco Kid has just traversed
An arroyo to find his cheating lover,
And next to me a gaunt woman mouths
Lyrics, slowly, to a song I cannot hear.

A Story with Sand

(after James Dickey's A Birth*)*

Inventing a story with sand,
I find gray anklebones broken
By the shore and not a horse
To graze upon my sand.

Better off. I haven't a lasso
And my trousers are too tight.
Like one side of a medallion
The sand clarifies the point

That these lines cannot hold.
Afternoon beats its tom-tom.
The shore gathers gull-cries.
Contingency is the new god.

Not an umbrella on the beach.
Wheels of clouds cross the sky.
That that happened, this does.
Mouths murmur ears of shale.

Waves came to the shore.
From before came the sand
And the sand lacked a horse.
The afternoon held no plan.

Driftwood sprains the shore.
You had to be here for this.
We could have been different
But past shapes still remain.

Driftwood and anklebones.
Afternoon beats its tom-tom.
Not an umbrella on the beach.
Elsewhere horses ruminate.

Lucia

My hair, voluminous from sleeping in
six different positions, redolent with your scent,
helps me recall that last night was indeed real,

that it's possible for a bedspread to spawn
a watershed in the membrane that keeps us
shut in our own skins, mute without pleasure,

that I didn't just dream you into being.
You fit like a fig in the thick of my tongue,
give my hands their one true purpose,

find in my shoulder a groove for your head.
In a clinch, you're clenched and I'm pinched,
we're spooned, forked, wrenched, lynched

in a chestnut by a mob of our own making,
only to be resurrected to stage several revivals
that arise from slightest touch to thwart

deep sleep with necessities I never knew
I knew until meeting you a few days
or many distant, voluptuous lifetimes ago.

The New Transcendence

The last time I was blindfolded, led from the city
by Mitzvah tank, Venus in retrograde eclipsed the moon.

Silicone was up, the Dow down, the season's rage reality
television. Later I would learn there was Teffillin on board,

but by then it was too late, more Republicans had ascended,
wiry hairs had begun to peek from my palms, the spring

breeze chockablock with burnt wieners and aerosol.
When squads of surgeons quit Mount Sinai to practice

laser vaginal rejuvenation, there's bound to be a fuss
that reaches far enough into Florida to upend bingo,

to turn the links into a place Camaros go to rust.
See: we're all in this together. It's up to us to insure sailors

have less to spend during Fleet Week and more time
to perfect salvos that can turn heads. Indeed,

the current rate at which both manifestos and limericks
are being produced is precipitously low, plus no one

besides those daft with reenactment thinks to wear
a tricorn hat. Instead, stitched for three dollars a day

in refurbished bunkers off the coast of Saipan,
sneakers that enhance support without compromising

breathability leave sole marks on the reflective floors
in the new line of gastropub's paperless bathrooms.

Remember when all we had was our wits and a piece
of jagged shale? When a keening in the bloodstream meant

to hunt? Now click a mouse and dinner's at the door.
Not that I'm against evolution, but in a certain sauce,

progress tastes like regression, the construction of space
with natal ease of access, everything amniotic and near

at hand. In fact, I recently stuck velcro to the universal
remote control and installed a beer jockey in the couch.

Charity after all, like gingivitis, begins at home.
Plus, toys have become the new transcendence:

mp3s, dvds, lcds, SUVs, palm pilots, Pentium processors,
rechargeable digital megapixel flat screens, they've all

conspired to replace heaven with a notion that daylight
is a zero-sum game, fodder for the latest distraction.

So it spins and as they say in Malta, to destroy the web,
squash the spider. I'd rather drink beer and bust caps.

Hedged in by nudniks on all sides, what's a blade to do?
Moshiach, it turns out, is no fan of hot dogs or klezmer.

BIBHU PADHI

(*b.* 1951)

Born in 1951 in Cuttack, Orissa, Bibhu Padhi was educated there at Ravenshaw College and at Utkal University in Bhubaneshwar. He is the author of six books of poetry. His poems have the numbed conversational tone of someone who has been so long in mourning that he has forgotten the origin of his grief. The melancholia is filtered through American speech that is tactile with soft voices, breathing and slowness. He and his wife Minakshi co-wrote *Indian Philiosophy and Religion: A Reader's Guide* (McFarland, North Carolina, 1989). He is a reader in English at Dhenkanal University in the small town of Dhenkanal, Orissa.

Stranger in the House

Someone is watching us, always,
from a place which the sun never touched
nor ever will, inside this house.
Words are sometimes faintly heard,
or just remembered from a distant year
when I was small. Modest words,
easy to understand, but which
I no longer use.
They have their times.

Sometimes, during hot and humid
afternoons, when nothing seems to move,
there're sounds which seem familiar –
an infant's tender mouth sucking
a careful breast, or small feet shuffling across
a dark room on the upper floor.

I see the dust of my father's year rise
from that corner where my son plays
with toys and slow time.
Whose lean fingers run through
his casual hair so affectionately?
Is someone, homeless and distant
over the years, watching him too?

Midnight Consolings

These are different in tone and theme
from the ones that we prepare
so discreetly during the day.
More from the heart, from
that corner where it keeps its
dark promises secure from our
habitual wishes. The cry
that wakes from sleep couldn't be
left alone so easily.
At a different time, it would've
found its end, perhaps in a game
of words or a play of eyes.
But now, in the dark, it is
different. Louder, less precise,
asking for nothing.
Our voices soften at these times,
as if they had learnt something
from the night –
its slow meditative course over
houses and streets, its pure spontaneity.
The residual dreams hover before
our invisible eyes, urging us
to pause and listen
to the reasonless cry, now diffusing
into our nights. Our bodies
are half-dreaming still, while
our generous words issue from
a place far within this night.

Something Else
Remembering Raymond Carver

There's always something else to these lines,
always someone behind you, watching.

You and the women and men who are elsewhere, sharing
our children's request to be near them, always.

The things that you use every day
without prior thought, the bed on which

every night you await your sleep,
your very own hours of the night,

your ill-timed sleep, desired rest of a lifetime –
there's always something else to these,

something other than ourselves
or objects we pretend to possess.

There're times when we feel something else
slowly coming to its fruition and flourish

through us, accomplishing its greenness
in the leaves' abandon, smiling

through the lean dead branches of an old
banyan tree, now waiting for its conclusion.

At the end of a period of defiant cheer, when
we lie exhausted, thinking what other line

might return us our plain human pride,
it hangs above us, smiling at our absences.

Who are we to think of others anyway,
or even ourselves, our children and friends,

our days and nights? It seems
all of them belong elsewhere, only

faintly nurturing that place's true character,
maturing into nothing beyond their own frail forms.

Something is always missing in the things
we use, the persons we care for –

something that teases us to believe
that we've come to the end of things

in its absence, amid its withdrawing ways.
Something which caused these lines,

pushed every word to a place that was
a lie long before it took its stanzaic place.

At this time, elsewhere, a lone sparrow
is calling out for someone who isn't

anywhere around, a slight voice speaking to
itself, consuming each moment of its mistaken time.

You know, it's always something else,
something other than the words in these lines.

from Sea Breeze

1

Hold your breath and watch:
the strong whisper runs over
the total blue uninterruptedly.

Now, don't think about it, spare a moment:
it shows itself at where your eyes can go;
the final blue shakes a little at its touch.

It sails over the seawater, its large features
hover, fall, melt, and then are born again;
it fulfils its slow dance towards the beach.

Look how it makes the last waters feel
the love of my waiting fingers,
how the sun filters a rainbow.

I hold the colours wrapped round my fingers.
Suddenly they are blown away; I wait for your touch.

2

It plays over the patient water
in little waves of sight; near the land's end
and the water's, it sucks in the quiet of the sea.

Slight unremembered hills
emerge like wishes and dissolve
in my eyes and the next blue.

At a different place, it visits
the dark deep green where a thread of light
is left alone; the forest roars.

Here, it arrives at my lips
with a salty solid touch; love's tears
are referred back to their old places.

With a loud trick it sends the landscape into my mouth;
I munch it as I would grapes or kisses.

Grandmother's Soliloquy

Now, within me, the blood moves
into the heart of my years,
where memory is so alive,
so persistent and alert.

Now it seems as though I might not know
the shape of tomorrow's wind,
through the coconut tree that I planted
with loving care not long ago.

Although, during the sluggish first hours
of every morning, a hope is quietly born –
that I might live on to name your
unborn son, hold his small voice in mine.

But your private and abstract faces
seem to believe in different things,
as if this last breathing minute weren't
really mine, but somebody else's.

TISHANI DOSHI

(*b.* 1975)

Tishani Doshi was born in 1975 in Madras to Welsh-Gujarati parents. She was educated at Queens College, North Carolina, and Johns Hopkins University, and worked for five years with the dancer and choreographer Chandralekha. The poems in her first book *Countries of the Body* are formal evocations of dislocated private space, where no latitudes apply except those of the senses. The title sestina's rhyme words – *love life own dress country strangers* – are revealing insights into the poem's obsessions: '…like the ruin of a country / In such despair it cannot name the names for love. / Your wife steps in…' The book won her the Forward Prize for Best First Collection in 2006. She lives in Madras.

Countries of the Body

For the way the moon rose in the sky last night my love –
Orange and eerie like a scene from a parallel life
Where we are married with children of our own
And your wife is the lady with the crimson dress
With ruffles down her breasts, sleeping in a country
Of dreams while we dance through a room of strangers.

She's the stranger in the park, the stranger
Who follows me home, taking apart the loveless
Night. She sees me waver from country to country,
Adjusting the curtains so no one can see this life
Where the sky moves in and out of the world, dressed
Like a starlet in stockings on streets of her own.

Here are the adulterers playing games of their own:
Husbands and wives by river banks, unmasking strangers –
As in the movies where one body undresses
The other, strips it bare like a blue gum tree, loves –
With markings, territories; disconnects life
So it's impossible to put back the countries

Where they used to belong. These bodies of countries –
They are our tracks of line and dirt, our own
Set of timeless days in the park. They play out. A life
Always plays out with somebody watching. The stranger
In the shadows spying while a man and woman make love.
See, the fingers move up the seam of crimson dress,

Part, like bruised wings of a butterfly. And the dress –
Shorn of its layers – lies like the ruin of a country
In such despair it cannot name the names for love.
Your wife steps in, pulls the dress over her hips, her own
Discs of bone and flesh. *Where've you been to stranger?*
The dress mutters, as it slides under the floor of my life –

Cracks the thing apart, hinges on your wife; her life
Swimming back into the sky as the moon dresses
The night in orange. See how light falls, licks at the stranger;
How two women will lead each other out of a country
To sort out wombs, scars, faces. Exchange the other's for her own –
Pull two ends of a curtain open, empty out the rooms of love.

Pangs for the Philanderer

I miss you – your glittering life
And marcasite eyes.
Where I am now, it is all made of nylon;
Smelling of talcum powder and envy,
Maudlin curtains and stockings,
Serrated bed covers,
Rooms denuded from pleasure.

The day softens.
The whole day, now that I hold
It up in the cracked light
Of the windows, is legendary
And alone, making its way in haste
To the scene by the water.

If I remove one of the pieces
Where the shoreline of her face
Is unfolding like crimson branches;
The green swimsuit glowing –
Evanescent and sylvan –
You might still be here:
Distant, unattainable.

At the Rodin Museum

Rilke is following me everywhere
With his tailor-made suits
And vegetarian smile.

He says because I'm young,
I'm always beginning,
And cannot know love.

He sees how I'm a giant piece
Of glass again, trying
To catch the sun

In remote corners of rooms,
Mountain tops, uncertain
Places of light.

He speaks of the cruelty
Of hospitals, the stillness
Of cathedrals,

Takes me through bodies
And arms and legs
Of such extravagant size,

The ancient sky burrows in
With all the dead words
We carry and cannot use.

He holds up mirrors
From which our reflections fall –
Half-battered existences,

Where we lose ourselves
For the sake of the other,
And the others still to come.

Homecoming

I forgot how Madras loves noise –
Loves neighbours and pregnant women
And Gods and babies

And Brahmins who rise
Like fire hymns to sear the air
With habitual earthquakes.

How funeral processions clatter
Down streets with drums and rose-petals,
Dancing death into deafness.

How vendors and cats make noises
Of love on bedroom walls and alleyways
Of night, operatic and dark.

How cars in reverse sing Jingle Bells
And scooters have larynxes of lorries.
How even colour can never be quiet.

How fisherwomen in screaming red –
With skirts and incandescent third eyes
And bangles like rasping planets

And Tamil women on their morning walks
In saris and jasmine and trainers
Can shred the day and all its skinny silences.

I forgot how a man dying under the body
Of a tattered boat can ask for promises;
How they can be as soundless as the sea

On a wounded day, altering the ground
Of the earth as simply as the sun filtering through –
The monsoon rain dividing everything.

The Day We Went to the Sea

The day we went to the sea
Mothers in Madras were mining
The Marina for missing children.
Thatch flew in the sky, prisoners
Ran free, houses danced like danger
In the wind. I saw a woman hold
The tattered edge of the world
In her hand, look past the temple
Which was still standing, as she was –
Miraculously whole in the debris of gaudy
South Indian sun. When she moved
Her other hand across her brow,
In a single arcing sweep of grace,
It was as if she alone could alter things,
Bring us to the wordless safety of our beds.

Evensong
(after John Burnside)

It's moments like this
        when the animals down by the river
are singing their lament for rain –

when fractured pieces of Canterbury
        begin to show themselves in Madras

in cloisters and coconut husks
    miracle windows of glass

It's moments like this
    I hear you on Pilgrims' Stairs

pinning the day's despair
    to the underbelly of dusk

By nightfall
    when the mosquitoes have retreated

and you've parted the skies
    for cathedral spires to rise

You'll have chanted our promise
    of togetherness
repeated it like hollows worn in stone

But it is nothing –
    this song or our communion

Less than what the animals share
    as they walk to the river bank in slow repair

stopping to lick each other's wounds

No bonds to tie them
    to the smell of certain skin
        certain hair

EUNICE DE SOUZA

(b. 1940)

Born in 1940 in Pune, Maharashtra, Eunice de Souza taught in the English Department at St Xavier's College in Bombay for 31 years. Over four influential books of poems she invented a mode of address that prized immediacy above form. Her poems – with their dancing, epigrammatic punchlines – use short stanzas of seemingly unadorned speech to offer both sarcasm and tenderness, sometimes within the same sentence; and they have been imitated by a generation of younger poets. She is an editor of anthologies and a writer of novellas, and has come to represent a kind of writing by Indian women that is unsentimental, unconventional, and 'spiky with wit'. She lives in Bombay.

Eunice de Souza, Santa Cruz, Bombay, 1998

Poem for a Poet

It pays to be a poet.
You don't have to pay prostitutes.

Marie has spiritual thingummies.
Write her a poem about the
Holy Ghost. Say:
'Marie, my frequent sexual encounters
represent more than an attempt
to find mere physical fulfilment.
They are a poet's struggle to
transcend the self
and enter into
communion
with the world.'

Marie's eyes will glow.
Pentecostal flames will descend.
The Holy Ghost will tremble inside her.
She will babble in strange tongues:

'O Universal Lover
in a state of perpetual erection!
Let me too enter into
communion with the world
through thee.'

Ritu loves music and
has made a hobby of psychology.
Undergraduate, and better still,
uninitiated.
Write her a poem about woman flesh.
Watch her become oh so womanly and grateful.
Giggle with her about
horrid mother keeping an eye
on the pair, the would-be babes
in the wood, and everything will be
so idyllic, so romantic
so *intime*.

Except that you, big deal,
are forty-six
and know what works
with whom.

Miss Louise

She dreamt of descending
curving staircases
ivory fan aflutter
of children in sailor suits
and organza dresses
till the dream rotted her innards
but no one knew:
innards weren't permitted
in her time.

Shaking her graying ringlets:
'My girl, I can't even
go to Church you know
I unsettle the priests
so completely. Only yesterday
that handsome Fr Hans was saying,
'Miss Louise, I feel an arrow
through my heart.'
But no one will believe me
if I tell them. It's always
been the same. They'll say,
'Yes Louisa, we know, professors
loved you in your youth,
judges in your prime.'

This Swine of Gadarene

This swine of Gadarene
has stopped his hurtle
to the sea.
No. The demons
haven't lost interest in him.
He feels
posthumous.
Behind him
the dead land.
Ahead
the dead sea.
For a little while yet, he says,
let me chew stubble.

Women in Dutch Painting

The afternoon sun is on their faces.
They are calm, not stupid,
pregnant, not bovine.
I know women like that
and not just in paintings –
an aunt who did not answer her husband back
not because she was plain
and Anna who writes poems
and hopes her avocado stones
will sprout in the kitchen.
Her voice is oatmeal and honey.

Pilgrim

The hills crawl with convoys.
Slow lights wind round
and down the dark ridges
to yet another
termite city.

The red god rock
watches all that passes.
He spoke once.
The blood-red boulders
are his witness.
God rock, I'm a pilgrim.
Tell me –
Where does the heart find rest?

She And I

Perhaps he never died.
We mourned him separately,
in silence,
she and I.

Suddenly, at seventy-eight
she tells me his jokes,
his stories, the names of
paintings he loved,
and of some forgotten place
where blue flowers fell.

I am afraid
for her, for myself,
but can say nothing.

The Road

As we came out of the church
into the sunlight
a row of small girls
in first communion dresses
I felt the occasion demanded
lofty thoughts.

I remember
only my grandmother
smiling at me.

They said
now she wears lipstick
now she is a Bombay girl
they said, your mother is lonely.
Nobody said, even the young must live.

In school
I clutched Sister Flora's skirt
and cried for my mother
who taught across the road.
Sister Flora is dead.
The school is still standing.
I am still learning
to cross the road.

Unfinished Poem

I found your unfinished poem:
There's a sun in the sky
and you are near me
and all should be right with the world.
But something hasn't set
(and it had better not be the sun!)
I could pinch a line from Neruda for you:
'I want / to do with you what spring does /
with the cherry trees.'
There you have it: the apparent ease
of love and poetry.

Outside Jaisalmer

I

The sea receded. The dunes remember.
Trees have turned quietly to stone.

I watch two men bend intently
over a pawnbroker's scales

and think of you:

Walled city. Dead kings.
The tarred road melts where we stand.

II

Sixty miles from the border
stories:
the general on the other side
doesn't want war, he wants to
cultivate his poppy fields.

We're here to watch the sun set.
Birds fly in formation, and jets.

III

The life of the hero on the scabbard of a sword.
Faces in profile, erect penis in profile,
the colours raw, the rug in detail.

The milk he's washed in has turned a little sour.
Her hand touches her veil.
He looks into her eyes
she looks into his.
Behind the lattice work the waiting women
cry oh and stroke their breasts.

IV

We clatter over five river beds
broad, sweeping, dry
tour potters' weavers' villages
and Kuldera, deserted in protest
against a greedy king.
An old man brings out a few fossils
and says, Once there was a sea.
(A hundred and eighty million years ago
but he doesn't know that.)

The children say hello
and look at my shoes.

SALEEM PEERADINA

(*b.* 1944)

Saleem Peeradina was born in 1944 in Bombay. Like Dom Moraes, H. Masud Taj and
Amit Chaudhuri, he lived in Bandra, a Bombay suburb he has described in his work. He
published two books of poems and edited *Contemporary Indian Poetry in English* (Macmillan,
1972), before emigrating to the United States at the age of 44. His prose memoir, *Ocean in
My Yard*, with its bleak description of immigrant life in the United States, is a form of
'Diaspora Blues', in Bruce King's phrase. He teaches at Siena Heights University, in Adrian,
Michigan.

Still Life

Face-up in a crook of brown, the river
breathes. Out of the sun-lit air
from the rim of a small town's still repose

Her ankles ringing the quiet path
a woman descends.

The river mumbles, stirs
where the woman bends, as if
the ripples were shifting circles

Of some dream the pot displaced.
Her people wake, imagining she brings

The stream: unaware of the water's
separate consciousness swinging into shape
on her hip.

Behind her the river curls up
to the brim in heavy-lidded sleep.

Landscape with Locomotive

For the man under the bridge
Into whose vision two buffalo calves
Flung off the track, plunge from the sky,
The thud is like a jab in the crotch. His job

He knows is to raise a shout. In a joint
Flutter the storks jump as the wave
Of a tremor hits the ribcages of cows grazing.
Leaping out of sight, a shadow

Chases a dog. For the crows who make capital
Out of anything unusual, this is an event
To report. For children, it is an invention better than
Any play. Banging clothes on the stream's floor,

The women stitch a rumor in their talk:
Too muffled for the pile of houses
To cock their ears; too distant
For the blue mountain to show any changes in colour.

The sky exerts its weight in favour of
Not reacting at all. The trees saw it coming
But rushing to the spot was beyond their power.
The green tips the field has pushed up

Were sucking the light with their eyes closed.
The patch of sunflowers as a witness confuses fact
With melodrama. Having been there the longest, the stones
Prefer to hold their tongues knowing this to be

Keki Daruwalla, Napean Sea Road, Bombay, 1997

A well-rehearsed accident. The keeper of animals,
The mother of all calves sobs inconsolably:
The hurt has entered her like news
That happens elsewhere but belongs to her.

One chewing a fruit asks another shifting in his seat
What is wrong? In a hand-mirror held delicately
Between the toes, one examines the contents
Of his nose and tells another how it happened.

On a slope a mile away, a figure
With stick and blanket looks up to see people
Swarming round a train on the bridge. In perfect silence
He tells himself a story with two endings.

KEKI DARUWALLA

(*b*. 1937)

Keki Daruwalla was born in 1937 in Lahore into a Parsi family. His father was a professor
of English literature. He too read English at the University of Punjab, but, at the age of 21,
joined the Indian Police Service, and retired as a senior officer with Indian intelligence. His
poems – whether they are set in modern India or ancient Greece – take a forbidding view
of human nature. In an essay on Daruwalla's first book, *Under Orion* (Writers Workshop,
1970), Nissim Ezekiel wrote, '[s]uch a bitter, scornful, satiric tone has never been heard
before'. It was a tone Daruwalla refined over nine books of poems, three of short stories,
and a life spent in law enforcement. In later poems he tempered his severity with a grudging
acceptance of human frailty: 'Decay sets in with birth; / We rust like iron, we splinter like
glass.' He lives in New Delhi.

The Poseidonians
(*after Cavafy*)

> (*We behave like*) *the Poseidonians in the Tyrrhenian Gulf, who although
> of Greek origin, became barbarised as Tyrrhenians or Romans and
> changed their speech and the customs of their ancestors. But they observe
> one Greek festival even to this day; during this they gather together and
> call up from memory their ancient names and customs, and then lamenting
> loudly to each other and weeping, they go away.*
>
> ATHENIOS, Deipnosophistai, Book 14, 31A (632)

All it takes to blight a language
is another sun. It's not burn
that does it, or chill, or the way
woods straggle down the hills, or seas

167

curl along the shingled coast.
It is the women, cowering
in fear, whom the soldiers,
as they clamber down the boats,
first reassure and then marry.

They are faithful, good with grain,
at baking bread and fermenting wine
and unscrambling the fish shoals from the meshes.
They get the goddesses wrong sometimes (but so what?)
confusing mother with daughter.
And there are minor errors
in ritual and sacrifice,
in lustration oils and libations.

A few seasons teach the man
that his woman's omen birds are always right;
her fears travel down the bloodstream
and a new language emerges from the placenta.

What does one do with a thought
that embarks on one script and lands on another?
A hundred years go by, perhaps two hundred,
living with the Tyrrhenians and the Etruscans,
and they discover there is more to a language
than merely words, that every act,
from making wine to making love
filters through a different prism of sound,
and they have forgotten the land they set sail from
and the syllables that seeded their land.

What do they do, except once a year
at a lyre-and-lute festival,
Greek to the core, with dance and contests,
grope for memories in the blood,
like Demeter, torch in hand,
looking for her netherworld daughter?
And weep a little for the Greece they have lost
and reflect on this gulf of years which has proved
wider than the Tyrrhenian gulf,
and the hiatus between the languages,
wider than the Aegean?
What can they do, but weep for Agora
and Acropolis, for ever left behind;
and reflect, how three centuries distant
from the Ionian coast,
they have been barbarised by Rome?

Roof Observatory

He moved past the slab of damp air over damp ground,
past the two whining hinges of the rusted gate,
past rows of eucalypti with black leaves
and white leaves – moon on one, moon-shadow on the other;
past the duplicate patios, onto the double stairs
and into the hall of mirrors where he found himself
infinitely mirrored in a still moment of receding reflections.
Then onto the circular antechamber
with only himself and his shadow in attendance,
to the roof where the double desolation of the garden
and the circular silence of the villa interior
sank into him like nightwaters filling up a forgotten tank;
till stepping on to a ladder, bone and ladder creaking,
he climbed into the quiet of his observatory;
where the solitudes were so large
that all else diminished in scale,
where the telescope hummed with planets
and the firmament fermented with astral fires,
and the glass lid on the barrel
multiplied the black spaces between the stars;
where at last, he thought, he was at one with,
and yet confronting, the universe.

But even there, Borges, the universe of your mind
was as large as the universe you were looking into.

The Glass-blower

1

He knew about glass and its history:
beads of the vintage of Amenhotep;
the Niniveh tablets of Assurbanipal;
blowpipe, marver, pontil, each successive step

which fire took to make clay transparent.
'Glass is not in the family,' he said.
'My forefathers were alchemists, sublimators
of baser alloys like zinc and lead;

believers in a four-cornered universe
of water and air, earth and fire.
They spent a lifetime with bellows, furnaces.
They were metallurgists, but they aspired

to mysticism. Alchemy for them was not
some quack technique harnessed to greed of wealth.
The goal was transmuting the earthy
into the celestial, sickness into health.

Now things are changed; a philosophy slips out
as an age loses its teeth. Nothing holds fast.
Decay sets in with birth;
we rust like iron, we splinter like glass.

2

We walked past litter to his boiler room
where a reed-thin boy in a tattered vest
and a lost face dipped his blowing iron
into a small vat of silica paste.

The furnace fitted with fire-clay pot and flue,
crackled and hissed. The stilt legs of the boy
glowed faint red on the shin-bone as he put
the blowing iron to his lips and blew.

His cheeks turned to hemispheres, fully blown;
his neck corded and veined, struggled up to the nape
with his exhalations. A blob ballooned
at the pipe's other end and froze into shape.

A smell of burnt resin, fossil gum, miracles,
of just-fallen lightning came from the bowl,
as it should, with clay altered to replicate
the luminous transparencies of the soul.

The first time men saw this state of mist,
this veil that veiled nothing – O glorious deception –
and glass cool into color of space, did they cry out
'This is no object, it is thought, perception!'

Wolf

Fire-lit
half silhouette and half myth
the wolf circles my past
treading the leaves into a bed
till he sleeps, black snout
on extended paws.

Black snout on sulphur body
he nudged his way
into my consciousness.
Prowler, wind-sniffer, throat-catcher,
his cries drew a ring
around my night;
a child's night is a village
on the forest's edge.

My mother said
his ears stand up
at the fall of dew
he can sense a shadow
move across a hedge
on a dark night;
he can sniff out
your approaching dreams;
there is nothing
that won't be lit up
by the dark torch of his eyes.

The wolves have been slaughtered now.
A hedge of smoking gun-barrels
rings my daughter's dreams.

Map-maker

1

Perhaps I'll wake up on some alien shore
in the shimmer of an aluminium dawn,
to find the sea talking to itself
and rummaging among the lines I've drawn;
looking for something, a voyager perhaps,

gnarled as a thorn tree in whose loving hands,
these map lines of mine, somnambulant,
will wake and pulse and turn to shoreline, sand.

The spyglass will alight on features I've forecast –
cape, promontory – he'll feel he's been here,
that voyaging unlocks the doorways of the past.

And deep in the night, in the clarity of dream,
the seafarer will garner his rewards,
raking in his islands like pebbles from the stream.

2

Does the world need maps, where sign and symbol,
standing as proxies, get worked into scrolls?
You see them, mountain chains with raingods in their armpits
and glaciers locked like glass-slivers in their folds.
Desert, scrub, pasture – do they need shading?
They're all there for the eye to apprehend.
A family of cactus and camelthorn tells you
where one begins and the other ends.

These questions confound me, I'd rather paint
for a while – a ship on the skyline,
or cloud-shadow moving like a spreading stain.
Yet they live, pencil strokes that speak for rain
and thunder; and die – maplines ghosting round
a cycloned island that has gone under.

3

Forget markings, forget landfall and sea.
Go easy Man, I tell myself; breathe.
Gulls will mark the estuary for you,
bubbles will indicate where the swamps seethe.
Map the wrinkles on the ageing skin of love.
Forget Eastings, Northings – they stand for order.
Cry, if you must, over that locust-line
flayed open into a barbarised border.

Mark a poem that hasn't broken forth, map the undefined,
the swamp within, the hedge between love and hate.
Forget the coastal casuarina line.

Reefs one can handle. It's lust that seeks
out its quarry that one cannot map, nor that
heaving salt of desire that floods the creeks.

4

If you map the future, while a millennium
moves on its hinges, you may find
the present turned to an anachronism.
This too is important – what is yours and mine,
the silk of these shared moments. But having stuck
to love and poetry, heeding the voice of reason;
and experiencing the different textures of
a season of love and love's eternal season,

I put a clamp on yearning, shun latitudes, renounce form.
And turn my eye to the far kingdom
of bloodless Kalinga battling with a storm.
Dampen your fires, turn from lighthouse, spire, steeple.
Forget maps and voyaging, study instead
this parched earth horoscope of a brown people.

JANE BHANDARI
(*b*. 1944)

Jane Bhandari was born in Edinburgh in 1944 and has lived in India for four decades. There is nothing recognisably British about the poem selected here. Others are recognisably Indian, they are situated on the streets of Bombay or in the city's apartment blocks, and they 'cross' – or make gestures at crossing – 'all cultural lines'. She lives in Bombay.

Steel Blue

1

The sea under rain-clouds
Was blued steel,
And the black boats
Flying orange and magenta flags,
Cut silver streaks in the blue.
A white line of rain
Divided the islands from the sea.
The sea milk-white
The sea dark blue
The sea carved by boats
Into silver scimitars against the dark.
The lighthouse rising
Out of the dark and woolly blue,
The horizon a blue line,

The far islands clear and blue,
Then fainter, diminished by mist,
But still blue.

2

I have not enough blue
To describe the boats
Canopied in bright cobalt
Against the drenching rain:
The big water-tank of the harbour
Also bright blue, to signify holding water,
And the sky shot with the burnished blue
Of heated steel. *Watch*, my father said:
*At a certain temperature, the steel
Colours straw, then blue, and finally,
Black. Nothing will change it back.*
And I, watching the glowing steel
Of the clock hands being blued,
Understood the significance
Of an irreversible change. That change
Was magical, the silver changing to straw,
And suddenly flashing iridescent blue
That became the navy of a raven's wing.

3

The polished steel of the sea darkens
To the colour of the alchemist's stone,
Brushed by the cold fire of sky,
And shadowed by clouds
Walking tiptoe across water
Blue as the steel; small islands
Floating densely, hard little rocks
Suspended from a shifting horizon.
A sky pillowed with clouds
And shot with blue:
Against the sky, birds scatter blue
Into the sea from their wings
With every shift and turn,
Carve their own scimitar lines in the air
Above the boats that cut
Through the steel-hard sea:
The effort palpable below, but above
The lines cut effortlessly
Into the blue, glance off the billows
Of the cotton-wool cloud pillows
Foaming along the horizon.

Blue, too, in windows reflecting sky,
And one tall building, the glass building
Full of sky, broken by other buildings,
This too, blue, and blue, and blue.

4

I have run out of blue.
But the alchemist sky
Still transmutes the sea
Into blue steel, dented by sun,
Then wiped out by rain,
A wet sponge leaving only
A blank page, emptiness,
Soft whiteness wiping across the steel blue:
But when clouds darken the water
After the sky has fallen into it,
And the horizon
Advances and retreats with the rain,
The sea is the alchemist of the sky,
Transmuting colour and time.

5

My father prepared the whitely shining steel,
Rubbing it till it shone like a cloud,
A soft sheeny white that belied the steel.
The blue suddenly spread across
Like a jay's wing, a peacock's tail,
The alchemy of heat on steel
Transmuting the cloud-white sheen
To the dark intense blue of the sea under sun.

6

I wish not for the unchanging blue of the steel,
But for the possibility of change: to reflect
The blue of the sky within my waters,
And change as the sea changes, eternally.
The little boats are tethered to the shore
By invisible strings, returning endlessly to the land,
Like young goats to their mother.
Thus I return to my old haunts, drawn
By those invisible threads casting a spider's web
Across half the world, their pull as strong
As the strongest rope, but as delicate
As the spider's thread, and as sticky –
They do not let go easy, each pull is pain,

Taking me back to my childhood
To parents, to old loves, to children, again
Back to old memories I would rather forget.
But I remember: unwilling, I remember
The child that went far away,
But always returned to the memory of blue.

The clock-hands were set in place.
The clock was wound.
Time moved along blued-steel tracks,
Around and around.

ARUNDHATHI SUBRAMANIAM
(*b*. 1967)

Born in 1967 in Bombay where she still lives, Arundhathi Subramaniam's poems commute between home and the world. Many are set in her native city, for instance on a 5.46 Andheri local as the narrator returns home. In these poems *home* is a complex idea, not necessarily the sunny dwelling associated with an Indian householder, but a place of some ambiguity – 'like this body, / so alien when I try to belong, / so hospitable / when I decide I'm just visiting.'

To the Welsh Critic Who Doesn't Find Me Identifiably Indian

You believe you know me,
wide-eyed Eng Lit type
from a sun-scalded colony,
reading my Keats – or is it yours –
while my country detonates
on your television screen.

You imagine you've cracked
my deepest fantasy –
oh, to be in an Edwardian vicarage,
living out my dharma
with every sip of dandelion tea
and dreams of the weekend jumble sale...

You may have a point.
I know nothing about silly mid-offs,
I stammer through my Tamil,
I've worn lipstick to protest meetings,
and I long for a nirvana

that is hermetic,
odour-free,
bottled in Switzerland,
money-back-guaranteed.

This business about language,
how much of it is mine,
how much yours,
how much from the mind,
how much from the gut,
how much is too little,
how much too much,
how much from the salon,
how much from the slum,
how I say verisimilitude,
how I say Brihadaranyaka,
how I say vaazhapazham –
it's all yours to measure,
the pathology of my breath,
the halitosis of gender,
my homogenised plosives,
about as rustic
as a mouth-freshened global village.

Arbiter of identity,
remake me as you will.
Write me a new alphabet of danger,
a new patois to match
the Chola bronze of my skin.
Teach me how to come of age
in a literature you have bark-scratched
into scripture.
Smear my consonants
with cow-dung and turmeric and godhuli.
Pity me, sweating,
rancid, on the other side of the counter.
Stamp my papers,
lease me a new anxiety.
Grant me a visa
to the country of my birth.
Teach me how to belong,
the way you do,
on every page of world history.

Home

Give me a home
that isn't mine,
where I can slip in and out of rooms
without a trace,
never worrying
about the plumbing,
the colour of the curtains,
the cacophony of books by the bedside.
A home that I can wear lightly,
where the rooms aren't clogged
with yesterday's conversations,
where the self doesn't bloat
to fill in the crevices.

A home, like this body,
so alien when I try to belong,
so hospitable
when I decide I'm just visiting.

5.46, Andheri Local

In the women's compartment
of a Bombay local
we seek
no personal epiphanies.
Like metal licked by relentless acetylene
we are welded –
dreams, disasters,
germs, destinies,
flesh and organza,
odours and ovaries.
A thousand-limbed
million-tongued, multi-spoused
Kali on wheels.

When I descend
I could choose
to dice carrots
or dice a lover.
I postpone the latter.

ANJUM HASAN

(b. 1972)

Born in 1972, in Shillong, Meghalaya, Anjum Hasan received an MA in philosophy from the North-Eastern Hill University. She lives and works in Bangalore, in South India, a sub-continent's distance from where she was born. In her poetry and fiction, the fact of travel affects only the traveler's immediate surroundings, for 'the expectation of the senses remains the same' and '[a]lways the 'where' of where you are is a place in the head / established through skin.' The poems in this selection convey a sense of conflicted nostalgia, of memory mixed with the recollected desire to leave a place where '[l]ife's not moving'.

Shy

I remember the urgent knocking of the
heart's small fist before a school elocution,
or running into a nun round a corner
and made idiot by that prim mouth,
those flawless skirts. There were
agonised deputations to the sitting room
at home, to ask some muddy-booted,
cigarette-smelling visitor about tea.

Shy.
That quivering emotion belonged perhaps
to quiet bedrooms on winter afternoons
in near-forgotten, hill-encircled towns
where children lisped tentative answers
to the questions of some serene matriarch,
and ate, anguished by undisguisable crunching,
the brittle butter biscuits from her tins.
That slow ordeal between the window's lace
and the fire burning in the grate
was the established manner of being young.

To be shy now is odd or impolite: no one
expects it. There's no longer the implication
of grace in being reserved. Yet doggedly
I remain the girl once bent over a shirt
on Sundays, ironing alone through afternoons
ill-defined by the monsoon's whimsical light.
It was only when coloured dream matched
the pressing to perfection of stiffened cuff
or pleated skirt, that I possessed all the clarity,
all the beauty in the world.

To the Chinese Restaurant

(for Daisy)

We come in here from the long afternoon
stretched over the town's sloping roofs,
its greasy garages and ice-cream parlours,
its melancholic second-hand bookshops
with their many missing pages.

Life's not moving.

We sit at a red table, among the dragons,
near the curtained-off street-facing windows
with their months-old orangeade.
Out in the streets there are schoolboys with
their ties askew and the garish fruit-sellers.

We eat more than we need to. We eat
so that our boredom's no longer dangerous,
so that from the comfort of soup,
with the minor pleasures of chopsuey,
we can fend off the memory of cities unvisited,
unknown and unknowable affairs,
people with never-fading lipstick and
confident gestures who we will never be.

One day soon we'll be running,
our lives will be like the blur seen from a bus,
and we won't read each other's letters thrice.
But right there we're young, we count
our money carefully, we laugh so hard
and drop our forks.

We are plucked from sadness there
in that little plastic place with the lights
turned low, the waiters stoned from doing nothing,
the smells of ketchup and eternally frying onions.

March

Between the gravestones,
going with flowers,
newspapers, minutes
in its teeth,
the March wind
suddenly returns
and then starts off again,
with some other
fragment of life
pressed to its thin chest.
Its mad rhythms
confuse the trees.

This wind is the
language
of indecision that
winter speaks when
it opens its slow mouth
to let April in.
Dark vacancies of forest fire,
shifting planes of pollen:
cold fills one window,
a sort of spring the other.

Jealousy Park

Clumsy, gleeful, accident-prone, running
from two-wheeler parking lots to the green-
as-jealousy park, with swings and seesaws
that come to them in their afternoon naps,
where determined walkers march in circles
in the rain-mottled September evening light.

They move in an animal sort of dreaming
that can leap out at a twitch of danger
and return at once to innocence and greed.
Everything else is suddenly in contrast –
traffic roaring past their fragility,
adults hardened by their somnambulism.

My baby hunger melts into those other
faces of unfinished childhood: the longing
to teach geometry to one's 13-year-old
self, give a haircut to oneself at 10.
I am a pretend adult who wants the upside-
down world of both to be and have a child.

So when we talk about *them*, the quiet,
imaginary ones, the clarified versions of
our cluttered selves, we are already jealous
green like the green-as-jealousy park
about our secret reciprocity,
the code-words and the solitude.

And I walk past jealousy park with its
orange seesaws and its subtle contests,
watching them, knowing that nothing
prepares one for this freedom to extract
from one's memories and confusions,
something this exact, this real.

Rain

You will hear it waking to the roar of a ceiling fan,
in the rustling of dry palm leaves, in pebbles
pouring from a lorry onto the dusty street.
You will hear it in the last aeroplane of night
(whose sound you will mistake for thunder),
in the alphabets of the birds, in indignant pressure cookers.
You will look for it in the evening, searching for one cloud
among tremendous shadows, and at night when it might come
from a great distance and touch the city with a new light.

You won't find it in the few grey leaves of March
or behind the thin red crescent burning itself out
on a fevered patch of sky. Your hair will
grow electric with the dry heat of the day,
your dreams shot through with the silver lightning
of monsoon nights, the blue-green nights celebrated
by crickets, the mountain nights where fate
is linked to umbrellas.

But Venus' eye is clear here.
You will look for it in refrigerators at night,
slice water-melons with its taste on your tongue –
unfeeling, red-hearted fruit – and buy cucumbers in despair.
You will almost forget the sadness of mist, but remember
how quickly mirrors darkened and streets turned grim,
and wait for the same blanket to be fastened over the sky
and change the quality of this harsh, unvarying light.

Always the 'where' of where you are is a place in the head
established through skin, and you recognise the address
not in numbers or names but through familiar patterns
of bird-song, traffic, shadows, lanes.

And when you go away only envelopes speak of
the city where everyone thinks you now stay,
for the expectation of the senses remains the same,
for years remains the same: bewildered by dry winds
in April, aching for rain.

AMIT CHAUDHURI

(*b.* 1962)

Amit Chaudhuri's parents left East Bengal when Independence split India into two nations. He was born in Calcutta in 1962. For a time his family lived in the North Bombay suburb of Bandra, on St Cyril Road, where 'all the lanes that ran parallel to it were also named after saints, most of them as obscure as St Cyril'. He revisited the neighbourhood in a 2005 book of poems, a delayed debut volume that appeared after he had published five novels and established his reputation. His poetry and fiction share at least one quality: they are made in moments of stillness, with a rapt extremity of attention to the world. He is the editor of *The Picador Book of Modern Indian Literature* (2001) and lives in Calcutta.

from St Cyril Road Sequence

1 *Midday*

The incantatory beating of a hammer
against a rock, and two birds cleave the field of air.
The sun sits in the garden, while the gardener
cuts and piles up grass, and leaves the flowers
secure, untouched. A woman sweeps a courtyard,
unsettling bedded, impermanent blankets of dust
and silence. And I'm lulled by the sound of workmen

delving the road. Their cloudy, metal clanging
apotheosises rest, like a recurrent Chinese
gong. I can't see them – I think of their silhouettes
flashing in the heat, bodies bent like ciphers.
Each sound lacks permanence, each wakeful image,
in its sharp flowering and slow fading to a zero
in this white, sunwhite noon, is a constant loss
of itself, and then a recovery, a glowing echo
surfacing from a dark, centreless well.
Twice, with my sense-heavy eyes, I notice,
among a muffled world of toylike objects,
the tangent outline of a dragonfly
against a leaf, its wings whirring so fast
you can hardly see them unless you imagine
their balance between urgency and composure.
Catch one, and knot a thread around its end,
and you can fly it like a kite. Let it go,
and it'll glide off, diminishing with mournful elegance,
the thread lagging behind it like a vapour-
trail spuming from a jet ribboning the sky.
Meanwhile, I fall asleep. Like a film of dust
that's absorbed the seven colours, quietly, the dragonfly,
the cut grass, the echoing workmen, and a reticence
settle imperceptibly on my black pupils; these
are twice-born in my sleep; when I wake
the lonely road crumbles before my eyes.

2 *Sunday*

Morning, and the mist ripples back to the unexpected roofs
              like a flock of endless, white
gulls circling to rest. And a galaxy of dew and insect
              glistens, as trees arrive briefly
out of the moist darkness, and this slow-flowering steam
              wavers from my coffee cup. Then
the single bread of peace is broken and distributed this
              Sunday, peace broken into
pieces, and the fine, too-delicate crumbs rain on the earth
              where the earth opens like
a grateful palm. Never to have lived is best. And the second best
              is to grow old with the morning into
afternoon, and then to evening, when sundry shadows and gestures marry
              like the vanished divisions of a shut fan.
              This Sunday raptness, this biblical
quietude unlabouring in waves, the crows pre-arranged on the boughs, the leaves
              a parrot-green, and the flies relearning

a disciplined dance... No movement but this dance, no movement
but a mimicry of shadows. And no voice
to be heard but the newspaper's, as it crackles peremptorily in
an old man's tangled fingers.

5 *After Midnight*

Last night, the medallion moon was caught oddly
between sleek, glowing channels of telephone wire.
No one stirred, but a Pacific of lights went on burning
in the vacant porches, the garages. I imagined
an impassioned movement beneath the still surface,
as if ants were travelling by hidden routes under
the sleeping earth, or a fin was dipping again, again,
past the calm skin of water. Twice, I sensed hands,
behind windows, strike a match, and a swift badge of flame
open and shut like a hot mouth. Later, ghosts
of dead Christians, dead animals, returned to displace
a leaf, to push a gate, and to knock on the silence
of the living. A worried wind scuttled past the schoolyard,
shadows slept on gaping church benches. Meanwhile,
the stars blinked, small, valedictory beads of moisture
on a surface of melting glass. Then the watchman
sojourned through the lane, tapping the walls and the lampposts
with a stick straight and mutely resonant, startling,
no doubt, frogs and bandicoots in their undergrowth
by the gutter. Around him, the heavy trees bent their necks –
swans at the edge of a dark lake. I stood and listened
to the slow and solitary rhythm of his stick, as it spoke
and spoke again, then again, each brief pellet of sound,
insufficient, but accurate as a metronome keeping
time, while a reluctant child practises scales.
Eloquently, it faded, dim, repetitive, metallic,
tick... tick... tick... tick... in the purblind darkness
then nothing. Only the faint, circular ticking of my wristwatch,
where the white, radium-pointed arms on the grey dial
changed from minute to minute, conceiving morning

Nissim Ezekiel

This man, in a room full of papers
in the Theosophy Building,
still young at fifty-five
the centre of his small universe
told me, for fifteen minutes,
that my poems were 'derived'.
I was seventeen.
I listened only to the precision
of his Bombay accent, juxtaposed
in my mind with the syllables of his name.
In some ways, he did not disappoint.
I went out and had a cup of coffee
at an Udipi restaurant
and did not see him again
until seventeen years later in Paris
when he recognised my name
but had forgotten who I was.

SUBHASHINI KALIGOTLA
(*b*. 1969)

Born in 1969 in Visakhapatnam, Andhra Pradesh, Subhashini Kaligotla left India when she
was nine. She was raised in Kuwait and the United States, where she studied electrical
engineering and worked for a decade in the telecommunications industry. She gave up that
career to read for an MFA. The selection below includes a sequence of poems addressed to
god 'without a capital G', who may be a Hindu deity, or, just as likely, an Old Testament
one – silent, unforgiving, masculine. If India appears at all in these poems – *'my country?'* –
it is a blur of sense impressions glimpsed in passing, and the speaker's sense of it is conflicted,
complicated by distance. She is a doctoral student in art history at Columbia University in
New York City.

In Freezing Light the Chrysler Building

looks down this scrap of avenue, cold air churns
incense and *garam masala*. The immigrant *français* returns
to La Maison du Chocolat, Les Mignardises; I Curry

in a Hurry. Whorling in bins prodigal with rice,
daal from the peninsula, pistachios impastoed with spice
like Vincent's yellow house, turmeric,

186

fenugreek, saffron, *heeng* (*Stinkendes* in German), odors
I banned years ago from clothes, apartments, and hands,
redouble, rise up. Why can't my country – *my country?* –

conduct itself less exuberantly, aloofly,
like Chanel No. 5? Something withheld, say,
to lure the lover home.

Lepidoptera

(after El Greco's The Crucifixion with Two Donors*)*

You can't stop trawling his belly
for the navel pooled there like a fish;
the eye now follows the fallow cloth
yoking the hips to the swell

of calf on the lifted and twisted leg –
twisted (you remember) in pain;
the mind considers *mounted*, recalls
the display of Blue Morpho in a shop

on Valencia Street, the one you first
walked away from, where row after row
of glass cases lined the walls, a phalanx
of moths; but then you stepped in

(had anybody noticed?) as if to stroke
one arrested head and another, staining
your fingers lapis to compliment
the dead, fooled by mere simulacra:

straining thigh muscles, pinned arms
reaching skyward, and the body
already rigid from the ache.

from The Lord's Prayer

You see advantage in this recent gazing in your direction.
Nothing could be closer to falsehood. Since collecting

the faithful is vital to your traffic, perform
an easy feat. Why don't you?

Not one of your phony miracles. Not a stay
against memory or a nostrum for blindness.

No, a simple thing for one so used to ruining.
Learn, simply, to talk back.

At least consider my shame. Stop showing by not showing.

*

I wouldn't be flattered if I were you. There's no one here,
and these nights – cataracts, which pillars of tallow

couldn't melt or warm – show no relent, atomising
into filaments that outline the bridge. So I turn to you, and call…

No answer. Not even the dispatch of an echo.
Lord, how poor you are. How indifferent

to bulletins transmitted daily from this place.

*

Is this how you picked up your other acolytes?
Starve an animal and he will obey: learn your tricks,

jump through rings of fire, prance and, if you whistle,
pirouette on hind legs in a fluff pink tutu.

*

Talk is cheap, lord, and yours has grown cheaper by the hour.
Bargain basement. A flea market vending other people's junk.
But I won't let you keep me on souvenirs and garage sale glories.
I want to know. What have you done for me lately?
Send me a sign, a compass, a silver Corvette, anything,
lord, even an unreadable, inscrutable boy will do. I need you.

*

I took the bus from town. Traveled all day
in the heat without so much as an ice chip
for comfort. Then another two hours

to climb the hill. This is how you test devotion.
The nice black dress I put on for you
might as well be made of dust. And the other

desperate souls? Morons. Pushing and shoving
like cattle, as if this was some kind of cheap
fair or carnival. And you? You only listened

to the cripple – dragged up here by a friend,
wobbly on his knees, crying at the top of his lungs
(Who does he think he's fooling?), intruding

on the rest of us praying quietly: *Look at me,*
look at me, me, me, me, as if shouting
your pain means you suffer more. Father

in heaven, save me. Make me whole. Cure
my afflictions.

*

Build me a house, you said, fill it with oil lamps and keep them burning.
   Let the flowers be fresh and fragrant, pile the sweetmeats high
on silver platters, ring the bells and burn the camphor. Weave me

silks and muslins, fashion me girdles and armbands, powder the vermilion,
   paste the sandal and gather the cassia, compose eulogies, lord
you said, tune the instruments, beat the drums, caparison the beasts

of burden, polish the brass. Send in the dancing girls, invite the priests,
   light the sacred fires, pour the ghee and let the singing begin, call me
you said, beautiful wandering, call me blue-black, call me handsome

lord of the mountains, call me almond, call me thief, call me heart,
   call me honey, call me lover. Call me. Call me lord.

How Versatile the Heart

Moralising one instant; howling for a companion the next; then scheming – for
sex, wanting to snatch it anywhere, from anyone; also whining, like a teenager
... *whether I am thick, thin, or pimply, who would notice.* And yes, chirping.
Sometimes she chirps: she's grateful, for the life she has, the one she's lived,
et cetera. Ouf! What a metamorphoser. What a poseur. What a mess. Charting
such movements isn't easy. Astronomers couldn't do it. Call in the astrologer.
Find out which of her stars is ascending, and when.

How Xenophobic the Heart

How like a mad politician railing against the auslander. Keep him out, keep
him out, it hollers. Protect this sacrosanct. Smash that minar and stanch his
lust, let it not grow like a rogue in this soil. O, stop, stop, stop this pollution.
Offer fire-flower and camphor to the four directions. Where's the holy water?
Let it wash down from the mountain, flow from matted locks... O, protect this
Hindu woman from the Muslim invader.

Ascent to Calvary
(After Hieronymus Bosch's Christ Carrying the Cross*)*

He gives you two choices, the artist. In the right hand he holds
Deny the body. In the left: *Sink into the muck*. One hand holds up

Christ and the other points a finger at the senses. For god's ears,
he's made a cushion of hair; and sealed his eyes and sealed his mouth.

For those who chose the body he has given a different air –
The mouth sticks in a leer; the eyes have grown big as bullfrogs;

and the ears curl open like the nautilus. The script is filmic,
the hero beautiful and the villain easy to spot. A story

about light and dark, how one is complete without the other,
how one promises heaven and the other leaves you grasping,

how one shuts out this world to live in a better one, how the other
knows no better. So what of Bosch, who asks that we read our world

in his small one? Give him two choices. Let the right hand hold *body is all*;
let the left hand hold *body is all*. The music should be rousing.

DEEPANKAR KHIWANI
(*b.* 1971)

Deepankar Khiwani was born in 1971 in New Delhi. The poems in his first book *Entr'acte*
– published by Anand Thakore's Harbour Line – are 'animated by secret narratives of loss'
and by an 'oceanic nostalgia for the present'. He lives in Bombay and works for a business
consultancy firm.

Delhi Airport

Both close and distant as a fading dream,
this day now nearly gone. My sleepless eyes
rest on that single sign that makes it seem
I still am in this city; then realise
how it could well be any other name
on this departure screen, for these bright halls
in every airport begin to look the same,
the same grey polished floors, the same white walls.

And yet this city somehow clings to me
in smells, exhaustion, dust yet in my hair;
I glance at my watch, rise and stretch, then see
the restrooms down the hallway, and head there.
It was a day's stopover, and I found
no time for memories, but summon here
into the rancid stillness, tense, around
this large bare room, the anger, hatred, fear:

But these bright halls, although as dirty white,
these basins, mirrors ageing just the same,
were different that adolescent night
I vowed not to return, though still I came...
Here, in this hour I have, my flight delayed,
I wait to be unmanned by bitterness,
splash water on my face, and feel betrayed,
as looking up, I blink at emptiness.

Night Train to Haridwar

Now past midnight the train stops with a jolt.
Twelve twenty-two. My friend sleeps, unaware
of both this journey and this sudden halt
and gently smiles, as if he could not care;
As if he knew no halt to smile about,
nor ever had a journey he could doubt.

I smile at myself: Journey, halts indeed!
I should have been a poet, adrift at sea,
asking the questions that could nowhere lead
except to more uncertain ways to be.
All it could be is engine trouble that
detains us, or some station we stop at.

We should reach there tomorrow by, say, eight.
The first time there, for both me and my friend.
Perhaps an unconscious unacknowledged wait
now hopes its sleepless questioning will end...
I close my eyes, as if to lose my will,
then realise the train is standing still.

In this air-conditioned still compartment, lit
by dim white light, I stretch, then try to see
what is outside the window, but find it
impossible to look outside of me:
there in two panes reflected, clearly seen,
two panes of glass, with a vacuum in between.

Collectors

These coloured stones are what we treasured then,
and here's the last you found that June. It was your birthday,
and on the beach, racing with me, you cried out at its blue.

The base of this little pyramid's still as orange. We were both ten
that year; and in this box, that hot and brittle day,
we added one more stone to twenty-two.

Now thirteen years long past that boyhood when
we chose what we collected, and what we found would stay,
I count these twenty-three and look at you

for what we were before we were the men
that close our fists round things we wish away:
Here, open your hand – you can feel it too.

LEELA GANDHI

(b. 1966)

Leela Gandhi was born in Bombay in 1966 and educated at the Universities of Delhi and
Oxford. Her theoretical work deals mostly with the postcolonial period, but her poems go
back to an earlier time. They return to the Elizabethan sonnet and sing, in grave measures,
of love and loss, of 'passion confined / to small hours, the darkened stair', and of the un-
shareable consequences of desire. Her books include *Measures of Home* (Ravi Dayal, 2000)
and *Postcolonial Theory* (Columbia University, 1998). She lives in Australia and teaches at
La Trobe University, Melbourne.

Sex

Our desire wanting we tried our love
and found it good enough without
this sex thing, this hip and lip thing.
Let other lovers sweat and grind,
our love's refined, raising virtues from necessity.

More than these hands, eyes, fingertips,
your voice, taxing the telephone,
equips my shabby days with grace,
and brings me home to certainties –
food, drink, conversation, this place.

Yet, in the night's grim abrasions,
this body suffers sense and taking sleep for death,
begs awakening, contests evasions,
turns craven – no better than the rest,
no worse, drawing blood, drawing breath.

Homage to Emily Dickinson, after Pain

Our formal feeling when it comes, comes belatedly,
like a chill on a good night, a season's afterthought,
the end of history, savage, contumely, overwrought
with pain, the flat refrain of casual years, casually
defeated.

Until, too late for these tight-lipped arrears,
the language of equity, hard-fisted, appears,
polite, policing, juridical, ill at ease,
a harsh civility of anxious words, anxiously
repeated.

This is the cost of sorrow, the price of dignity; our testimony,
speaking as strangers should in hostile company,
stammers its excuse, attempts amnesia,
in the place of love, a quarantine, hopelessly
conceited.

Noun

Let me call you lover once
and I'll agree this love's a tenancy.
Just one tenacious arrangement
of our mouths, some tactile synergy
– you're good at that – to announce
the vowels, corporeally, with tongue's fluency,
then lips, catching the sharp descent
of teeth and sound. For this small bribery,
my lover-turned-landlord, overnight,
my occupancy will be light.
I'll pay what rent I owe in kind,
behave, keep passion confined
to small hours, the darkened stair,
and what gets damaged, lover, I'll repair.

Copula

I

Your face is figured in the mortar
such as it is. The peeling walls weather
extremity, the shallow bricks hold true,
but you don't live here anymore, and I do.

II

At sundown our city stretches her smoky limbs.
I envy her ligaments – even the broken roads,
the rusting girders, creaking as I made my way to you
once, when we lived here, more than we do.

III

Then, too, this copula was forbidden –
we were fugitive, even from those who knew
some bending in the sequence of desire.
Now I don't live here anymore than you.

IV

Or rather, you've flown and I've become the girl-next-door,
keeping home like Dido and that lot before.
If I lived here anymore than I do
perhaps you'd come back too.

On Reading You Reading Elizabeth Bishop

You lend me Bishop to improve my mind,
trusting yours, I turn the pages, find,
this poet is your confidant and friend,
while I, consigned to where her margins end,
must annotate your litany, with apologies:
it wasn't me, I wasn't mean, I didn't mean
to stammer in mid-flight; the weather intervened,
a dark brown land turned green, I was across the sea,
I tried, I couldn't make it over the Brooklyn bridge.
Sweet plaintiff, I am powerless against the
influence you wield, cannot sing in self-defence.
Why use the poets for advocacy?
Let us quarrel in our own words, edge to edge,
choosing conversation over bibliography.

On Vermeer: Female Interiors

You could take these pictures as the same
old theme: happy women, happily shelling peas
(reading, writing – same difference), inane,
before evening brings the sweaty masonry
home, on heavy knees: thick male shapes, thickening
the air with petulance, slamming windows, appeal,
demanding drink, until the women, sickening,
look up, breaking their reverie, the colours congeal.
Except, Vermeer didn't do evening scenes this way,
the chiaroscuro intervenes, taking light for play,
leaving officers, husbands, in the dark, unseen.
Alone, untaught, these women are pristine,
the corpus preserves interiors; a bright continuum
of female heads, conspiring to still life, live on.

A Catalogue for Prayer

For prayer, a room accustomed
to the shape of need, a sense of ease.
An honest room, well worn, well thumbed,
where love has been allowed to please

small beginnings, still conclusions of despair,
your footfall agitating the supple air,
home, conversations with my family,
images, pictures, moved across the sea,
a night of dreams, the habit of God
in a day's routine.

A.K. RAMANUJAN

(1929-93)

Born in Mysore, Attipat Krishnaswami Ramanujan went to the United States at the age of 31. As a professor of linguistics at the University of Chicago, he taught Shakespeare, Yeats, Whitman, Joyce and Eliot. (Saul Bellow said he was 'astonished that Ramanujan (had) such a grasp of British and American poetry. He really gets inside those poets'.) At the same time, he became identified with the university's Department of South Asian Languages and Civilisations, where his work as a translator and interpreter of Indian epics, oral narratives, and devotional poetry won him, among many honours, a MacArthur fellowship, or 'genius' award. He lived in many spaces at once – Indian and Western, Brahmin and Rationalist – and was not entirely comfortable in any one location. (He described himself as the hyphen in Indian-American.) This tension is apparent in poems that allude to a dizzying range of philosophies, poetries, and cultures; and in an allegiance to the small, the provisional and the disenfranchised.

He has had a prolific record of posthumous publication, including, so far, *The Black Hen* (1995), from which most of the poems in this selection are taken, *The Flowering Tree and Other Oral Tales from India* (1997), *Uncollected Poems and Prose* (2000), and culminating in the monumental 2004 *Oxford India Ramanujan*, edited by Molly Daniels-Ramanujan. He died in Chicago.

The Black Hen

It must come as leaves
to a tree
or not at all

yet it comes sometimes
as the black hen
with the red round eye

on the embroidery
stitch by stitch
dropped and found again

and when it's all there
the black hen stares
with its round red eye

and you're afraid.

Foundlings in the Yukon

In the Yukon the other day
miners found the skeleton
of a lemming
curled around some seeds
in a burrow:
sealed off by a landslide
in Pleistocene times.

Six grains were whole,
unbroken: picked and planted
ten thousand
years after their time,
they took root
within forty-eight hours
and sprouted
candelabra of eight small leaves.

A modern Alaskan lupine,
I'm told, waits three years to come
to flower, but these
upstarts drank up sun
and unfurled early
with the crocuses of March
as if long deep
burial had made them hasty

for birth and season, for names,
genes, for passing on:
like the kick
and shift of an intra-uterine
memory, like
this morning's dream of being
born in an eagle's
nest with speckled eggs and the screech

of nestlings, like a pent-up
centenarian's sudden burst
of lust, or maybe
just elegies in Duino unbound
from the dark,
these new aborigines biding
their time
for the miner's night-light

to bring them their dawn,
these infants compact with age,
older than the oldest
things alive, having skipped
a million falls
and the registry of tree-rings,
suddenly younger
by an accident of flowering

than all their timely descendants.

Love 5

Though, at night, or anytime at all
in bed, he flashes lightnings, strips stark
naked, won't even wait for the half-dark
to watch her watch him rise and fall,

wants the lights on when she takes off
her underthings, to see her resume
her natural curves and catch the waft
of colours transcending all perfume,

to kiss her deep, say unspeakable things
to her back and front in whisper and joke,
taste her juices at their sources, stoke
the smithy all hours to hammer rings

of gold out of touch and taste – he's stunned by
daylight, he stammers and his looks are shy.

The Day Went Dark

I bought a carpet
with orange flowers
and green leaves

but all my furniture
looked bilious yellow
in its gorgeous light.

I loved a woman
with turquoise eyes,
navel like a whirlpool

in a heap of wheat

and the day went dark,
my hands were lizards,
my heart turned into a hound.

To a Friend Far Away

Between official letters, I doodle the wet
wild tendrils of a familiar alphabet:

I leaf through telephone books, watch the sand
run as I read small print inked on your hand:

breathing the sulphur of city fumes,
I sense your faraway breathing rhythms

quicken as you turn round and round
looking for a child in the market crowd:

hear oceans lash between now and now,
groping in the mist for what I can know,

do, or be, when affections find a bird,
tiny, button-eyed, city-bewildered,

green-yellow, hopping on the yard: I take it
home in a kerchief to a checkered blanket

maybe only to find it dead
by morning in the twist and fold

of my confusions, my absent presence,
faraway rivers amok in my continents.

Mythologies 2

When the clever man asks the perfect boon:
not to be slain by demon, god, or by
beast, not by day nor by night,
by no manufactured weapon, not out
of doors not inside, not in the sky
nor on earth,

               come now come soon,
Vishnu, man, lion, neither and both, to hold
him in your lap to disembowel his pride
with the steel glint of bare claws at twilight.

O midnight sun, eclipse at noon,
net of loopholes, a house all threshold,
connoisseur of negatives and assassin
of certitudes, slay now my faith in doubt.
End my commerce with bat and night-
owl. Adjust my single eye, rainbow bubble,
so I too may see all things double.

Second Sight

In Pascal's endless queue
people pray, whistle, or make

remarks. As we enter the dark,
someone says from behind,

'You are Hindoo, aren't you?
You must have second sight.'

I fumble in my nine
pockets like the night-blind

son-in-law groping
in every room for his wife,

and strike a light to regain
at once my first, and only,

sight.

BRUCE KING

2004: Ezekiel, Moraes, Kolatkar

For the national and international community of Indian poets who write in English, 2004 was a sad year; three major writers died – Nissim Ezekiel (*b.* 1924), Dom Moraes (*b.* 1938) and Arun Kolatkar (*b.* 1932). Each was an excellent poet, a well-loved individual, and significant on the Indian cultural scene. Each was known abroad and has left work which will continue to be read and anthologised. If it were not for the deaths of the three writers, 2004 would have been a vintage year with the publication of Moraes' *Collected Poems 1954-2004*, Kolatkar's two volumes – *Sarpa Satra* and *Kala Ghoda Poems* – and a new edition of Ezekiel's *Collected Poems* at the printers. Both Moraes and Kolatkar knew they were dying; the former consciously wrote poems about the experience, the latter worked to have the two books in print before his death.

Nissim Ezekiel was perhaps the central figure in the evolution of Indian poetry in English to a more modern idiom than the amateurism and windy, shapeless, overblown spiritualist epics prevalent when he began to write. He made Indian poetry up to date. His poems were about urban life, economical, well crafted, often filled with ironies, and they communicated directly to the reader. Although recognisably about an Indian and India, they were on the same wavelength as poetry then being written on both sides of the Atlantic. An intellectual, his reading and interests ranged from the existentialists, W.C. Williams and African art to the still lively factional disputes of Marxism and Socialism.

While holding various full-time jobs, Ezekiel was a leader of those writing poetry in English when politicians and most intellectuals were trying to impose Hindi as a national language and when Indian literature too often consisted of wrenching stories of peasant life, romanticised tales of nobility, the cultural conflicts of those returning from education abroad, and, best, quiet comedies of provincial society in which tradition prevailed. In using his own disquiets as subject-matter, Ezekiel shifted the focus of Indian poetry to contemporary life in India, especially Bombay, the nation's largest, liveliest, and most culturally productive city. He remained a central figure in Bombay's literary community and he wrote and published throughout his life.

Born into the ancient Indian but then impoverished Bene Israel community of Jews, his parents were highly educated teachers: he was raised with a largely secular outlook and took an early interest in politics and ideas. By 1948 he joined the after-the-war migration of former citizens of the British Empire to London where he shared a basement room, barely supported himself with odd jobs, attended lectures in philosophy, and published poems in literary journals and his first book of poetry, *A Time to Change* (1952). The title refers to what was to be a theme of his early books, the need for moral decision when faced by opposing attractions, especially those of the body and a settled, productive life. This would take various directions, usually involving sexual desire or love in contrast to marriage, and was often resolved in poems about art giving form to the conflict. 'London' is about those formative years:

> Sometimes I think I'm still
> in that basement room,
>
> a permanent and proud
> metaphor of struggle
>
> for and against the same
> creative, self-destructive self.

After three and a half years of intellectual and sexual adventure, he worked his way back to Bombay scrubbing decks and shovelling coal on a steamer.

He soon had a job on *The Illustrated Weekly* of Bombay, where his responsibilities included reading the manuscripts of and advising other Indian poets, such as the soon-to-be famous Dom Moraes. Whereas most Indian poets in English were amateur versifiers, Ezekiel, influenced by Rilke, insisted poetry was a career which a writer worked to master. He later quarrelled with P. Lal (whose Writers Workshop was then the only significant publisher of Indian poetry in English) over what he felt was a lack of critical standards, and he became the leader of those who were aiming to write as well as English-language poets abroad. His decision to return to India (he could have stayed in London or emigrated to Israel), his active involvement in Indian literary and intellectual life, and his setting his poems in Bombay, made him India's equivalent to New York's Jewish cultural community, someone whose minority status made him especially conscious of the contradictions of modern life. Although his outlook was secular, he never severed his connections with the Bene Israelis and at times, such as when asking his mother to arrange his marriage, he unexpectedly showed his need to be linked to a community. As the country's cultural and financial energies shifted from Delhi and Calcutta to Bombay, India's most cosmopolitan and modern city, Ezekiel became one of the nation's more important cultural figures. He represented the opposite of the Hindiising, peasant-idealising, Soviet-sympathising, nationalist cultural assertion of the government and many intellectuals.

He contributed to the intellectual life of India as a poet, literary critic, art critic, editor of literary magazines, playwright, advisor to publishers, newspaper columnist, university professor, and in oppositional politics. He seemed to know everyone and be everywhere, shaping opinion as well as poetry. Besides becoming a university professor, he was an editor of PEN's newsletter and his office at PEN was practically his home. Perhaps because after his stint on *The Illustrated Weekly* he had managed some businesses, and perhaps because he helped to edit political journals, he somehow managed to get money, at least for short periods, to support the publication of poetry; the years during the mid-1950s – when he was editor of *Quest*, a general publication of arts and ideas which was associated with the Congress for Cultural Freedom – encouraged a generation of poets. It was the Indian equivalent of the British *Encounter*. The six issues he edited of *Poetry India* (1966-67) are still regarded as a high point for the translation of excellent poetry from other Indian languages into English verse by bilingual writers. A social democrat and humanist who disliked the way India was leaning during the Cold War, he was one of those who brought the study of American literature to Indian universities. When Mrs Gandhi proclaimed an Emergency, in 1975-77, and the nation's political journals shut down, he started and edited *Freedom First*.

Many of the poets who are now thought of as the canon of modern Indian poetry in English were his friends, studied with him, were published by him, recommended to publishers by him, or were influenced by him for a significant time – Dom Moraes, A.K. Ramanujan, Eunice de Souza, R. Parthasarathy, Adil Jussawalla, Saleem Peeradina, K.D. Katrak, Gieve Patel and Arvind Krishna Mehrotra. Arun Kolatkar's poetry was first published by him. He is the subject of many poems by Indians, some seeing him as a model, some replying to his views, some, by women, mocking him as a famous poet-seducer.

While he was an example of a writer engaged in the world, Ezekiel remained primarily a poet who kept publishing poetry of variable quality throughout his life. Many of his poems, such as 'Enterprise', 'Night of the Scorpion', 'Poet, Lover, Birdwatcher', 'Marriage', 'Philosophy', 'Background, Casually', and, 'Goodbye Party for Miss Pushpa T.S.', are often and rightly anthologised. While some of the better poems concern the conflict between desire and ethics, others take an amused look at situations when cultures and languages come into conflict. He remains one of the few Indian poets (in contrast with those who lived abroad, such as A.K. Ramanujan and Agha Shahid Ali) whose poems are known and taught in other countries.

Ezekiel's best-known poem outside of India is probably 'Night of the Scorpion', written when he was a visiting professor at Leeds University, and meant to be read to Commonwealth Literature students. The poem tells of the reactions of two parents when their child is bitten by a scorpion, and humorously reveals a conflict between the father's education and his reversion in an emergency to peasant superstition. But even this poem which is consciously written for English students concludes with what might be described as a Jewish mother joke, the effect of which is to universalise the emotions, characters, and the conflict between cultural traditions and modern knowledge. Ezekiel's well-known 'Background, Casually', another example of his nationalism, was written for the 1965 Commonwealth Arts Festival:

> I have made my commitments now.
> This is one: to stay where I am,
> As others choose to give themselves
> In some remote and backward place.
> My backward place is where I am.

Many years later in 'The Egoist's Prayers VII' he wrote:

> Confiscate my passport, Lord,
> I don't want to go abroad.
> Let me find my song
> where I belong.

Ezekiel always had the desire to roam, whether sexually or to move on to another job, another place, another literary manner, and his best poetry contrasts such urges of renewal and creativity with his considered judgment that a settled, dedicated life is better. But the temptation was always there, and in 'The Egoist's Prayers III' he asks God, 'But do you really mind / half a bite of it?'

Although a father of modern Indian poetry in English, he was not a radically original poet. Rejecting the long-winded spiritualism and twee aestheticism of much contemporary Indian poetry in English, he began by writing formal, tightly rhymed verse in iambic pentameter in which he expressed his search for a balanced way to live. He increasingly became the poet of Bombay, using it as the backdrop for his poems, at times imitating its use of English, and making it a symbol of modern anxieties and confusions. In this he was a post-colonial heir of such writers as Baudelaire and Eliot, although his actual verse manner was somewhere between post-1939 Auden and the Movement.

The Unfinished Man (1960) is an impressive, short, tightly written volume in which the conflicting attractions of freedom and moral responsibility are crystallised in the libido and marriage, and set in a city, Bombay, which figures as both backdrop and projection of the self. He evolved as a poet with the times. In the late 1960s and 1970s he used LSD and wrote poems to go with posters, increasingly used free verse, and turned to meditation to soothe his soul. As he became less critical his poetry sometimes became slack. While there are interesting poems among the long later sequences, they seldom are as good as the ironic, wry, tight poems in which he created what has come to be thought of as the model for the Bombay poets. Such Bombay poems are often short, ironic, witty monologues or conversations about an ethical problem, or observation of and moral reflections on some emblematic character or situation. Whether it is a newspaper report, meeting a friend, a social event, or describing a scene, the context is clearly Bombay in its varied aspect, though the background is present more as an image or allusion than filled in.

Ezekiel's achievement as a poet was complete by the time of his *Collected Poems 1952-1988* (1989), although he continued to contribute poems to literary journals. The new edition of his *Collected Poems* (2005) contains only one new poem. The last decade of his life was a terrible period. He was on his own and suffering from Alzheimer's disease. He did not wash, wore smelly clothes, lived among filth, and was frightened, under-nourished, ashamed and unwilling to be helped. He feared returning to his house and begged to stay with friends; he gave what he and others had to beggars.

The story of his early years, his continuing relationship to the Bene Israelites, why he never divorced and his wife's revenge, and especially his pitiable old age, can be followed in R. Raj Rao's *Nissim Ezekiel: the authorised biography* (2000), a useful although badly written and malicious book. Rao, a poet whom Ezekiel helped, and now a university professor, claims that his mentor did not sufficiently appreciate his poetry. Now that he has uncloseted himself, Rao wishes he had spent ten years of his life collecting material about a gay or lesbian poet rather than a womaniser.

Although from another of India's minorities, **Dom Moraes** was almost Ezekiel's opposite. Born into a Roman Catholic family, his father, Frank Moraes, a famous newspaper editor of Goan origin, his mother a medical doctor, Moraes might be thought of as a product of the late colonial anglophone elite. His father was one of those both promoted by the British as they prepared to leave India and one of those who challenged them, a friend of many of the nationalist leaders. When Dom was seven his mother began to go insane. She developed a religious mania, would scream, throw furniture from windows, lock Dom in a room and burn him with cigarettes. For the remainder of her life she would be in and out of mental homes. At first her husband tried to ignore the problem. He went to his office and left Dom alone with her and the servants. Later he escaped for some years as an editor in Sri Lanka and Australia, taking Dom with him, at times sending Dom back to India in the hope that somehow this would make his wife calmer. He would continue to think that, and plead with Dom to take care of the mother, even when Dom was an adult and had a career of his own abroad. Dom came to associate India with his mad, violent mother and hated it. After attending school in Bombay in 1954, he studied Latin in England as a preparation for Oxford and travelled in Europe. He was already a writer, having published a book on cricket when he was 13; through his father he had met Stephen

Spender and other visiting poets in India, and had been published in literary magazines in England and the USA.

In London he soon became part of a then and still famous Soho bohemia; his circle of drinking friends and acquaintances included the painters Lucian Freud, Francis Bacon, the poets George Barker, W.S. Graham, David Gascoyne, the publisher David Archer, and Henrietta (born Audrey Wendy Abbott), the beautiful, amoral, witty, foul-mouthed, hard-drinking, thieving, drug-taking Queen of Soho. Archer's famous Parton Press (Dylan Thomas' publisher) would publish his first book of poetry, *A Beginning* (1957), while Moraes was still a student at Oxford (1956-59). It won the Hawthornden Prize, the first time it had been given since the war, and Moraes remains the only Indian as well as its youngest recipient. Henrietta, who had already been married and had children, seduced him when he was 18 and became his first wife, living with him in Oxford, and in London in a house in Chelsea she had been given by a rich admirer. Moraes eventually left her, as he did his second English wife, and later his third, this time Indian, wife. For a decade he was very much in fashion, the lover of many beautiful women, a highly profiled poet, journalist and magazine editor, and acquaintance of such famous poets as W.H. Auden, T.S. Eliot and Allen Ginsberg. He was the author of *Poems*, which was a Poetry Book Society Choice (1960), *John Nobody* (1965) and *Beldam Etcetera* (1966). *Poems 1955-65* was published in the USA by Macmillan. *Gone Away* (1960), the first of his three autobiographies (republished under the collective title *A Variety of Absences* [2003]), appeared when he was 22; the second, *My Son's Father* (1968), when he was 28.

As a poet Moraes began as a dreamy romantic heir of the English verse tradition. He was more likely to echo Spenser, the Cavalier poets, Keats, or early Yeats in contrast either to the Movement poets, the remaining modernists, or the Imagists. By the mid-60s he was clearly influenced by Auden, but he never was an experimenter, avant-gardist, or influenced by American verse although he knew many good American poets in England, including Allen Tate and Sylvia Plath. He was, like Derek Walcott, one of those writers from the former colonies who had a better ear for the harmonies of English verse than most British poets, but, unlike Walcott, he had nothing to say about colonialism, nationalism, racism, cultural conflict, the Cold War, existentialism, or any of the major political and intellectual themes of the time. His apparent lack of engagement was not from lack of knowledge – as a reporter he covered the Eichmann trial in Israel and as a journalist wrote about the Congo, the brutal conditions under which Communist prisoners were held in Indonesia, and many of the world's problems – but such writing was in prose; his poetry was about himself, his mother, his hurts, or used conventional love themes addressed to some woman with whom he was then involved. Allen Tate incorrectly

206

told him that no 20th-century female could be seduced with such old-fashioned poetry.

Eventually his muse left him, he wrote no poetry for 17 years during which time he worked for the UN in New York and was, ironically, sent to India as a UN gift to Mrs Gandhi, who claimed she needed him to write educational television scripts. Actually she had no use for him, although he was later to write her biography. Stranded in India he would learn that he had been away from London too long and from now on would need to support himself in Asia which, after a period in Singapore, concluded with him unhappily stuck in Bombay as the highest paid journalist in India, grinding out daily newspaper columns, writing coffee-table books, and drinking far too much. Moraes at this point of his life was a formerly successful poet in England who was barely remembered there and, although he had been one of the first modern Indian poets, he had written no poetry in India for decades.

Then unexpectedly, but significantly during a time when he was out of work and no longer writing much prose, the muse made her appearance again. A privately printed volume, *Absences* (1983), showed him tentatively trying out new verse manners, a less ornamental reporterish style as he attempted to write about his experiences abroad as a journalist. His *Collected Poems 1957-1987* sold extremely well in India, followed by *Serendip* (1990), both published by Penguin India. He was a poet once more. He remained haunted by his early success in England, and many of his later poems looked back on that time with nostalgia and a sense of loss. But other tones and themes were starting to appear, often with the use of masks especially of ancient warriors, or when addressing Leela, his third wife, a Swiss-born Indian who was previously a movie star and model, and who had walked out of a brutal marriage to a wealthy heir of a hotel chain. Some of these poems allude to a harsh godless world only made significant by activity, while the love poems are conscious that Dom and Leela are ageing, alone, have had disappointments in their lives, and will eventually die. 'Future Plans' concludes with him and Leela 'A little tired, but in the end, / Not unhappy to have lived.'

Moraes even points to the oddness of his poems in that they seem personal and confessional, but actually he is not there: there is always a distance, a reserve, a mask, between poet and reader, as if there were an emotional shell around the speaker – a habit, we know from the autobiographies, that he developed as a youth. 'Babur', one of his historical warrior figures, speaks of himself as 'lonely in all lands', claims 'my books are where I bleed':

> If you look for me, I am not here.
> My writings will tell you where I am.
> Tingribirdi, they point out my life like
> Lines drawn in the map of my palm.

Soon after Moraes promised in verse to grow old and remain with Leela until death, he fell in love with someone else, a younger married woman with children who was separated from her husband. This led to emotional renewal, an intense period of writing, and some of his best poetry in years. *In Cinnamon Shade* (Carcanet Press, 2001) was the first volume of his poems published in Britain since 1966, and is modelled upon those Renaissance sequences in which poems of desire and complaint form an implied narrative about the problems faced by the two lovers, their psychology, their moods, their pains, their past, the poet's love and the woman's departures.

In Cinnamon Shade begins with a cankered, snail-infested garden, representing the poet's past life, to which the concluding poem returns as the lady has left him:

> Because of the moon, you have left my side,
> for the moon made you different and afraid.
> But wherever you are, I imagine you still,
> Sedated into sleep, long eyelashes sealed,
> moist lips bereft. Rest in cinnamon shade.
> Deep tides of darkness will cover the wound.
> But of two once made one, what will be left?
> Only footprints on water, handmarks on wind.

The mixture of sensual longing, erotic, almost pornographic desire ('moist lips bereft'), conveyed in such romantic poeticisms and formalism, would be mockable if it were not so excellent. Indeed, many of the poems seem to be part of a canon of an invented former age of poetry which spoke differently than we do, although the emotions are recognisably universal and applicable to Moraes. 'Alexander' proclaims:

> Write, scribe, I was my army. The world was mine.
> Exiled from two countries I hated and loved.
> At the end of the day I was my own enemy.
> But, scribe, write: at the end of it I had lived
> a life so crowded others envied it; also
> my path would not have been gladly chosen
> by most. Look at me. I am my own ghost.

There are poeticisms, unnatural word order in places, but also a mastery of technique, literary echoes, phrasing and phrase making, tone and sound, drama, and contrast of form and breath groups. The history of English poetry is behind and has made this stanza.

In *Typed with One Finger* (2003), Moraes continued to write about the drama of his new woman, his renewed sense of self that came with being in love once more, and his pride in his past. He hoped that Carcanet would publish an updated version of his collected poems. But he was suffering from cancer, was operated upon, and, rather than change his ways and take treatment to prolong his life he decided to live as he had, although he knew this would soon lead to his death. The powerful new lyrics in *Collected Poems 1954-2004* were written with such a consciousness. The final sequence of twelve sonnets are magnificent in their range of emotions and memories, their variety of dictions, their compression, their recall and reinterpretation of earlier poems, their wit and puns, their literary echoes, their explicit reference to events that had shaped his life, their lack of self-pity, and their acceptance that life has no purpose except to be lived fully. These are remarkable poems that should be given detailed explication; they belong to the classics of our time. Suddenly at the end of his life Moraes became a great poet.

From the first of the sonnets:

> From a heavenly asylum, shrivelled Mummy,
> glare down like a gargoyle at your only son,
> who now has white hair and can hardly walk.
> I am he who was not I.

Moraes always had the useful ability to assume that his readers were interested in him, his pains, his past, and his self-pity. There were even a few poems in which he unexpectedly tapped into the world of nightmares and the horrific. But he never before expressed such a wide range of emotions or commanded so many different attitudes and dictions in one volume, let alone a single poem. While each of these final twelve sonnets is amazing, the other new poems in *Collected Poems 1954-2004* are also impressive. Those who do not already know Moraes' poetry should begin by reading his later work. It is like discovering a Sylvia Plath, but one who could compress many poems into a sonnet.

In the *Times Literary Supplement* 'International Books of the Year' for 2004, the well-known novelist Pankaj Mishra claimed that 'Indian poetry in English has a longer and more distinguished tradition than Indian fiction in English, and may finally become better-known in the West when **Arun Kolatkar**'s narrative poem, *Jejuri* (1976), is published by the *New York Review of Books* in 2005. Kolatkar published two volumes of poetry, *Kala Ghoda Poems* and *Sarpa Satra* (both by Pras Prakashan) before his untimely death this year. Moving deftly from street life in Bombay to Hindu myths, these last poems confirm his cult reputation as the greatest Indian poet of his generation' (*TLS*, 3 December 2004: 10).

Kolatkar was that good a poet. Although his work was known only by those who sought it, he was a poet of world class with a very individual way of looking at the world. In his writing every cliché is transformed into something new and unexpected, a transformation by imagination, language, and tone. If Moraes is a master of older verse idioms, Kolatkar's realm is street talk, the colloquial, the poetry of the ordinary and anonymous.

Take, for instance, 'Pi-Dog', a nine-part sequence which begins

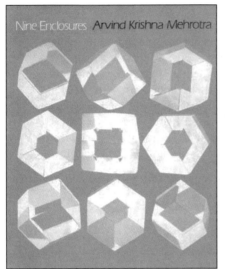

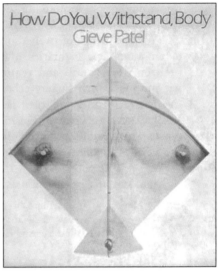

POETRY COLLECTIONS WITH COVER
DESIGNS BY ARUN KOLATKAR

TOP LEFT: Arvind Krishna
Mehrotra's *Nine Enclosures*
(Clearing House, 1976).

TOP RIGHT: Gieve Patel's
How Do You Withstand, Body
(Clearing House, 1976).

LEFT: Jayanta Mahapatra's
The False Start
(Clearing House, 1980).

Kala Ghoda Poems (2004), a volume of thematic connected poetry. Here a mangy street dog rests on a traffic island thinking of its ancestors and circumstances while Bombay sleeps. There is the quiet humour, physical realism, colloquial speech, subtle contrasts of registers and linguistic invention, and unobtrusive harmonies typical of Kolatkar's verse. It all seems so relaxed, the kind of seeming free verse to which prose aspires, yet behind the first five stanzas is familiarity with a great range of the world's poetry, the kind of distant echoes, allusions, and structures that would make a scholar's paradise. I find myself murmuring Horace, John Dryden, Thomas Gray, T.S. Eliot, W.C. Williams, knowing that any source or influence could be right or wrong as this is written by a poet who has absorbed such sources and influences to make them his own. The poem rapidly moves by way of whimsy to the history and mixed culture of the city. The dog claims his body looks like 'a seventeenth-century map of Bombay' with its seven islands black irregular spots 'on a body the colour of old parchment'. According to 'a strong family tradition' he is a descendant, 'matrilineally / to the only bitch' among thirty hounds which survived the sea voyage from England, imported

> by Sir Bartle Frere
> in eighteen hundred and sixty-four,
> with the crazy idea
>
> of introducing fox-hunting to Bombay.
> Just the sort of thing,
> he felt the city badly needed.

Kolatkar is a master of the incongruous and the absurd. Sir Bartle Frere actually existed. He was a British colonial administrator and famous in his time; there are mountain peaks, fruits, and other memorials in former British colonies. It is typical of Kolatkar to focus on the importation of hunting hounds to show both the British influence on Indian culture and some of its inappropriateness.

The classical, Sanskritic, Hindu tradition was little better. On his paternal side, the pi-dog claims descent from the dog in Mahabharata who remains with Yudhishthira long after such warriors as Draupadi, Sahadeva, Nakul, Arjuna and Bhima 'had fallen by the wayside'. The epic roll call contrasts with the physical description of the journey into the Himalayas ('frostbitten and blinded with snow, / dizzy with hunger and gasping for air') which itself jostles with the conclusion in which the epic 'flying chariot' appears in the same context as the colloquial 'airlift', 'get on board', and 'made it to':

> ...help came
> in the shape of a flying chariot
>
> to airlift him to heaven.
> Yudhishthira, the noble prince, refused
> to get on board unless dogs were allowed.
>
> And my ancestor became the only dog
> to have made it to heaven
> in recorded history.

In still another version of 'man's devotion to dog', Harlan Ellison's 1969 science fiction short story, 'A Boy and his Dog', which is described as 'a cultbook among pi-dogs everywhere', the boy sacrifices his love,

> and serves up his girlfriend
> as dogfood to save the life of his
> starving canine master.

The range of literary allusions continues with an explanation of the pi-dog's name, 'Ugh', which is supposed to come from Sanskrit, 'the U pronounced as in Upanishad'; Ugh is 'short for Ughekalikadu, / Siddharayya's / famous dog'. Such literary allusions are supposedly part of the dog's thoughts as he meditates in the morning sun surrounded by the concrete highrises of Bombay knowing that soon the city will awake and he will 'surrender the city / to its so-called masters'.

The choice of science fiction is not just for its story. Kolatkar suggests that the Sanskritic literature of ancient India, the literature which is allegorised, spiritualised, treated as moral and historical truth, and used as a foundation for Hindu nationalism, really is little different than present-day science fiction, a collection of amusing, often sophisticated invented tales, meant to entertain, amuse, shock, a world of fantasy. In doing so he is making a cultural statement that is also political. His is a poetry of reality, of pi-dogs, of saying the world is as it is, a place of colloquial language and the present, in contrast to the idealisation of the past, its literature, and ancient Indian languages, symbols of both official Indian cultural nationalism and of the Hindu revivalist movement with its radical, often fanatic politics. Kolatkar is often thought an aesthete, someone detached from notions of literature as engagement, but throughout his career as a poet he was creating a body of work which in its unique way is a tribute to the sceptical here and now as opposed to the dogmatic, idealising, and ideological.

The long 31-part 'Breakfast Time at Kala Ghoda', at the centre of the volume, mostly observes for an hour the various people, objects, and actions around Flora Fountain in Bombay. Throughout the city people are eating but here the main attraction is an old lady selling from 'a jumbo aluminum box full of idlis' with 'a bucket full of sambar / fit for fire-eaters.' She is 'Our Lady of Idlis' and sits on one of the many concrete blocks surrounding the traffic island, where the pi-dog slept and meditated, around Flora Fountain. This is another version of or symbol of Bombay:

> Each and every hungry and homeless soul
> within a mile of the little island
> is soon gravitating towards it
>
> to receive the sacrament of idli,
> to anoint palates
> with sambar,
>
> to celebrate anew, every morning,
> the seduction and death
> of the demon of hunger
>
> (threatening the entire world)
> at the hands of Gauri
> in the form of a humble idli.

They come from all over;
walking, running, dancing, limping, stumbling, rolling
– each at his own speed.

Besides the many characters described ('the laughing Buddha', 'the old pirate', 'the shoeshine boy', 'that old paralytic in a wheel-chair / made by cannibalising two bicycles', 'the legless hunchback', a 'scruffy looking stranger') there are also crows, dogs, and other species who join in the communal feast of idlis until the seller departs and the street drama, this urban, part-comic, part-realistic version of romance, ends and all we are left with is an awareness of how art and imagination invest the ordinary with interest.

The pop-up cafeteria
disappears
like a castle in a children's book

– along with the king and the queen,
the courtiers,
the court jester and the banqueting hall,

the roast pheasants and the suckling pigs,
as soon as the witch
shuts the book on herself –

and the island returns
to its flat old
boring self.

Arun Kolatkar was born in Kolhapur, Maharashtra, to Hindu, Marathi-speaking parents. He was educated bilingually in Marathi and English, took a diploma in art in Bombay, and was one of India's best-paid graphic designers. He pointedly had no portfolio and claimed that those who did not know his work could not afford him. He designed the covers and layout of his books, which are a treat, simple yet eye-catching works of visual art. When he wanted special effects he would write his poems in affective shapes. He was both an English- and a Marathi-language poet, publishing in both languages, and is better-known for his Marathi work. He was also something of an eccentric. He had once been a heavy drinker and as a consequence lost his first wife; he lived in a tiny apartment with his second wife, a place so small it was necessary to eat outside to sit at a table. The apartment was, however, filled with books, especially volumes of poetry from around the world. Kolatkar had no telephone: it was necessary to leave messages with an upstairs neighbour. If you wanted to see him he could always be found on Thursday afternoons at Bombay's Wayside Inn, a café near Flora Fountain, seemingly left over from the late colonial past. It served fish and chips, fried eggs and bacon, and tea, and Kolatkar could be found there once a week with a group of Marathi-speaking friends, writers and intellectuals. He was at least as much immersed in Marathi as English and world culture. He spent more than 15 years translating the work of a popular Marathi entertainer and storyteller. Nothing came of the project during Kolatkar's lifetime.

Kolatkar's poetry continued a Marathi modernist tradition best-known for B.S. Mardheker (1909-56), who had fused Surrealism, the Imagists, Eliot and what is called Indian medieval or Saints' poetry. (Saints' poetry directly addresses the divine in a colloquial, often erotic language with similar kinds of paradox and wit to those found in European religious and metaphysical poetry. Such poetry, in India, was written for many centuries in regional languages by men and women long after and in contrast to the Sanskritic classics.) It is a lively regional modernism that has produced several good bilingual poets, including Kolatkar's friend Dilip Chitre and Ranjit Hoskote. Kolatkar early explored the possibilities of the highly imagistic and its opposite, the anti-poetic. His best-known early poem is 'Three Cups of Tea', supposedly originally written in Bombay-Hindi and translated into an amusing American tough-guy realism that sounds like something written in the 1930s or 40s:

> i want my pay i said
> > to the manager
> you'll get paid said
> > the manager
> but not before the first
> > don't you know the rules?

While 'Three Cups of Tea' has attracted much attention in India because it was in a very local form of Hindi before being translated by the author into a particular kind of American realism, I think it really shows Kolatkar's love of parody, tone, postures, and language; this is a poet with a sense of humour and a delight in pastiche.

Kolatkar's 'the boat ride' tells of a touristy trip around Bombay harbour, as both incredibly dull and yet surreal, as the bored eye and imagination invests uninteresting material with the amazing.

> because a sailor waved
> > > back
> to a boy
> > another boy
> waves to another sailor
> in the clarity of air
> the gesture withers for want
> of correspondence and
> the hand that returns to him
> the hand his knee accepts
> as his own
> > is the hand
> of an aged person
> > a hand
> that must remain patient
> > and give the boy it's a part of time
> > > to catch up.

A similar purposeful flatness, mixed with occasional free associations and sudden intrusions of the author, can be found in *Jejuri* (which was awarded the Commonwealth Poetry Prize), which recounts a day trip to a famous ruined temple complex near Pune. The tone of the sequence of poems is argued over by Indian critics, probably because there are many possible attitudes, as seen in 'The Doorstep':

> That's no doorstep.
> It's a pillar on its side.
>
> Yes.
> That's what it is.

The speaker (in 'A Scratch') has an eye for realistic detail and mentions seeing underpants drying on a temple door, a calf in what might be a temple or cowshed,

> what is god
> and what is stone
> the dividing line
> if it exists
> is very thin
> at Jejuri
>
> [...]
>
> there is no crop
> other than god
> and god is harvested here
> around the year

When an old woman wants to be paid for taking the tourist to a shrine, she says 'What else can an old woman do / on hills as wretched as these?'

Jejuri offers more than a sceptical, bored, tourist's perspective. Three of the poems allude to Chaitanya, a Bengali saint who tried to reform Jejuri.

> he popped a stone
> in his mouth
> and spat out gods.

After Chaitanya left, the holy place returned to cow-like mindless faith, 'the herd of legends / returned to its gazing.' Contrasted to the lack of dynamism in the shrines, there is the life the poet sees around him in butterflies and in chickens dancing. (This is also visually a great poem. Kolatkar, a graphic designer, was an excellent concrete poet.) When the poet tries to leave, he is faced by all the inefficiencies of India. The train station indicator and clock do not work, no one answers his questions, there is no way of telling when the next train will come. *Jejuri* is less a poem about loss of faith than, indirectly, about a national loss of the kinds of dynamism that produced the saints and their shrines, an energy found in

215

nature (which some Hindus would claim is the actual source of religion).

As much as Kolatkar was interested in life's dynamism, a characteristic he found in the streets of Bombay as well as in nature, he also carried on a running battle with the ways that India's classical Sanskritic culture had been ossified by brahmins and scholars or used as a basis for social injustice, Hindu extremism, and for an unintelligible poetic diction that was meaningless to most people and resulted in bad art. *Sarpa Satra*, one of the two final volumes he published knowing he would soon die, retells from an alternative perspective the snake sacrifice performed by King Janamejaya in the *Mahabharata*. If, by the way, you do not know this section of the *Mahabharata* (Book VI, 90, 1–27) you should read it as it is great, a wild precursor of both *Star Wars'* futuristic space battles and Uccello's stylishly patterned manneristic scenes of warfare. The sacrifice is intended to annihilate the Nagas, or Snake People, and, like much of the *Mahabharata*, uses war between various groups to teach a spiritual message. Such wars and stories are usually allegorised as alluding to actual historical battles. Unfortunately, most translations of the *Mahabharata* are barely readable. *Sarpa Satra* modernises and makes colloquial the often incomprehensible language common to translations of Sanskrit into English:

And I think it's your job,
Aastika.
I mean who else is there to do it?

Kolatkar's version is also a story about ending revenge; revenge breeds further hatred, more battle, and continued death:

You belong to the human race.

Don't forget that, ever.
And that's the reason
why you'll have to stop this sacrifice.

Not for Vasuki Mama's sake,
or mine.
Not for anything else –

but to make sure
that the last vestige of humanity
you are heir to,

your patrimony, yes,
does not go up in smoke
in this yajnya.

Kolatkar does not need to make explicit the application of this story to contemporary India with its intense religious, caste, and other communal conflicts. In modernising the language and tones of the *Mahabharata* he is also offering a liberal or common sense revisioning of what in India has become a text used to justify the violence of reactionary Hinduism. It is like putting the Bible into contemporary speech and retelling it to give emphasis to its message of Love.

If Indian poets in English are less well-known abroad than the novelists it is probably because their concerns are personal, local and yet universal; they do not write, at least not directly, about the nationalist and postcolonial political and cultural themes that the West patronisingly expects, even demands, from the formerly colonised. Several of the earlier novelists whose texts are sometimes used in university courses to illustrate the meeting of cultures, social injustice, or cultural assertion, are dull and obvious. It would be difficult to treat Ezekiel, Moraes, or Kolatkar, as exotics who need be protected by cultural relativism, babble about different national poetics, or other apologies for the second-rate. Their work stands on its own as literature, while contributing to and helping to shape the many strands and different views that comprise Indian culture. Although the best Indian poets can be read in terms of postcolonial critical theories, they are too good and too interesting for such a limited approach.

BIBLIOGRAPHY

Nissim Ezekiel: *Collected Poems: 1952-1988* (Oxford University Press, Delhi, 1989; second edition, 2005).

Dom Moraes: *Collected Poems 1957-1987* (Penguin, Delhi, 1987); *Collected Poems 1954-2004* (Penguin, Delhi, 2004).

Arun Kolatkar: *Jejuri* (Clearing House, Bombay, 1976; sixth edition, Ashok Shahane for Pras Prakashan, Mumbai, 2006); *Sarpa Satra* (Ashok Shahane for Pras Prakashan, Pune, 2004), cover and book design by Arun Kolatkar; *Kala Ghoda Poems* (Ashok Shahane for Pras Prakashan, Pune, 2004), cover and book design by Arun Kolatkar. These and other volumes of both Kolatkar's Marathi and English poems are available through Pras Prakashan, Vrindavan-2B/5, Raheja Township, Malad East, Mumbai 400 097.

Dom Moraes, Bandra, Bombay, 1997

DOM MORAES

(1938–2004)

Dom Moraes was born in Bombay into a Roman Catholic family. His father was the journalist and editor Frank Moraes. His mother Beryl DeMonte was a doctor whose mental breakdowns and violence he obsessively revisited in poetry and prose. He began writing at the age of 10, and, three years later, published his first book, a collection of essays on cricket titled *Green is the Grass*. His first book of poems, *A Beginning* (Parton Press, 1957), appeared when he was 19. It won him deserved if disastrous early fame, via the Hawthornden Prize. He published two more collections before running into 'a writer's block, but only about poetry.' Despite the block – which lasted 15 years – he published 10 volumes of poems, two of translations from the Hebrew, and more than 20 books of prose. In 'Figures in the Landscape' from his debut volume, a character says: 'Dying is just the same as going to sleep.' The poem ends, 'I long to die.' Between the assured romanticism of this early poem and the stripped-down sonnets of his last work, 'After the Operation', there occurred a world of travel, prose writing, resurgence, and regret. He died in Bombay.

'Another Weather' appeared in the July 1959 number of *La Revue Bilingue de Paris*. It was never collected or republished.

Another Weather

Winged things move in the fleecy pelt of heaven.
The horses stroke the grass with their great hooves.
Often this weather, when a wind has driven
Insects and dust through air, the landscape moves,
Tilting itself one way, until this wind,
Shifting the world, has purified my mind.

For this weather I think I see things clearer.
All spring I drank until my money went,
Weeping for the horizon. Now I'm nearer.
Things happen here without my full consent.
And I accept them all. What is my choice?
I have few muscles; I must trust my voice.

My voice calls out in darkness, but it is calm
And very gentle: and it tells me this
Only: that it will come to no great harm
For the cathedral where its lodging is
Was built far off, and should the world get worse,
Two friends alone will find it: death and verse.

At Seven O'Clock

The masseur from Ceylon, whose balding head
Gives him a curious look of tenderness,
Uncurls his long crushed hands above my head
As though he were about to preach or bless.

His poulterer's fingers pluck my queasy skin,
Shuffle along my side, and reach the thigh.
I note however that he keeps his thin
Fastidious nostrils safely turned away.

But sometimes the antarctic eyes glance down,
And the lids drop to hood a scornful flash:
A deep ironic knowledge of the thin
Or gross (but always ugly) human flesh.

Hernia, goitre and the flowering boil
Lie bare beneath his hands, for ever bare.
His fingers touch the skin: they reach the soul.
I know him in the morning for a seer.

Within my mind he is reborn as Christ:
For each blind dawn he kneads my prostrate thighs,
Thumps on my buttocks with his fist
And breathes, Arise.

Visitors

The tireless persuasions of the dead
Disturb the student of the dark.
Hunched over derelict hands, they rock.
Cobwebs and pennies stop their eyes,

Dishevelled creatures, still unready
To be dead, heard only by his mood,
Casualties of a commonplace event:
The surprising conclusion of it all −

Needs for liquor, the moaning bed,
Oblivion in orchards, memories
Of smells, voices: the hand at work,
The mind at work, denying death.

Warned, they could not believe –
Clarities drawn from the known flesh:
Clutched at crosses when it came,
At hands, at the slipping world.

From earth, air, water, fire,
Hewn stone, welded words,
Coloured shapes left on canvas,
Breath from the nostrils of flutes,

The dispensation of absolutes
Disturbs the student in the dark,
Listening to the whispers in his work:
Knowing the impermanence of moon and star.

Absences

Smear out the last star.
No lights from the islands
Or hills. In the great square
The prolonged vowel of silence
Makes itself plainly heard.
Round the ghost of a headland
Clouds, leaves, shreds of bird
Eddy, hindering the wind.

No vigil left to keep.
No enemies left to slaughter.
The rough roofs of the slopes
Loosely thatched with splayed water
Only shelter microliths and fossils.
Unwatched, the rainbows build
On the architraves of hills.
No wound left to be healed.

Nobody left to be beautiful.
No polyp admiral to sip
Blood and whiskey from a skull
While fingering his warships.
Terrible relics, by tiderace
Untouched, the stromalites breathe.
Bubbles plop on the surface,
Disturbing the balance of death.

No sound would be heard if
So much silence was not heard.
Clouds scuff like sheep on the cliff.
The echoes of stones are restored.
No longer any foreshore
Nor any abyss, this
World only held together
By its variety of absences.

Two from Israel

1 *Rendezvous*
(for Nathan Altermann)

Altermann, sipping wine, reads with a look
Of infinite patience and slight suffering.
When I approach him, he puts down his book,

Waves to the chair beside him like a king,
Then claps his hands, and an awed waiter fetches
Bread, kosher sausage, cake, a chicken's wing,

More wine, some English cigarettes, and matches.
'Eat, eat,' Altermann says, 'this is good food.'
Through the awning over us the sunlight catches

His aquiline sad head, till it seems hewed
From tombstone marble. I accept some bread.
I've lunched already, but would not seem rude.

When I refuse more, he feeds me instead,
Heaping my plate, clapping for wine, his eyes
– Expressionless inside the marble head –

Appearing not to notice how the flies
Form a black, sticky icing on the cake,
Thinking of my health now, I visualise

The Aryan snow floating, flake upon flake,
Over the ghetto wall where only fleas
Fed well, and they and hunger kept awake

Under sharp stars, those waiting for release.
Birds had their nests, but Jews nowhere to hide
When visited by vans and black police.

The shekinah rose where a people died.
A pillar of flame by night, of smoke by day.
From Europe then the starved and terrified

Flew. Now their mourner sits in this café,
Telling me how to scan a Hebrew line.
Though my attention has moved far away

His features stay marble and aquiline.
But the eternal gesture of his race
Flowing through the hands that offer bread and wine

Reveals the deep love sealed in the still face.

2 *Spree*
(for Yosl Berger)

Tonight I see your blue protuberant eyes
Following your angry wife, who sweeps away,
With their perpetual look of mild surprise.

'No, have another drink for luck,' you say.
I settle back to let your swift talk flow
Freer with drink through the small hours till day

Reddens the bottles in your studio,
While, still unchecked, a rapid spate of words
Explains some brush technique I did not know.

A Polish boy, you took cadaverous birds,
Perched in a burnt-out Europe, for your text,
Then came here, but kept sympathy towards

Creatures with wings, for you chose angels next,
Though different from those flaming ones that flew
Into the bible: yours are too perplexed

Even to fly, waifs without work to do.
Yudl reproved you once, in the Cassit:
'Your angels are not Israelis, Jew.'

No: but they are the images we meet
In every mirror: so I understand
Those helpless angels waiting in the street

For somebody to take them by the hand.
Still, hangovers won't wait, so now we walk
Past herons down the beach towards liquor land.

223

There's not much left to talk of: but you talk,
Waving both arms, eccentric, Yiddish, free,
In your new home where tall winged creatures stalk

Between the ancient mountains and the sea.

from After the Operation

I

From a heavenly asylum, shrivelled Mummy,
glare down like a gargoyle at your only son,
who now has white hair and can hardly walk.
I am he who was not I. It's hot in this season
and the acrid reek of my body disturbs me
in a city where the people die on pavements.
That I'm terminally ill hasn't been much help.
There is no reason left for anything to exist.
Goodbye now. Don't try and meddle with this.

Why does your bloated corpse cry out to me
that I took from the hospital, three days dead?
I'd have come before, if the doctors had said.
I couldn't kiss you goodbye, you stank so much.
Or bear to touch you. Anyway, bye-bye, Mumsie.

III

Death will be an interruption of my days, of
all matters pertinent to me, and the private
intimacies I have that cannot be taken away.
It will interrupt my talks with my dead father,
moribund friends, and bent, witchlike trees;
and most of all interrupt what I have with her
who lives and saves me from my lost countries.

But whose feet are these that crush new leaves
on the lawn outside the mansion I once imagined
I inhabited, with the cadaverous butler Craxton?
He feeds me blood, and grieves for me each day
in his own way. But the feet? Whose are they?
The curtains rustle with the presence behind.
Are they feet, or the hooves of a hideous God?

V

Monster who unmade man, masturbate, leer
through whatever window you see the world
as though at some woman you watch undress,
unknown to her, stripped to her last privacies.
Then, God, leave me alone. I don't want any more,
I'm drained by death. Dust blurs my spectacles.
Craxton will fetch me nightly doses of blood
which I'll accept and swallow, mild as a child.

My throat was split open by a surgeon's knife.
Though he was a pleasant man, whom I liked,
when he took the tumour out, he invaded all
the private places in my head, and you, God,
giggling, watched. I shall choke on my blood
but not to toast you, monster made by man.

IX

I was good at school, though what I learnt I found
useless for all the rest of my life. But I learnt it
and I learnt to be lonely. Still, I liked my solitude.
Through it, in my own way, I learnt about the world.
At home my mother suffered from clinical insanity.
Her clear eyes became wild. I shrank from her touch.
After some months, strange nurses took her away.
My father did his best for me, but was not a woman.
I developed several masks, and have worn them since.
Sometimes I am not sure which one I have on, or even
what I am underneath. Neither do most others know,
apart from her I love. For thirteen years she has known
what I am, and made me know it. Whether I want to,
except when I am with her, is another matter.

XI

My raven locks Time hath to silver turn'd.
The growth in my throat makes itself felt.
Each day I wonder how much time there is.
I flinch from mirrors, raddled in the face.
I start to think when I see all those lines;
but not to think much is now necessary.
Hardest are these slow, tidal afternoons
that, ebbing, slide me out, not quite to sea.

The grinding gears of an absurd machine
recycled many friends whom I knew well.
They, as they went, stayed calm and cynical.

If my upper lip should slip, even for seconds,
and the sheer terror in my face were seen,
I should feel guilt that I betrayed my friends.

JEET THAYIL

(*b.* 1959)

Born in 1959 into a Syrian Christian family, Jeet Thayil was educated in Jesuit schools in Bombay, Hongkong and New York – cities in which his father worked as an editor and writer. In early poems marked by 'Christian romanticism' and a 'slurred surrealist drawl', he favoured song-like rhythms and invented structure over strict verse forms. The poems below are taken from his fourth collection *These Errors Are Correct* (Tranquebar, 2008), in which there is a wider formal arrangement – ghazals, sonnets, the sestina, the canzone, terza rima, rhymed syllabics, stealth rhymes – of history and grief. In 2004 he moved from New York to New Delhi, and currently lives in Bangalore.

To Baudelaire

I am over you at last, in Mexico City,
in a white space high above the street,
my hands steady, the walls unmoving.
It's warm here, and safe, and even in winter
the rain is benign. Some mornings I let
the sounds of the plaza – a fruit seller,
a boy acrobat, a woman selling
impossible fictions – pile up in a corner
of the room. I'm not saying I'm happy
but I am healthy and my money's my own.
Sometimes when I'm walking in the market
past the chickens and the pig smoke,
I think of you – your big talk and wolf's heart,
your Bonaparte hair and eyes of Poe.
I don't miss you. I don't miss you when
I open a window and light fills the room
like water pouring into a paper cup,
or when I hear a woman's white dress shine
like new coins and I know I could follow
my feet to the river and let my life go
away from me. At times like this,
if I catch myself talking to you,
I'm always surprised at the words I hear
of regret and dumb boyish devotion.

The Heroin Sestina

What was the point of it? The stoned
life, the chased, snorted, shot life. Some low
comedy with a cast of strangers. Time
squashed flat. The 1001 names of heroin
chewed like language. Nothing now to know
or remember but the dirty taste

of it, and the names: snuff, Death, a little taste,
H – pronounce it etch – , sugar, brownstone,
scag, the SHIT, ghoda gaadi, #4 china, You-Know,
garad, god, the gear, junk, monkey blow,
the law, the habit, material, cheez, heroin.
The point? It was the wasted time,

which comes back lovely sometimes,
a ghost sense say, say that hard ache taste
back in your throat, the warm heroin
drip, the hit, the rush, the whack, the stone.
You want it now, the way it lays you low,
flattens everything you know

to a thin white line. I'm saying, I know
the pull of it: the skull rings time
so beautiful, so low
you barely hear it. Itch this blind toad taste.
When you said, 'I mean it, we live like stones,'
you broke something in me only heroin

could fix. The thick sweet amaze of heroin,
helpless its love, its know-
ledge of the infinite. Why push the stone
back up the hill? Why not leave it with the time-
keep, asleep at the bar? Try a little taste
of something sweet that a sweet child will adore, low

in the hips where the aches all go. Allow
me in this one time and I'll give you heroin,
just a taste
to replace the useless stuff you know.
Some say it comes back, the time,
to punish you with the time you killed, leave you stone

sober, unknowing, the happiness chemical blown
from your system, unable to taste the word *heroin*
without wanting its stone one last time.

Malayalam's Ghazal

Listen! Someone's saying a prayer in Malayalam.
He says there's no word for 'despair' in Malayalam.

Sometimes at daybreak you sing a Gujarati garba.
At night you open your hair in Malayalam.

To understand symmetry, understand Kerala.
The longest palindrome is there, in *Malayalam*.

When you've been too long in the rooms of English,
Open your windows to the fresh air of Malayalam.

Visitors are welcome in The School of Lost Tongues.
Someone's endowed a high chair in Malayalam.

I greet you my ancestors, O scholars and linguists.
My father who recites Baudelaire in Malayalam.

Jeet, such drama with the scraps you know.
Write a couplet, if you dare, in Malayalam.

The Art of Seduction

When the flooding in the basement got worse
she slipped into a silly dress

and danced to *The Best of Nirvana*.
The way she fell on the divan, her

arms open – *The best thing for stress* –

you could have been some guy brought home
to read *Confessions of an English Opium*

Eater louder over Kurt's guitars,

some guy who would spend the evening
cross-legged on a tatami mat,

listening for the words between the words.

Youth is wasted on the young
and wisdom on the old, you know that,

like the call of a rare flightless bird.

Poem with Prediction

Because he's old and unsure,
he counts on your faith in images
and your fear, which is as pure
as when you were a child, turning the pages
of the illustrated books. He intones castrato *symbol* & basso *portent*,
reveals the unexpurgated blood truth of fairy tales, pretends
his closed, unchanged-in-2-millennia judgments
are improvised and no 5-star
disaster
awaited you. He gives you viral in exchange for Sister
Tree and calls it fair trade. You're allowed to whine
if you stay in key and watch your rhyme.
But your innocence
will be punished, this is a rule of the Great Gagadong.
Another is, You will love and obey him and let him lick
your wound with his infected tongue.
He brings you the good news – your tick
is erratic,
you are uninspired, dear
idiot, and no meaning will adhere
to you or your dead. His wide hand will rain
with blessings and good sense.
He'll translate the world into plain
language for you who are without ability. Your need for money
is as banal as it is weak.
The real work
is his to accomplish – in a week.
Your demands are too many,
your skin too soft. You deserve the paddle of his handmade violin.

Superpower

Leap tall buildings in a single bound? Forget
you, buddy, I
leap years, avenues,
financial/fashion/meatpacking districts, 23
MTA buses parked end to
end. I leap Broadway,
yoyo to
traffic light, to
bus top, to Chrysler, to jet.
You need a mind of sky, of rubber,
to understand I. You need
silence, cunning. Exhale!
You need to know that everything is metaphor,
that poems sprout
in my hands
like mystic confetti, like
neural string theory.
My brother, Mycroft, is tiny, but a genius,
oh a tiny genius, whose
'art is subtle, a precision of hallucinatory brilliance',
– that's serious talk, boy –
he's 'furthermore' and 'however', I'm
'know what I'm saying?' and 'whatever'.
He is the ghost ant, the one who is not
there, unseen until he stops
moving. I am
companion to owl and peregrine,
emperor of air, and I'm loyal
to you my loyal subject, whose hard-won
pleasure I perform,
and though I'm not rich it takes a lot
of cash to keep me
in the poverty to which I'm accustomed.

You Are Here

The bees of summer sail the avenues
like lovers. It's June but cool, and the news

isn't new: no change in your fortune,
not in the proximate future,

not for the better. You talk of cities
you won't see again. One, to the East,

is pounded by rain for half the year,
for the other half it stews in fear

of its own dialects. Its Victorian stations,
water stained, are eye-catching ruins,

like the six-legged monuments
to British adulterers. Sex and violence,

casual as the monitor licking lunch from the air,
scraps the estranged mind will share.

Led by One Law for Aliens and your own lack
of foresight, you do a dance: two steps back,

best foot forward. A future races the street,
draws even with the corner, you in pursuit,

following like another Orpheus,
his three friends still friends, his voice

intact, no plans for a moonlit headlong swim,
his wife at the window waiting for him.

The New Island

Once, carried by the rains of September,
a boat lifted free of its mooring place,
of a shed become part of the river,
    and floated past
    the porch, where I caught her.

Somehow the house kept itself clear of the
river that had made it a new island,
but everything around us was water.
    I made the stern
    seesaw with every step.

You were lining up the prow with a tree
I thought too far upstream in the blurred tides
of current to be trusted. Now I'm sorry
    I held the sides
    as we climbed the water.

Your hands, as you moved us forward, were sure
in their shaping of water, your eye true,
and our few feet of hammered wood, our floor,
    took us in to
    lamplight, voices, the shore.

PRAGEETA SHARMA
(*b.* 1972)

Prageeta Sharma's parents arrived in the US from Rajasthan (Jaipur and Bharatpur) and she
was born in Framingham, Massachusetts in 1972. Her poems take on the big subjects: love,
death, faith, power. But they are obsessed with the minutiae of language and the mechanics
of miscommunication between lovers or family members. Her system of reinvented Chinese
Whispers ('You say marred and I say martyr'; 'you stand out like a sore thumb in Bethlehem')
takes her from the landscapes of North America to the forests of the Vedas to somewhere
indistinct and unique: 'it seems / I am holding the bread for a Hindu Eucharist, confused
about / origins and art-making'. She teaches at the University of Montana in Missoula.

On Rebellion
(for Katy Lederer)

It was not a romantic sentiment, nor self-determined; rather, it was embarrassing.
My love of spearheading, from introvert to extrovert,
from cowardice to consequence, from the enjambment to the unspecified dunce.
It was a sabotage, a reckless moment: a purulent, tawny decree.
All temptation puzzled me and drew me in.
I dropped out of a large life,
I flew over exams, I punched out breakfast teachers with lunch money,
toiling over the idea of belonging rather than over upward mobility.
I understood how power flung outward
into the troves of the cursed (I felt cursed or troubled all of the time).
I wasn't bearing oranges, limes, or even lemons.
All of it blurred together so that a mere suggestion made by
an outside force was something to be freely ignored.
I could nod off, I could misinterpret, it could be reconfigured as a negotiation.
The fog felt like an aphorism. Never lifting, always dull,
always an added pull. The tribunal cloud judged below, judged my direction.
There was lying, conning, faking, elucidating in order to get away with undoing.
I was interested in preserving yet I can't tell you if it felt
sacred or befallen.

Your anxiety might have represented a crushing faith
or a character assassination, my own or someone else's.
Or a lack of grip on reality: the wet rip of the grocery bags

all of it falling –
your body on all fours.
Accumulating soot upon retrieval.

There were downsides to feeling different so I huddled
in the corner (not a ball, not rocking). I felt friendless and yet social.
I felt no aptitude towards refining a skill.

However, words cut my brain into two brains with their precipice
their demarcations, their incisions (too strong a word).

They held me captive against their edge,
their influence: I felt like insinuating something delicate or dear.

Now – I am holding on – trying to pay attention to the collusion that I must
        be playing over
and over in my mind, and it was my mind,
it needed me to leave everything outside, on the steps or in the sky,
to feign exhaustion in order to meet an aberration,
the one in the corner that felt large and carefree with its
own vernacular sprawled with whitewash on bricks or floors or that ghastly
far above that kept me standing very still but perhaps I wasn't inactive,
I was just interpreting what had already been an assumed boundary,
immersed in its insularity and in what stuck to its roundedness.

Blowing Hot and Cold

What does it mean to say that faith alone works?
Or that faith in itself can drag a whole mountain to the other side.
Of course faith rests its laurels on the impossibility of the fleet
of dreadfuls worshipping a magnetic bounty of light in
the neutral distance. I am tired of so much confusion,
of dreary, ugly ideas, of nonsense.
Now to strangers and friends – of columns of stars organised for the onlookers
        here,
any several of the tropical trees, any several hocus-pocus earth-
muffin types. You should just stay clueless amongst your granola
huts and your failed relationships. I was told everything
does go back to one's miserable family, and it's true it's
the root of all odes to neurosis. Look here
between the cherry, the sugar maple, and the shagbark hickory
you stand out like a sore thumb in Bethlehem. Accept that nature
itself wouldn't have you and your former sport of death of life
of foul-mouthed abuse, it is all egregious and against clairvoyance,
charitable dreams groomed for a billion swine.

The Silent Meow

Under the parts of the Brooklyn Bridge, I was with Hedi and Angus.
We were discussing his cat's mute mewing.
Hedi and I perked up: What a metaphor for a woman we said.

This was a little off the cuff, because we are off the cuff
and were not that kind of feminist –
not to make such a drab and pathetic metaphor
likening a woman to a cat.
But we liked the persistence that the mute cat exhibited,
its mewing, demonstrative yawns with nothing coming out –

it was the kind of perfect caption we had for such obvious things
and obvious needs for day-to-day living.

Birthday Poem
(after Bill Luoma & Barbara Guest)

When that boat soars off, my lover is full of
magnetic sensibilities, but there are French chemists
who've made pills for this. I tell my lover of just one week that
there are museums drunk with people.
Headrushes are lovely when cured,
as one cups an illustration of the densely crowded man who is my lover.
My lover is strangely seductive and punishing,
I can tell. On his birthday, I wish him a Happy Birthday
but I think he has a complicated head, it seems to frustrate
him. For I have seen him swoon and
has he spun around a bit too quick? And this may not be him.
My lover of one week swims with small finned fish and cypress
in the shape of oceans. And yes, I am in a stranger ocean
than I fished and my lover is just beside, with a possible foil,
curing me for a moment of all possible intricate characterisations.

Release Me from This Paying Passenger

There is nothing to really note in this world
you might say. But since crescent moons
frame brittle grass all over the world,
I won't stop at this philosophy. I won
the argument yesterday when we were nearby
the park and the day before when you ran me over.
I have run away from you with accidental
fortune in hands not all of your bank statements.
But I am not a Calvinist in the true sense I only
lowered it to ahistorical terms. I believe in principles
prophetic principles. You say marred and I say martyr.
I drink two liters; you don't drink anything.
There are pests roaming the floorboards.
There are animals all around us now.
Save the foolhardy measure for your male companions.
They desire this more readily
more enigma, shall we say, to entertain them
barren matadors or empathetics.
I need neither Grand Marnier nor vodka
to wash my throat or collapse my senses to tiny
careless obliterations. The way this ended shut you out,
so drop the lensatic compass and lavish gift, and please, run.

Underpants

My sweetie's underpants have argyles on them and grip his thighs.
O his European underpants with pastel colors,
how they illustrate his unassuming ways.
His secrets are feasts and traumas
and he is sometimes the loneliest under blankets.
His underpants represent the unconscious,
innocent, nervy, and true.
I can't help feeling eager.
O how he is an old man in his underpants.
When he is sleeping he has the softness of a child,
unquestioning and quietly fitful,
I kiss his head and wings,
for he in his underpants travels like a Griffin
to himself, a fabled monster of certain sadness,
when he sleeps it all goes inward,
in his lion and eagle.

Ode to Badminton

Today my sixth sense tells me to play Badminton: a game of yielding,
of volleying a shuttlecock back and forth. A game named after a chair,
named after the Duke of Beaufort's country seat.
This game imitates tennis but our birdie
is much more exquisite, the obligations of a ball are somehow graceless
when compared to a piece of rubber with a crown of fine feathers.
This sport where the signature is the flight
of a bird. A backhand is as necessary as the yield it purports.
We know intuitively that the meaning of the game is that it is not the sideline
        of tennis,
not an observer resisting participance
but rather for the mischievous or creative sorts that need duplicity
to determine a sound trajection. Also it is a pretty thing to go up in the sky
as sweet as stellar, bespangled with small stars. As well as yourself if
you are hit in the head with the racket.
Alas the birdie itself is never a painful hit, like its replacement,
the tennis ball, the birdie
is a Florence Nightingale, if you will – only do not get her in the eye.
It will soar to the light base of the racket, above the long thin handle,
I hit firmly as it continues to engage me. I stand in the backcourt
between the service line and the base line, as in some country
chair that was, perhaps, soothing under a nighttime of clear stars.

Miraculous Food for Once

I put you in writing and put you in speaking
all about you until you disappeared into the haystack.
A fire then smokestack thus ending my selected works,
of my barnyard wants, to my treaty of hay bail.
You vanished and my farm appeared again the way I wanted it.
I thought, what a gift, what a rake –
this fate was mine again – I bask in perpetual joy.
The snow falls and I think it's marvelous.
The parkas of suitors look sensible and exciting.
The categories are multiple; I am off the ball and chain
of unrequited love – onto the seduction
theory wrapped in overalls and archives
of new things; how provocative and alluring
verse and tree; lamb and locket,
gently daring without a pull of resignation –
not a hot oven, not branded in doom

or silence, my valentine is forthcoming,
Basque, on horses and on time.
There is no unease and we live here for a while
closing in with a great gray fog that allows
for its own density to draw everything mildly and
gently out, so that it's never, ever trickery.

The Fantasist's Speech on the Fifteenth of August
(for Salman Rushdie)

Whether or not the two of us had anything to do with our parents' independence.
We were children of independent thinkers.

We were not bribed into the business of the Hindustani as much as to the
business of the fantasist, which was the real business of the Hindustani.

This reality does not rest on the face, apparent and jutting as bad light
when cast over a villain's face.

A knife is stud in the heart of the mother-in-law.
For the daughter, there is the companionship with herself.

The mother does not love discovery anymore;
her independence takes as long as will,

when the arms become fantastic sources
when we pull down books, throw away plates.
The wonders become, the mother surprised,

the independence eminent, there are now children's poems about independence.

ANAND THAKORE
(*b.* 1971)

Born in Bombay in 1971, Anand Thakore studied Hindustani classical vocal music from
the age of seven. He was educated in Britain and in India, and the two cultures feed his
work. His poems have a line and weight reminiscent of mid-20th century British verse; his
music reaches to Indian antiquity. He lives and performs in Bombay where he runs a
publishing collective, Harbour Line, and a music collective, Kshitij.

Departure

I see them across the rim of a fogged lens,
Amidst the swivelling glare of party lights –
Too bright now, now too dark,
To do what they have asked me to: these two,
Arm in arm, their eyes aslant with impatient poise,
Awaiting the brief redemption of a flash –
Now? Perhaps, but I am a poor photographer,

And prefer to see what open eye and shutter
Conspire so closely to conceal:
Her fastening her seat-belt three nights hence,
Content to believe, as she leans to the left
To watch grey buildings grow tiny below her,
That her flight home is also a journey out.
She is not thinking of the man who wades

Through the familiar spaces of her absence,
Into the exquisite hovel of his home,
Floundering, lip-deep, in the gravy of speech,
As he reaches out for the lost island of the flesh:
Words that may conjure the ghost of a caged green bird
Who never answered back, even when alive – Quick –
My fingers say, as they tighten, and click.

Chandri Villa

His name was Chandri – my grandfather once said –
Who was to live here, but died of plague. Each of us fails
In the end, but I was born in a house built for the dead:
On the red gate they hammered his name with nails.

Nineteen Nineteen. These bougainvillaeas
Have grown since then; the dead leave us, leaving no trails.
Deep in the banyan-grove at Chandri Villa,
A secret sense of loss prevails.

And the very stillness of these trees carries me past an April
Long dead, newly strewn with banyan-leaves; thick roots dangle
Above my head – ancient, knotted roots I cannot untangle,
Till I am a child once again though against my will,

The wide grove closing its arms as if to kill.
My veins so many banyan-roots twisted into one,
And all their tangled knots come undone,
Till almost I see him, the plagued man I never will.

Creepers on a Steel Door

Three months now, creeping up this door,
Half-open, between myself and the garden-yard.
I wonder why, at times, it is so hard
To reach the wide world across the narrow floor.

Space must have its bounds, I suppose;
Though the heart's first impulse be to leap.
The creeper does not wish to move, it simply grows –
It is the eye that makes these broad leaves creep.

But see how tight each tendril grips the grill,
Where the highest leaves, translucence-shy, peep inside.
I can tell what makes them want to hide.
Could they hear, I would tell them: looking in can kill.

What I Can Get Away With

Let me get this down before I forget –
Time may not recover a forgotten rhyme;
But what I can get away with you can never get.

There will be time to think things over, time for regret,
Time for other lovers and hangovers at dawn;
But let me get this down before I forget.

I should have told you this when we first met:
I'm a performing seal without a soul –
So let me get this down before I forget.

The bet unmade, the truth unsaid, the unpaid debt,
And the same black lies blanched by new moons –
What I can get away with you can never get.

But let's not get upset, my pigeon, my little pet,
Not being a poet, or in love, isn't all that bad;
Though I can get away with what you can never get,

My muse may not wait for the perfect pirouette
Of a half-meant phrase flawlessly turned;
So let me get this down before I forget,

Before you spread your charms about me like a net;
Though your arms have a way of making me feel small,
And your eyes are adept at making me forget

The rent I could not pay, the heart I would not let,
The lines I do not mean but think it fine to say –
What I can get away with you can never get.

But Damn, it's gone again. My brains are too wet.
This whiskey's pretty good, though the waiters aren't too bright,
And what they will get away with I will never get.

Another cigarette? No, my little friend, no need to fret,
I'll be with you in a minute, but not just yet;
Just let me get this down before I forget –
What I can get away with you will never get.

Ablutions

Each morning, lying back in bed, I sing my first note.
My demon sings his, standing at my door.

He never stops when I start,
Though I close my lips soon enough

To take in his finer trills and smoother arpeggios,
His steadier rhythms and bolder flourishes.

He is a better singer than I am,
I concede.

His vowels are rounder,
His humming more audible,

His frills are more decorous,
His tremolo more subtle.

He has a broader tone, a huskier bass,
A more stentorian upper octave,

An instant mellifluous retort
To the most arcane musical question

I can think of posing, a louder bellow,
A sharper twang, purer pitch and yet,

He remains completely dumbfounded,
Each time I ask him

Why he never dares follow me into the shower.
Does he flinch from water because he fears –

For all his bravado and brash virtuosity –
That being drenched in something more tactile

Than he can ever hope to be,
Might be too much for him,

That he would perish at its touch?
Or can he simply not bear to see

How comfortable I now am
With my own nakedness,

How willing I turn
To be seized by water

And give myself to the stark and craftless rapture
Of this chill awakening?

I muse, pacifically, upon the sober comforts
Of being human, perishable, and clad in my own flesh;

And ask of all that host of demons,
That have made their homes

In the frenzied nerves of this world's singers,
Since the first song sprang forward

And the first note broke from the human throat,
Who, amongst them, can rob me now

Of this growing presence,
This minute's reprieve?

RUTH VANITA

(b. 1955)

Born in 1955, Ruth Vanita was educated in Delhi. Her sonnet-like love poems derive enormous energy from their hidden meanings. Her books include *Sappho and the Virgin Mary: Same-Sex Love and the English Literary Imagination* (Columbia UP, 1996), and she is the editor of *Queering India* (Routledge, 2002). She teaches at the University of Montana.

Sita

From being the perfect wife, there's only one way out –
Not one you planned. Or imagined, even.
You'll see her suddenly in the laughing eyes
Of some stranger turned lover, or lover stranger –
The woman you never quite believed in,
The abandoned woman, the temptress, stealer
Of others' spouses. You'll conceive her
Some drunken evening, take her into your eyes,
Find her again next morning, in the mirror,
Born of sight. And then you'll call on the earth
To swallow you, hide you from light.

Sisters

Always there's a Martha – there has to be –
Who dusts the furniture and makes the tea,
Wakes on time and runs to catch the bus,
Who smiles and sends out cards, who counts the cost.
And sometimes, sometimes Mary at your knee,
Drunk on your words and innocent of art,
Without answers, not seeing that all is lost,
Choosing the better part.

Swayamvara

Anything is easier –
To do without, to wither,
Serve, and slave, to let
Choices be made that turn

Blood sluggish – anything
Rather than see your eyes
Become the other's
And say, I want this. Nothing
Is harder than to say, Yes, this,
This face, this stone, this sky, this song,
This, this, and not another.

Fire

It occurs to you, off and on,
That it could happen some time.
Idly you wonder what you'd grab
If you had five minutes flat –
What would be priceless, after all?
Yet it takes you by surprise
When it explodes – hands, mind and feet
Run different ways, grope to recall
Which moment lies embalmed where,
In what toy – until that joyful
Flaming skyward brings release:
Knowing that everything can only turn
To ash, except what lives in you, and burns.

Effluence

After the ups and downs of the day
Manufactured alone in this small room,
Aching in more than one way, I press
Seven buttons, and am at last in heaven.
Who is to be praised like Graham Bell
For the greatest, kindest imagining,
For knowing that no song can please so well,
So heal, as one voice saying two syllables
In a tone not reproducible?
Thanks to an era that may blow us both
Up any minute, my heart is lifted,
I see the stars again, bless a world
That has you in it, and that makes you mine
Along a line so tenuous, vibrant, fine.

KERSY KATRAK

(1936-2007)

Born in Bombay, Kersy Katrak was ordained as a Zoroastrian priest at the age of 12. He published one book of prose and four of verse while running an advertising agency. The poems in this selection circle around the numerous physical breakdowns that occur with ageing, and with the way the body's 'bright arterial jungle' articulates its misgivings in 'the wide throat at night.' He died in Bombay.

from Malabar Hill

4

The bone prevails. Always I have found this.
The flesh exists upon it, breeds,
Proliferates, turns to itself for love:
Creates its bright arterial jungle and undergrowth of nerve,
Pap, genital and thigh;
Suffers its own agony and dies.
Somewhere beneath,
Interior and unlit, the bone remains
Inexorably white.

Opposed to it is something
Animal and profound. The body's dark
Instinctive fondling of itself. The snare of blood.
Something that ties
Metaphor and flesh, dreams of paradise
And breasts of real women. Something that shouts,
Screams or sings alternately
In the wide throat at night.

Yet the bone prevails. Always. Partaking nothing.
Immovable to all that blood commands,
It does not bend,
But witnesses the body's barefaced lusts,
Watches the mind's hidden and prolific lusts
And stays in the end
Itself.

5

To know the bone and know it well:
Its inner hard compulsions and complexities;
To eat, make love,
To defecate and sleep, holding it near
May be perhaps a vocation:

A way of life requiring
Fortitude and love to make it true.
I think I have it now –
Love – because of you.

I used to come here often. December was my month,
Now coming here with the first rain in May
I find that I have grown remote from pain
And have something to say.

6

I do not know much about love.

My father shaped my head and handed down
His large distinctive nose. My mother taught me facts
But left me little else. Of their first act
That made me
Swaggering and shy, nervous, afraid of love,
Nothing was said. Whether it was
Quiet or passionate, trivial or profound
My eyes know nothing. Nothing is left
Of their first sound.

I used to come here looking for love, alone.
And now that it is found
I see the old division of its ground
Between the antagonists of flesh and bone.
I think I know now why lovers laugh
Obsessively against the cold;
Compelled to see even in love the old
Powers that divide the world
Half and half.

Ancestors

I followed him as he left the body, every limb
Turning to anthracite, his mind half conscious and arctic
As the late October night closed like a thick gas around him.
The cancer turned quickly rampant, now the opposing
Spirit had withdrawn; lymph and gland,
The stopped arterial flow, now all turned iron,
Eyes to dull stones, the skin in thirteen minutes

A visible brown green. The body at last
Become triumphantly itself, not him. And he
Turning slowly from the thing he had become
For fifteen minutes was now himself:
Trudging painfully away from us under a sky like iron
Blazoned with eight o'clock Bombay stars,
Remembering us a little, waving his handkerchief
Shyly almost, his last pennant. They stopped him at the pass
Before the five peaks.

Often he returns now, not always remembering
Himself as dead, only half aware
He was once my father. He comes, simply familiar
As one who has the right:
No door is closed against him, no circle drawn.
I drop my magic breastplate as he enters
To claim his due of friendship,
To talk as we could never talk in life,
Exert affection for a four-year-old grand daughter,
Or simply watch bemused
A pattern magical to him, as time flows round us.

I saw him again yesterday (having learnt to distinguish
Fantasy from the true Imagination
Which alone brings inwardly
Us to the returning dead) and at his word have set this down
A memorial not to him nor to his vanished past
But to what survives:
This strange haunting of Love.

IMTIAZ DHARKER

(*b.* 1954)

Born in 1954 in Lahore, Imtiaz Dharker 'grew up a Muslim Calvinist in a Lahori household in Glasgow and eloped with a Hindu Indian to live in Bombay'. She is a documentary film-maker and visual artist. Her poems and line drawings are complementary studies of women in spiritual purdah, and of the 'rare genius for revenge' visited upon them by men. She lives between Bombay, London and Wales.

Living Space

There are just not enough
straight lines. That
is the problem.
Nothing is flat
or parallel. Beams
balance crookedly on supports
thrust off the vertical.
Nails clutch at open seams.
The whole structure leans dangerously
towards the miraculous.

Into this rough frame,
someone has squeezed
a living space

and even dared to place
these eggs in a wire basket,
fragile curves of white
hung out over the dark edge
of a slanted universe,
gathering the light
into themselves,
as if they were
the bright, thin walls of faith.

Its Face

A woman getting on a plane.
This is how it will happen.
A bird that has stopped singing
on a still road. This is how it will sound.

This cloth belongs to my face.
Who pulled it off?

That day I saw you
as if a window had broken.
Sharp, with edges that could cut
through cloth and skin.

You wrapped my mouth in plastic
and told me to breathe in free air.
This is how it will feel.

I remember heroes.
Figs, dates, a mango.
This food, your enemy's food.
This is how it will taste.

It will not come
slouching out of the ground.
It walks along a street
that has a familiar name.

This is how it will look.
It will have my face.

Before I

This is what was happening
before the planes came in.
She woke early,

switched on the songs,
fetched milk and put it on to heat.
Bare feet slapped across the floor.

She shook the children awake,
her voice a little hoarse
from sleep.

She was thinking about
what she would pack
for them to eat

at school, something
cooling in the heat.
And now, the water.

The water spilling
out of a steel glass.

All this happened
before.

Dreams

I write down his dreams,
pulled in to the sleeping
and waking of his night,
punctuated by the light switched on,
switched off.

They had to look around to find
the vein that would be strong enough
to hold the dreams
they were going to put in, the people
he would gather up and take with him
along a stream
of country roads that lead
to unknown
imagined towns, polished cities,
squares in civil geometry.

My blood turns round with his
till we break through, into the clearing
of his heart, and stop, amazed,
struck by light, the sight
of tables laid, glasses he has filled,
making, dreaming, waking
to unexpected wine.

Purdah I

One day they said
she was old enough to learn some shame.
She found it came quite naturally.

Purdah is a kind of safety.
The body finds a place to hide.
The cloth fans out against the skin
much like the earth that falls
on coffins after they put the dead men in.

People she has known
stand up, sit down as they have always done.
But they make different angles
in the light, their eyes aslant,
a little sly.

She half-remembers things
from someone else's life,
perhaps from yours, or mine –
carefully carrying what we do not own:
between the thighs, a sense of sin.

We sit still, letting the cloth grow
a little closer to our skin.
A light filters inward
through our bodies' walls.
Voices speak inside us,
echoing in the spaces we have just left.

She stands outside herself,
sometimes in all four corners of a room.
Wherever she goes, she is always
inching past herself,
as if she were a clod of earth,
and the roots as well,
scratching for a hold
between the first and second rib.

Passing constantly out of her own hands
into the corner of someone else's eyes...
while doors keep opening
inward and again
inward.

Object

Desire can be a delicate thing,
or so the punishments
suggest.
Who needs as much as the naked
breast? Lust
is aroused by a wrist
revealed,
the hollow at the neck,
the ankle-bone
half-concealed.

The guardians of our need
patrol the streets, fired
with pure passion,
eager to find the flesh

unsealed, frantic
to mete out justice,

Oh delicious,
exquisite pleasure, to punish
the object of our desire.

RUKMINI BHAYA NAIR

(*b*. 1952)

Born in 1952 in Vishakhapatnam, Andhra Pradesh, Rukmini Bhaya Nair teaches at the Indian
Institute of Technology in New Delhi. Her academic fields are literary theory and cognitive
linguistics. Her poems rhyme Hindi words with English ones, and they may mention Tarski
and Ong – by one name only – as often as Ashbery and Whitman, or Baudrillard and Lacan.

Genderole

Considerthefemalebodyyourmost
Basictextanddontforgetitsslokas I

Whatpalmleafcandoforusitdoes
Therealgapsremainforwomentoclose I

Spacesbetweenwordspreservesenses
Intactbutweneedtomeetineverysense I

Comingtogetherisnoverbalmatter
Howeveroursagespraise*pativrata* I

Katavkantakasteputrasamsaroyam
*Ativavichitra*waswrittenformenbyaman I

Theworlddoesnotseemsostrangeseen
Throughgentlereyesnorwomensoalien I

Nalinidalagatajalamatataralamtadvat
*Jivanamatishayachapalam*changeability I

Isinthenatureofthingsandespecially
Femalebutsankarayayouoldmysogynisttellme I

Whatssocontemptibleaboutfleeting
Splendour?andwhileyouareaboutitthink I

Wehavewrungpoemsfromhouseholdtasks
Carryingwaterchildsorrowcanyoudoasmuch? I

Itmaybebeneathyoutopriseapartthisgimmick
Butrememberthethingawomanchangesbestishersex I

Opposingyouischildsplaybecauseyoufail
Torealisethisandwecanbeatyouatyourowngame I

Muchhardertoconvertourselveshaving
Labouredlongatbeingmenwepossessnothing I

MyworstfearissankarathathadIindeedbeenyou
Imightnotafterallhaveconceivedanythingnew I

Renoir's Umbrellas

This woman looks straight at you
Her dark hair hectic

Imprisoned in a cage of water
Une triste lunatique

When the rain beats down across
The world's asylums

She negotiates small puddles
In the afternoon sun

Lifts high that froth of skirts
Over netted pantyhose

And waits for summer's downpour
To shimmer to a close

Holds out her hands to you
Through bars of rain

Grey pearls and luminous pallor
Her enraptured pain

You see each tiny thing about her
Gleam with disorder

Taut stretch of madness overhead
Like a parabola

On some damp morning when a woman
Looks straight at you

Victim of a painted liquefaction
Whom you do not rescue

Usage

To use another, even to be used to her, seems
Insufficient, as if love's way remains the same.

So you left much unspoken when you said
My soft, fissured body was a habit you had.

That ploy's worn out, the shoe fits loose
Small wonder then we stray, footloose.

Among your secret thoughts (of which such
Quantities exist, some spill), one's about touch.

Because the form's thickened you called 'petite'
And my arms, on the inside, turned to putty.

The swan-shape of my neck, once a single span
Now quite escapes this measure of your hand.

Before I did, you noticed new lines cut me up
In the rough contours of an unfamiliar map.

Therefore these minefields are dangerous.
Memory may blow us up like enemies, strangers.

If all we remember is a firm bend of thigh
And the toss of limbs, we could fight shy.

Blundering, we must track our subterfuge,
For love's foot-soldiers, the last refuge.

Survivors say courage matters, not luck
Passionate argument, and the will to laugh.

It is better the sag-folds of my skin
Amuse you, than sadness haunt your ken.

Otherwise lust gains cover, and the dark signals
Only fugitive activity, furtive kiss and snuggle.

Escaping love's predictable range, we pursue
Ourselves, aliens we are entirely used to,

With weapons unknown in early combat, minds
Naked and sharp, their latitude undefined.

Custom endures, endears, that's the secret
Of the many you've kept, the most indiscreet.

Hope's bubble, effervescent Alka Seltzer,
Useful too, the trick is to change, to alter.

Give everything away, hidden sentiment, thought,
And love's self returns, via a different route.

Convent

The coloured light burning
In her colourless hair

High, high above the snare
Of the sinful world

Glides Mary, mother of god
Pure as plaster, and as unaware

From her perch in the scented air
She sees small faces

Giggling, and the fair
Nuns from Ireland, kneeling

And she wonders about prayer
The pity of it, the point...

GOPI KOTTOOR

(*b.* 1956)

Born in 1956 in Trivandrum, Kerala, Gopi Kottoor has been an officer with the Reserve Bank of India for 25 years. In his short illuminated poems, the strange and the sacred combine in unexpected ways: 'This is pure god, the flowing water... As about Him the dark nuns build / Their rosary of ice.' He lives in Bombay.

Penguins

Down the grand slopes in monastic treble,
Their feathered arms conducting a church choir in the air,
They turn up at the riverfront waiting,

Like souls in the sky,
In expectation of grand heaven. Always in pure black
And white,
They climb, one by one in gifted queues,
The steep kingdoms of ice; then from their steppes
Let themselves fall as perfect swimmers

Into the wetness of the fishing seals;
This is pure god, the flowing water,
As around rising foam they build a circle of love,
As about Him the dark nuns build
Their rosary of ice.

Old Time Friends

Perhaps this is after all a season
And will pass.
Friends die. In strange unfamiliar rooms
They turn over and become so quiet.
Their painted wagons roll off the long wet sunset,
Jolting us, sometimes
Making us cry. Just how easily they peel away,
One by one,
Each face going out like a wet balloon,
And all its bright colours nowhere,
In the centre of the carnival
Under the big floodlights,
Beside the playing children.

KAMALA DAS

(b. 1934)

Born in 1934, in Punnayurkulam, Kerala, Kamala Das was raised in Calcutta. Her mother was a poet in Malayalam and her father the editor and managing director of *Mathrabhoomi*, a leading Malayalam-language newspaper. She has published six books of poems and several novels and short stories in Malayalam and English. Despite this, she is probably best-known for a racy autobiography, *My Story* (1976), and an eventful life that has included a period in politics and a conversion to Islam. The autobiography became something of a publishing sensation in its time, drawing readers who had possibly never before read a literary memoir. But the writing may have little bearing on the life. The speakers in her poems, and the speaker in her autobiography – 'unhappy woman, unhappy wife, reluctant nymphomaniac', in Eunice de Souza's words – may be nothing more, or less, than various personae. She lives in Pune.

The Descendants

We have spent our youth in gentle sinning
Exchanging some insubstantial love and
Often thought we were hurt, but no pain in
Us could remain, no bruise could scar or
Even slightly mar our cold loveliness.
We have lain in every weather, nailed, no, not
To crosses, but to soft beds and against
Softer forms, while the heaving, lurching,
Tender hours passed in a half-dusk, half-dawn and
Half-dream, half-real trance. We were the yielders,
Yielding ourselves to everything. It is
Not for us to scrape the walls of wombs for
Memories, not for us even to
Question death, but as child to mother's arms
We shall give ourselves to the fire or to
The hungry earth to be slowly eaten,
Devoured. None will step off his cross
Or show his wounds to us, no god lost in
Silence shall begin to speak, no lost love
Claim us, no, we are not going to be
Ever redeemed, or made new.

Luminol

Love-lorn,
It is only
Wise at times, to let sleep
Make holes in memory, even
If it
Be the cold and
Luminous sleep banked in
The heart of pills, for he shall not
Enter,
Your ruthless one,
Being human, clumsy
With noise and movement, the soul's mute
Arena,
That silent sleep inside your sleep.

A Request

When I die
Do not throw
The meat and bones away
But pile them up
And let them tell
By their smell
What life was worth
On this earth
What love was worth
In the end.

The Looking Glass

Getting a man to love you is easy
Only be honest about your wants as
Woman. Stand nude before the glass with him
So that he sees himself the stronger one
And believes it so, and you so much more
Softer, younger, lovelier... Admit your
Admiration. Notice the perfection
Of his limbs, his eyes reddening under

Shower, the shy walk across the bathroom floor,
Dropping towels, and the jerky way he
Urinates. All the fond details that make
Him male and your only man. Gift him all,
Gift him what makes you woman, the scent of
Long hair, the musk of sweat between the breasts,
The warm shock of menstrual blood, and all your
Endless female hungers. Oh yes, getting
A man to love you is easy, but living
Without him afterward may have to be
Faced. A living without life when you move
Around, meeting strangers, with your eyes that
Gave up their search, with ears that hear only
His last voice calling out your name and your
Body which once under his touch had gleamed
Like burnished brass, now drab and destitute.

The Stone Age

Fond husband, ancient settler in the mind,
Old fat spider, weaving webs of bewilderment,
Be kind. You turn me into a bird of stone, a granite
Dove, you build round me a shabby drawing-room,
And stroke my pitted face absent-mindedly while
You read. With loud talk you bruise my pre-morning sleep,
You stick a finger into my dreaming eye. And
Yet, on daydreams, strong men cast their shadows, they sink
Like white suns in the swell of my Dravidian blood,
Secretly flow the drains beneath sacred cities.
When you leave, I drive my blue battered car
Along the bluer sea. I run up the forty
Noisy steps to knock at another door.
Through peep-holes, the neighbours watch,
They watch me come
And go like rain. And me, everybody, ask me
What he sees in me, ask me why he is called a lion,
A libertine, ask me the flavour of his
Mouth, ask me why his hand sways like a hooded snake
Before it clasps my pubis. Ask me why like
A great tree, felled, he slumps against my breasts
And sleeps. Ask me why life is short and love is
Shorter still, ask me what is bliss and what its price.

The Maggots

At sunset on the river bank, Krishna
loved her for the last time and left.
That night in her husband's arms, Radha felt
so dead that he asked, what is wrong,
do you mind my kisses love, and she said
no, not at all, but thought, what is
it to the corpse if the maggots nip?

The Old Playhouse

You planned to tame a swallow, to hold her
In the long summer of your love so that she would forget
Not the raw seasons alone, and the homes left behind, but
Also her nature, the urge to fly, and the endless
Pathways of the sky. It was not to gather knowledge
Of yet another man that I came to you but to learn
What I was, and by learning, to learn to grow, but every
Lesson you gave was about yourself. You were pleased
With my body's response, its weather, its usual shallow
Convulsions. You dribbled spittle into my mouth, you poured
Yourself into every nook and cranny, you embalmed
My poor lust with your bitter-sweet juices. You called me wife,
I was taught to break saccharine into your tea and
To offer at the right moment the vitamins. Cowering
Beneath your monstrous ego I ate the magic loaf and
Became a dwarf. I lost my will and reason, to all your
Questions I mumbled incoherent replies. The summer
Begins to pall. I remember the ruder breezes
Of the fall and the smoke from burning leaves. Your room is
Always lit by artificial lights, your windows always
Shut. Even the air-conditioner helps so little,
All pervasive is the male scent of your breath. The cut flowers
In the vases have begun to smell of human sweat. There is
No more singing, no more a dance, my mind is an old
Playhouse with all its lights put out. The strong man's technique is
Always the same, he serves his love in lethal doses,
For, love is Narcissus at the water's edge, haunted
By its own lonely face, and yet it must seek at last
An end, a pure, total freedom, it must will the mirrors
To shatter and the kind night to erase the water.

MENKA SHIVDASANI

(*b.* 1961)

Menka Shivdasani was born in 1961 in Bombay. Her family settled in the city following Partition, when her ancestral home in Sind became a part of Pakistan. She has worked as a journalist in Hongkong and some of her poems are set there, others on an unnameable expanse of sense- or spirit-conflict. Wherever they are located, the voice is cool and unsettling. She lives in Bombay and runs a communications company.

Spring Cleaning

That was your skull on the bottom shelf,
staring socketless at my ankle.
It was a surprise find among those
bunches of old clothes.
Once I would have screamed;
now I've learned to discard
what doesn't fit, and especially, all that's ugly.

Carelessly draped on a hanger, I found an arm
leaning bonily towards the perfumes;
in another corner, a dislocated knee.
Did you run away so fast you broke your leg?
I wish you'd wipe that foolish
toothless grin off your stupid face.
You needn't be embarrassed about
letting me down. Other men have too, and they
didn't disintegrate like you.

What the hell
does one do with human remains?
Should I put them in the waste basket,
let the sweeper see? Or, struggling under the weight,
dump a gunny bag off the beach?

You really are a nuisance, turning up
on a lethargic Sunday. Now go away.
When I want to say hello, I'd rather
walk up to the graveyard
with a sweet-smelling bunch of flowers,
look sad, and pretend
you are still below the earth.

At Po Lin, Lantau

In the monastery to which I do not belong,
high in the clouds where Buddha smiles,
a strange ferocious statue looks down on me
as the joss sticks lose themselves.
A shaven monk, going out of his mind,
slings a careless arm around me.
And I wonder what it's like
to make love to a monk,
wonder what it's like to make love to you

again. And you, once the god who did not belong
to me, have come back like a prayer wheel,
and slowly the thudding begins, drumming out
from the heart into the monastery of my mind.

Tourist voices bulldoze through stone,
high on the monastery where clouds converse,
before silences spread like joss-stick ash,
leaving their fragrance behind.
Were you the Buddha I used to know?
Why, then, did you teach discontent?
The eight-fold path we walked together
was so full of thorns and sediment.

Where are you now as the aliens pass;
are you gently rotating away?
Will you come back to this monastery,
teach me how to pray?

Epitaph

The thing to do
is feel the texture of the page
still white before the lines form,
touch the smoothness of its skin,
refined unlike the bark
once peeled away.

The trouble is,
we do not wear white
on the wedding day.

My religion calls for blood,
redness draped across the eyes,
wrapped tight around the skin.
But lines form anyway,
alphabets rounded like shoulders
or flat as hair upon the arm.
The story begins like a wrinkle on the face
and does not end
when the wrinkles freeze.

But that is when the surface
turns to white and I hold my pain
in its plastic tube,
let the fluid fall.

That's when the poem writes itself
like an epitaph.

No Man's Land

What did it take for bone
to crack, like dry leaf or a match
pressed too hard on its back?
When was the line drawn
in the toe? Which side of the border
do you need to go? How far
are red rivers beneath the skin?
See that swelling? What ghosts
hide within? What do they share
in that silent snare, tucked away
inside that leather shoe,
a mess of dead nerve and human glue,
where nails turns upon the flesh
and distances run through a wire mesh
that clamps down upon the broken toe,
through which you see how far to go,

except that the metal burns the skin,
the chains rust slowly, and within,
the foot that could take you across the shore
has turned to dust; you can walk no more.

When will the crack begin to heal?

GOPAL HONNALGERE

(1942–2003)

Gopal Honnalgere was born in Bijapur, Karnataka, the grandson of a well-known Vedic scholar. His father, an engineer, died when Honnalgere was still a boy. He was raised in his grandparents' home in Mysore and later in Bangalore. He taught art and writing at the Oasis School in Hyderabad in the early 70s, where he met the woman who would become his wife. The couple travelled widely, teaching in schools in Panchgani, Vijayawada, and the Punjab, and taking their two children with them, a boy and a girl. It was a time of travel and productivity, and it ended when Honnalgere's son was killed in an accident while cycling to school: his marriage broke up. He spent the last years of his life in an old people's home in Bangalore. Diagnosed with cancer, he was taken to Delhi by a nephew. He died in a hospital there.

Honnalgere published at least six books, all of which are out of print. They include *Zen Tree and the Wild Innocents* (1973), *Gesture of Fleshless Sound* (1975), *Wad of Poems* (1975), *The Fifth* (1980) and *Internodes* (1986). Now mostly forgotten, he was an enigmatic figure who corresponded with some of the major poets of his time. 'If you use thoughts so violently to reject thoughts, why do you write a poem using your head?' asked Robert Lowell. Auden wrote of a Honnalgere poem that it was 'simple but powerful. I liked it.' William Stafford read out poems from *Zen Tree and the Wild Innocents* to his family, and, he wrote, 'We were immediately elated.' It is impossible to paraphrase a Gopal Honnalgere poem, one can only point to the freshness of the humour and the reckless originality of the thought.

The City

I

She
   with her
   finger tips
   touched his
   tailbone
   and waited for a reply
   he said:
   'we have lost something else
   with our lost tail.'

She
   with her
   finger tips
   tickled his
   tailbone
   and asked him to see:
   he saw a calendar
   with a semi-nude picture
   hanging on the wall.
   and outside the room
   he saw male and female

monkeys, naked monkeys,
eating ticks from
each others armpits.
they were so quiet, so saintly
they were sitting like digambaras
without a thought of sex.

She
    with her
    finger nails
    scratched his
    tailbone
    and asked him
    to make a statement
    he said:
    'We have gained death
    when we lost our immortality.
    we have gained our nudity
    when we lost our nakedness.'

    II

The trees caged in the park
Still flower in the spring.
The caged peacock in the zoo
Has four peahens in stock,
Still he opens his wings and dances,
Wooing a mate.

I have come to the city
I have bought machines
My home machinery runs smoothly.

Only sometimes
I tried to kiss
Her in a restaurant
Before the waiter came
She refused, hissing:
'Our car's too old.
Your mother,
The old villager,
Should not come here to stay.'
Sometimes I said,
'Padma, there are sun-
Flower seeds in your eyes.'
And I promised her a new car,
A new fridge, a diamond ring,
And caressed her to excess.

III

The broken wine glass
In the city's dustbin
Glitters like a diamond
Glitters better than the diamond
Of our loving ring.

I wanted a child
I cried 'Child, child
Come here, stand
And watch
The broken wine glass
In the street's dustbin
Is glittering
Is glittering better than the diamond
Of our loving ring.'
But she was as cold
As dry fish in the fridge.

I wanted a child...
Kissing her
And caressing her
I cried 'Child, child
I shall come to the Eros womb
I shall take you out
From the Eros womb
Come and play with me
I shall stand on my head
Upside down
Like an Indian Yogi
And make you laugh
Laugh from your belly
Laugh like a laughing Buddha,
I shall see something new
Which is not here
In the tick-tack of my wrist-watch
And I shall see
The much important nothing
In your toothless mouth.
Child, child
Come with me and play.'
But she was as cold
As dry fish in the fridge.
She said: 'I love you
And if you love me
With the same intensity
Don't trouble me with love.

Love me
Give me a kiss
Without a child.
Bring me a sensation
Without a hangover.
Take me into anything you like
But for God's sake
Dope me into a deep sleep.'

Marriage is a refrigerator,
It freezes eggs, apples and bananas
But protects them from rotting.

IV

It is not the season
Nor the season's flowers
Or heat
But the efficient
Housewife's mind
Which decorates
The drawing room
And sets right the clock
Makes it run slow
Or fast
And regulates
The pet dog's heat
With injections.
My female companion
Sometimes she remembers me
And kisses me
With her painted green lips.

The opposite of beauty is
The human mind.

V

Pet dogs
And stuffed tigers
Still have their faces.

Men and women
Make faces
But really they do not
Have them
They wear the city's face.

Our self
Moves
Green
Behind our face
A green
Overcrowded
Double-decker
Which does not
Stop
To take us.

You Can't Will

I

You can't will sleep to come
You can only dream of it.
And prepare a bug-free foam bed
In an air-conditioned room.

Christ can't teach you
How to say
'Good Night' to your sleeplessness.

Saints can't teach you
How to sing
A lullaby to your insomnia.

Prayers and confessions
Are as useless as drugs
And a best-seller
On 'How to sleep well.'

II

You have to work
Very hard
For the simple happenings
Of sleep, God and atonement
You have to carry
Your self
On your shoulders
A child
Vehement in his crying
A sick child

Who has inherited
All your tension
Pat him affectionately
Tell him fairy tales
Sing nursery rhymes
Show him dark clouds
Playing with the moon
Show him stars
Through some summer trees
Stars glowing like
Glow-flowers in the trees
And also tell him
How to grow up
To be a good boy
And all about Rama, Buddha and Christ
Whether he understands or not
Tell him
Until you fall asleep.

A Toast with Karma

On the kernel
Of each grape
Its drinker's name
Is written.

Your ding-dong
Will can only
Crush, brew
And raise
A glass of wine
In the hand.

And you drink
If your name
Is written on the grape

Or you pass it on
To a friend
Which means
Christ's name
Is written on the fruit.

Nails

imagine and enact:
imagine that you lived in golgotha
imagine you were a blacksmith
imagine you loved jesus christ
more than yourself
imagine you were made to make
nails for his crucifixion
imagine that you could do nothing
but make good sharp nails
so that the son of god felt less pain

o son of man
now you are in golgotha
what do you do?

Theme

there is a possibility
of breasts
becoming a theme
with coconut hard shells –

      behind the nipples
      her bosom
      behind the bosom
      she, my wife
      with a large heart
      pumping greens to the palms
      and behind her
      nothing –

        a backyard with a slant
        mangalore tiled roof
        and two coconut trees
        one slanting 60 degrees
        the other 45
        they grew so
        she said, because
        coconut hates papaya
        and her mother
        was unwilling

to weed out two
papaya saplings
which accidentally
started growing
in the coconut beds
until the trees flowered
and she knew
they were male

How to Tame a New Pair of Chappals

don't leave them together
don't allow them to talk to each other
they may form a trade union

don't at anytime leave them near
a wall clock, law books, a calendar, the national flag,
gandhi's portrait, or a newspaper
they may hear about
independence, satyagraha,
holidays, working hours, minimum wages, corruption

don't take them to your temple
they may at once know you are weak
your god is false and they may bite you

don't let them near your dining table
they may ask for food
or cast their evil eyes on your dinner

first use them only for short walks
then gradually increase the distance
they should never know the amount of work they have to do

pull their tight straps loose
let them feel happiness
they are growing bigger
smear some old oil on the rough straps
let them feel they are anointed

now they are good subdued laborers
ready to work overtime
for your fat feet

The Donkeys

maybe it's a legend
I don't remember his name
a tibetan poet sat and wrote
poems poems poems all his life
when he was eighty-nine
and with a mirror-like bald
head approaching death
he had with him three
donkey-loads of poems
he wanted to give them away
to a prayer wheel turning monastery
he carried them on three hired donkeys
and began to walk thinking about life
it was a god-freezing winter
the old man started shivering
and couldn't walk
he made a bonfire of
one of his donkey-loads of poems
and warmed himself sitting near the fire
when he was about to start on the journey
a thought came into his mind –
he saw the donkeys, recalling one of his poems
on donkeys, the donkeys too were shivering
he again made a bonfire
of his two remaining donkey-loads
and made the donkeys stand
around the fire in trinity

　　　the critics say
　　　a single unburnt line of his poetry
　　　　　discovered by posterity
　　　　　is enough to express all his perception
　　　　　　　　　　　　you
　　　　　　　　　　　　　search
　　　　　　　　　　　　　　for the donkey
　　　　　　　　　　　　　　　you
　　　　　　　　　　　　　　　　ride
　　　　　　　　　　　　　　　　on

DALJIT NAGRA

(*b*. 1966)

Daljit Nagra was born in 1966 in West London to parents who emigrated from Nogaja, a village in the Punjab. His early poems appeared in British literary journals under the pseudonym Khan Singh Kumar, an invented Muslim-Sikh-Hindu persona. They are spoken in an exclamatory Indian English (like an updated, relocated version of Nissim Ezekiel's), by a cast of linguistically adventurous British Punjabis. His book *Look We Have Coming to Dover!* (Faber, 2007) includes a Punjabi to Ungrezi Guide which tells the reader, among other things, that a 'chum-chum' is a 'lusciously syrup-hearted, spherically challenged spongy delight enrobed in coconut shavings' and 'Rub' is 'GOD!' He lives in London and teaches at the Jewish Free School.

The Speaking of Bagwinder Singh Sagoo!

Why now not be naked, you naughty western woman?
Not four month since I Delhi–Heathrow to you,
already you lying in living room with catalogues
of Bombay passions, rolling into my praying father
to give him cardigan arrest! Mother still have her trunk
of dowry, each year from it she stitch a shiny couture'd
salwaar in minutes, and no one notice she stand out.
But your tightening of the dowry of the costume bottoms
is a punky drain-piping! Not *we* made for upping
cardboard base so ankle flashing, but *we* for baggy,
we for smiley wide-pride of pyjama leg,
puckered by you into bony lady's bellybutton!

Our peoples at the Sugar Puff factory, I overhear
poison their wives at night monster their heads
crazy with: *She was in film-star red*, one says.
No, no, another replies, *she's in chocolate sauce*.
The sweaty-necked boiler-suit boy, chicken-dancing,
even louder: *No, no, no, I saw her at market
with milky teeth, in the company of her doctor –
the Avon Lady. I swear by all the gods in my locker
she was in the Dulux of British poodle pink!*
They toss up their chapatti rolls, their Black Jack cards,
in this break for lunch – only at your toenails.
I make up constipation for shame of leaving the loo!

Turn off those sunglasses. Is it summer in this evening
of winter? Look at me, what is that cherry jelly
lumping the lash of your eyes? Are you bleeding upwards?
Those mascara scars? This half cut hair-mop?

How can this be a forehead for the special red bindi
when it's undressed by dirty-love bride (from college!)
who tie my arms with jockstraps from my B-team
hockey days. All night long – the pouncing, the tickling,
the lipstick and 'odour toilet'. My father blowing a cough
as you put my bottom up my backside! I cannot meditate,
pray, lock into my lotus position! I cannot close my legs!
Oh my Rub, what is England happening for us?

Look We Have Coming to Dover!

So various, so beautiful, so new...
                MATTHEW ARNOLD, 'Dover Beach'

Stowed in the sea to invade
the alfresco lash of a diesel-breeze
ratcheting speed into the tide, brunt with
gobfuls of surf phlegmed by cushy come-and-go
tourists prow'd on the cruisers, lording the ministered waves.

Seagull and shoal life
vexing their blarnies upon our huddled
camouflage past the vast crumble of scummed
cliffs, scramming on mulch as thunder unbladders
yobbish rain and wind on our escape hutched in a Bedford van.

Seasons or years we reap
inland, unclocked by the national eye
or stabs in the back, teemed for breathing
sweeps of grass through the whistling asthma of parks,
burdened, ennobled – poling sparks across pylon and pylon.

Swarms of us, grafting in
the black within shot of the moon's
spotlight, banking on the miracle of sun –
span its rainbow, passport us to life. Only then
can it be human to hoick ourselves, bare-faced for the clear.

Imagine my love and I,
our sundry others, Blair'd in the cash
of our beeswax'd cars, our crash clothes, free,
we raise our charged glasses over unparasol'd tables
East, babbling our lingoes, flecked by the chalk of Britannia!

Singh Song!

I run just one ov my daddy's shops
from 9 o'clock to 9 o'clock
and he vunt me not to hav a break
but ven nobody in, I do di lock –

cos up di stairs is my newly bride
vee share in chapatti
vee share in di chutney
after vee hav made luv
like vee rowing through Putney –

Ven I return vid my pinnie untied
di shoppers always point and cry:
Hey Singh, ver yoo bin?
Yor lemons are limes
yor bananas are plantain,
dis dirty little floor need a little bit of mop
in di worst Indian shop
on di whole Indian road –

Above my head high heel tap di ground
as my vife on di web is playing wid di mouse
ven she netting two cat on her Sikh lover site
she book dem for di meat at di cheese ov her price –

my bride
            she effing at my mum
            in all di colours of Punjabi
            den stumble like a drunk
            making fun at my daddy

my bride
            tiny eyes ov a gun
            and di tummy ov a teddy

my bride
            she hav a red crew cut
            and she wear a Tartan sari
            a donkey jacket and some pumps
            on di squeak ov di girls dat are pinching my sweeties –

Ven I return from di tickle ov my bride
di shoppers always point and cry:
Hey Singh, ver yoo bin?

274

Di milk is out ov date
and di bread is alvays stale,
di tings yoo hav on offer yoo hav never got in stock
in di worst Indian shop
on di whole Indian road –

Late in di midnight hour
ven yoo shoppers are wrap up quiet
ven di precinct is concrete-cool
vee cum down whispering stairs
and sit on my silver stool,
from behind di chocolate bars
vee stare past di half-price window signs
at di beaches ov di UK in di brightey moon –

from di stool each night she say,
> *How much do yoo charge for dat moon baby?*

from di stool each night I say,
> *Is half di cost ov yoo baby,*

from di stool each night she say,
> *How much does dat come to baby?*

from di stool each night I say,
> *Is priceless baby –*

Bibi & the Street Car Wife!

O son, I widow each day by netted windows
playing back days when my daughter-in-law
hooting over hot sands with chappal-less feet
would basket her head on fields of live carrot,
then cowed by courtyard wall with peacock sari
and mousy head, she would mould me dung
buns in caramel sun to pass our village audition.

Her boogly eyes would catch my fast grip ripping
the shokri hairstyle of each carrot, potting
the pan for Indian skinning the slices, tossing under
her buns to drama the screen of fire, *Don't watch it –*
water the carrots for sauce! Directing our fresh
bride, so like Madhur Jaffrey on telly
she soak my applause on praise of stuffing husband.

275

Ever since we loosened our village acres
for this flighty mix-up country, like moody
actress she buy herself a Datsun, with legs
of KFC microphoning her mouth
(ladies of temple giddily tell me her tale):
she manicured waves men, or honking horn
to unbutton her hair she dirty winking:
Come on friend, I like it letting you in!

What to make of wife who hawking late
from Terminal Two to bad blood me: *We*
no needing this car-park house you share,
in your name, clamping us to back-seat
of your cinema. In 'my' movie, old lady,
I meat you for boot of my Turkmenistani
departure! She propeller her fist
with drumstick, in landing light, then bite!

Beef-burgering her backside on our 5Ks,
what do we care for the toilet of her big
bank balance? O son, as you wheel the taco
meter of your lorry for days then sofa to me
as now, who does she her black-box film
shoot with to blow 'our' soaring name?
O my only son, why will she not lie down
for us, to part herself, to drive out babies?

My Father's Dream of Return

Booming the clouded mountains,
hurtling around and downwards –
the bird-like, plane-like jet
descent of his car speckling
the slant of goats, fast-brake
at the ceremonial elephants,
downwards for the cows mothering
on the plain, fourth gear
he hooters leathery skin
that climbs on husky trees,
some hands fanned into waves
from sunflower fields, some twisted
heads from the sugarcane. Soothing
his engine by the cesspool,
air-conditioned, he awaits
his audience.

My father then imagines
his old village as a ghost
home with its doors padlocked
creaking for the landlord profiting
abroad, yet men are stooped
to the point of his burgundy loafers,
with the old, in the dust who launch
prayers to ascend their stares
from the gold hooping him.
He raises the boot of his Ambassador –
nectars children with boxes
of chum-chums, or cool
sherbets in plastic pipes,
shares out tubs of powder
paints and gunned rainbow
liquids, and elastic party hats.
My father dreams of scattering
fireworks through the sun
on everyone!

I'm plonked on his overall'd knee
catching at scabs of cement
on his breast pocket after his return
from work, as he pictures his built
frame in pinstripes, with voice
blaster than the temple speakers
he'd summon them all to my
wedding with an alabastered
family we'd keep company.
He'd tell them we live over there –
on top of the married mountains
sipping mauve faludas, as we size up
queues of customers (side
by side, in the forecourt shade)
to our almighty BP
stop!

GIEVE PATEL

(*b*. 1940)

Gieve Patel's grandfather was a landowner in the village of Nargol, Gujarat. His mother was a doctor's daughter, his father a dentist. They moved from Nargol to Bombay, where Patel was born in 1940 and where he continues to live. He is a doctor whose clinic in Central Bombay has served the city's poor for four decades. His paintings – he is self-taught – hang in private and public collections in India and elsewhere. He is the author of three plays, one of which, *Mister Behram*, was published by XAL-Praxis in 1988; all are forthcoming from Seagull Books.

Post-Mortem

It is startling to see how swiftly
A man may be sliced
From chin to prick,
How easily the bones
He has felt whole
Under his chest
For a sixty, seventy years
May be snapped,
With what calm
Liver, lung and heart
Be examined, the bowels
Noted for defect, the brain
For haemorrhage,
And all these insides
That have for a lifetime
Raged and strained to understand
Be dumped back into the body,
Now stitched to perfection,
Before announcing death
Due to an obscure reason.

The Ambiguous Fate of Gieve Patel,
He Being Neither Muslim Nor Hindu in India

To be no part of this hate is deprivation.
Never could I claim a circumcised butcher
Mangled a child out of my arms, never rave
At the milk-bibing, grass-guzzling hypocrite
Who pulled off my mother's voluminous
Robes and sliced away at her dugs.
Planets focus their fires
Into a worm of destruction
Edging along the continent. Bodies
Turn ashen and shrivel. I
Only burn my tail.

Servants

They come of peasant stock,
Truant from an insufficient plot.

Lights are shut off after dinner
But the city-blur enters,
Picks modulations on the skin;
The dark around them
Is brown, and links body to body,
Or is dispelled, and the hard fingers
Glow as smoke is inhaled
And the lighted end of tobacco
Becomes an orange spot.

Their hands are wide
Or shut, it does not matter
One way or other –
They sit without thought,
Mouth lightly open, recovering
From the day, and the eyes
Globe into the dim
But are not informed because
Never have travelled beyond this
Silence. They sit like animals.
I mean no offence. I have seen
Animals resting in their stall,
The oil flame reflected in their eyes,
Large heads that though protruding
Actually rest
Behind the regular grind
Of the jaws.

Squirrels in Washington

Squirrels in Washington come
Galloping at you on fours, then brake
To halt a few feet away
And beg on hindquarters.
No one stones them,
And their fear is diminished.
They do halt, even so,
Some feet away, those few feet

279

The object of my wonder. Do I
Emit currents
At closer quarters? Are those
The few feet I would keep
From a tame tiger? Is there
A hierarchy, then, of distances,
That must be observed,
And non-observance would at once
Agglutinate all of Nature
Into a messy, inextricable mass?
Ah Daphne! Passing
From woman to foliage did she for a moment
Sense all vegetable sap as current
Of her own bloodstream, the green
Flooding into the red? And when
She achieved her final arboreal being,
Shed dewy tears each dawn
For that lost fleeting moment,
That hint at freedom,
In transit, between cage and cage?

MELANIE SILGARDO
(b. 1956)

Born in 1956 in Bombay to Roman Catholic parents, Melanie Silgardo read English at St Xavier's College. She was taught by Eunice de Souza, who became a friend and early influence, but Silgardo's poems are more violent and adrenalised than those of any other woman of the Bombay school. Her early work appeared in *Three Poets* (1978), published by Newground, a short-lived collective she founded with Santan Rodrigues and Raul D'Gama Rose. The selection here includes work from that book as well as newer poems. She lives in London and works as an editor.

Bombay

you breathe like an animal.

Your islands grained and joined
are flanks you kicked apart
when some dark god
waved diverse men into your crotch.

They built
your concrete-toothed skyline,
with kicks and dedications
to their gods.
They stuck a paper moon
into your carbon sky.
Your future scrawled ten storeys high
and inside sewage pipes.
Some live unwarranted,
their carpets thicker than their lawns.
Their children suck at pacifiers,
and other children suck their thumbs
to bone.

And Bombay, with your sluggish shore
reclaim your cunt from time to time,
then let the sea rush into you.

Sequel to Goan Death

All the people frozen in their places,
gaping at the spaces
that are mouth and eyes.
I bend over to kiss the face,
dead with last stubble,
cold as the marble church
across the road.

This death is stiff and proper
and self-contained.
This death is a Christian Duty,
slipping into eternity with the final prayer.

The coffin is long as a journey.
The grave looks like a grave.
Nothing special for father
who hated graves.
It saves an epitaph.

1956–1976, a Poem

Twenty years ago
they laid a snare.

I emerged headlong,
embarrassed, wet.
They slapped me
on my bottom,
I screamed.
That was my first experience.

Ambitions gutter now.
Afterthoughts glide by.
My special icicles
rifle through me. For diet
I scratch out eyes.

Under my pillow
a lever
to manipulate dreams.

The insane need
to roll up the sky.
Stand it up
in some convenient place,
hang a picture up instead.
A change from God's blank face.
The end.

Stationary Stop

This station has no name.
No king was born here.
No president died here.

This station breathes with people
who breed each other.

There are one way tracks
diverging at the signal 'go'.
No train has ever passed this way.
No commuters have tired

of waiting. They have lost
count of each other.
J. and K. are very much alike,
are they brothers?

Rats burrow through bones.
Scavengers are never hungry.
The perfume of dead flowers
stinks in compromise.
J. and K. *are* brothers, their
mother says so.

When the train arrives
it will be disastrous to say 'go'.
If the people had resources
they would build an airplane.
But the air is crowded too.
In fact J. and K. are identical
twins, they compare in every way.

Today there is hope.
Old men are dressed in
youthful attire. Babies are
still born. A train may come.
It is Sunday.

One man begins to walk.

from Beyond the Comfort Zone

1

Between Salthouse and the Arctic
a great, grey water stretches.
I run my finger along the horizon.
Holkham beach is the span of my hand.
I can bounce a message off that star
and reach someone in Bombay or Beirut.
Everything is within reach.

2

The housemartins, small and sure as darts,
bullseye into their mud huts under the eaves.
Birds of dual nationality, they winter in Africa

(ornithologists don't know exactly where)
and return for the summer, masons from another land.
This place is home and also a long way from home.

3

In London, Mrs Patel is laying
her Avon catalogues on the counter.
Beneath the scents of lavender and rose
lurk the base notes of asafoetida
ghosts of last night's dinner.
Her grandfather crossed from a small town
in Gujarat to a small town in Kenya.
Her cousin who never left Gujarat
works in a call centre. He knows
the weather in Derby, and all the names
of the new family in *Eastenders.*

5

There are no gods in Guantanamo Bay.
The scratching in the dirt and a glimpse
of prisoner orange is all you will hear and see for hours
– occasionally a lost prayer, a wingless dove.
A family in Kandahar who never knew their son,
or know him too well, are posting messages in the air.

9

The short-necked oil beetle has re-emerged in Devon after
sixty years. Where did it go to? We thought it was extinct
like the sea mink or Vespucci's rat. Will dinosaurs and dodos
and all the dead rise on our warming planet?
Meanwhile, in Taiwan every spring a busy motorway closes
to let one million purple-spotted butterflies pass.
A mass migration, a blizzard of wings.

DILIP CHITRE

(*b.* 1938)

Dilip Chitre was born in 1938 in Baroda, then the capital of the princely state of Gujarat. He was educated in Bombay and attended the International Writing Program in Iowa City in 1975. He is a translator and film-maker and has published more than two dozen books in English and Marathi, a bilingual career that parallels Arun Kolatkar's. In his poems – even when they are breakfast soliloquies – the time is always 3 A.M and the speaker appears to be a solitary man who has been up several nights running and is more than a little worse for wear. The voice is startlingly direct, offering unexpectedly intimate physical detail and a composite portrait of spiritual estrangement. Chitre lives and works in Pune, where he edits the journal *New Quest.*

The First Breakfast: Objects

This morning is tasteless, colourless, odourless:
I sit alone at the big table.
The waiter is watching me.
In the deadly white dish
Lie two fried eggs.
Two containers of salt and pepper.
A bowl of butter, a bowl of jam.
Two oranges. A heap of toast.

I pick up a knife and a fork
And see parts of my face reflected in the shining steel.
There are strips of bacon to go with the eggs.
I sense the finality of everything.

The whole world is cold and instantaneous this morning.
A certain chill pervades the silent ritual of breakfast.
I shall be served in silence.

The best service is the silent service.
I have been preoccupied with words for too long.
I must eat in silence now.

I must not name the colours, the aromas and the flavours.
I must not ponder the brief tingle of sensation.
I must be strict: I must be miserly:
I must not go beyond eating what I have ordered and am served.
A breakfast, then, is like one's own funeral
Marching towards a vigorous day.
Alienation begins with breakfast.
The waiter is watching me in silence as though I am God.
And I am the lord of my own breakfast.
This morning is tasteless, colourless, odourless.
I sit alone at the big table.

The Second Breakfast: Intimations of Mortality

I am asked, 'And what is the colour of this orange juice?'
It is grey. All is black and white, and falls within
The spectrum. Everything is a shade from the black rainbow.

I wake up in the morning of my mortality.
This is in the nature of the egg
That lies scrambled on my toast.
I have been given a fork and knife.
Earlier I was served with a grey vermouth
To wet my dry mouth. The first flavour that spread
On my tongue in the blank morning
Was the taste of ash.
Black aromas pervade the morning air
In the restaurant.
Night, on the contrary, had brilliant flavours and colours.
When it ended, a white sun rose over the horizon
Turning everything variously black.
Here, I break up the toast inside my mouth
And taste death, the elemental carbon.

Who was it I slept with last night?
I do not remember her face because I do not remember
Any colours. She was warm. It was a live flow of flesh.
Her blood made a lot of noise. Her breath was hot.
We were naked in a night without knowledge.
Stars burst upon the surface
Of the soda-water of the dark.
But I do not remember any colours.
I am colour-blind in the morning.
My memory is colour-blind now.
Was she a whore, was she a Yakshi?
Was she seventeen, or was she seventy?
I remember nothing.
I remember nothing at all.
It all happened before I was born.
It all happened when this great egg-shell burst open.
I do not want to go back to it.

The Fourth Breakfast: Between Knowing and Unknowing

Between knowing and unknowing
Lies the unchanging morning.

Nothing in this interval of black and white
Is coloured or named.

It is a morning such as one which lies
Between the *lingam* and the *yoni*.

It is the stillness that follows and precedes
A deluge. It is the suspension of cataracts
In a stilled symphony. It is this black coffee
Without sugar or cream that I sip. It is too bold to strike you,
Waiter. You, who do not know the true nature of your service.
Or my order, or this fatal menu,
You cannot understand the metaphysical aspects of a breakfast.

You who think that cutlet and sauce are reality,
You cannot understand how a man begins his day
Using the knife and the fork on himself.

I understand the nature of food, do you?
Or are you a woman, offering what you do not know?

Your service spells doom, then. You serve me
Because you are proud that you feed me,
And this food is your ego.
In that case, I cannot accept this breakfast.
I feed on no power; no, not even on love,
If it is a power game.

Meat, for me, is the beginning of death.
Life is a cannibal's breakfast.
This is my fourth. I have spent four nights
Inside myself. With women. Making love and war.
For four nights have been spent
On the ritual of the destruction of man and woman.

Between knowing and unknowing
Lies the sexless morning
In the posture of the foetus.

The *Brahman*, Waiter, is the sexless posture of the foetus.
Male and female is the conflict and the creation.
Shiva and Shakti are mutually mouth and food.

SHANTA ACHARYA

(*b*. 1953)

Shanta Acharya was born in Cuttack, Orissa, in 1953, to a family of academics. She went
to Oxford on a scholarship in 1979, eventually settling in the United Kingdom where she
took up a career in investment management. She lives in London and works at the London
Business School.

Shunya

It took centuries, the journey from nought,
cipher, invisible wedge, thing of no importance to

Zero, absolute reality, point of reckoning –
a piece of the unknown fathomed,
being counted, standing solidly on the ground,
three-dimensional, banishing mystery,
altering the lives of men forever;
establishing one's significance in space,
time, trade, science, lending the world order;
measuring phenomena,
not just the freezing point of water;
creating certainty,
absolute zero, devoid of all heat;
zero hour when battles commence,
at the centre, holding things together:

Shunya, vessel taking the shape
of whatever is poured into it,
godlike, containing everything and nothing –
pregnant with concepts of probability,
poised between positive, negative,
life and death; vanishing point, knowing infinity,
drawing down divinity, creating opportunity,
reflecting the sum of the universe,
reducing all to Itself, always transforming...

Bori Notesz
(for Miklós Radnóti)

If I placed my faith in miracles
     thinking there was an angel walking beside me,
do not judge me, for my thoughts were only of you –
I cannot die, and cannot live, without you.
I saw the blue of your eyes in the sky
shining like the angel's sword protecting me
as I fell, a ghost in the glow of dawn.
But I was lifted by invisible wings
and marched on ignoring the ditch's embrace.

As long as I knew my way back to you,
I was prepared to walk on live coals,
bear witness to the barbarism of human beings
for man is the lowest of all the animals –
setting houses, fields and factories on fire,
streets overrun with burning people, men twisted,
then like a snapped string they spring up again, dead;
twitching like a broken twig in the ditch.
Women screamed as children were dashed
        against walls: *What is the purpose of this, Lord?*
I asked. I survived, fixing my thoughts on you.
You were the constant in this churning, smoking mess.

I can only leave you my anger, my powerlessness
        at finding my world in ruins, left with neither
faith nor hope, compassion nor redemption;
for I know nothing can save me now...

If I placed my faith in miracles
thinking there was an angel walking beside me,
judge me only by my thoughts of you in a world rebuilt
where my song will live and be heard...
I cannot die, and cannot live, without this thought.

RANJIT HOSKOTE

(*b.* 1969)

Born in 1969 into a family of Saraswat Brahmins in Bombay, Ranjit Hoskote's preferred
manner is the elegy, a preference that is likely connected to his own heritage. He is descended
from Saraswats who left the Kashmir Valley in waves between the 8th and 15th centuries,
because they were invited to do so – they were scholars and priests whose skills were needed
by the Indo-Scythian rulers of the west coast – and because they wished to escape religious
persecution by rulers such as Sikander Shah. They settled in various parts of the country,
taking surnames from the towns they found themselves in. Hoskote came to attention in
the late 1980s as a writer of art criticism for a newspaper in Bombay. It was criticism of a
kind unseen in India – erudite, opaque, fiendishly obscure. Since then, his several books of
poetry and criticism have addressed a natural aversion to being 'too easily understood'. He
lives in Bombay where he works as a writer and independent curator.

Passing a Ruined Mill

(in memoriam: Nissim Ezekiel, 1924-2004)

His mind's gone blank as a fax
left untouched for months in a drawer,
his faded words a defeat
of grammar and the continuities we prize.

Passing Lower Parel, the train slows by a ruined mill:
my eyes settle on chimneys stripped down to brick,
look away from crippled sheds, twisted gantries,
rusting flues and cranes overrun by creepers
that loop across the city, explode in prickly flowers,
drape the windows of the room in which he breaks
his hoarded silence with visitors whose names
escape him. They pour tea into his hours,
waiting for the clouded marble of his eyes
to spark a relay in the burnt-out tungsten
of his thoughts.

*

Can you see the window through your fraying blindfold?
The window framed in straggling creepers,
a sunbird's nest dangling from the bougainvillaea,
the surly gardener retreating, his shears still drawn
to hack, and you in the window, fresh from the rescue,
waving your wave of welcome
that was always a goodbye.

Months of slow fades until at last the curtain
marks a patch of scrubbed violet
through which the sky used to glow.
My face is as good as another's,
the kind word acknowledged, soon lost to the clock,
a ticking device, awkward in an awkward room,
this minefield of objects that rituals alone
can restore to sense: morning bath
and towelling, bedpan and brush.

*

Clouds form his idea of afternoon. Having read
only the tea-leaves in his cup,
he dreams of books
stacked on shelves too high to reach.

Look, he's standing square in a frame
bleached by sun, peeled by rain:
he's never asked the weather's permission
to leave, now he lets go the window
in which the landscape's settled:
two shards of pane, a shred of maroon kite.

*

The sea outside his window, he knew that sea
long before God parted it for Moses:
he'd probed the edge where shelves drop
into trenches, he knew where
the oysters slept, their dreams growing
in rings around a stone.

Who would believe he'd begun to dream
the ebb would suck him in, that he'd forgotten
how to swim? One last time he dived.
When he surfaced, the havoc birds were waiting:
they swooped to peck
at the few pearls he'd retrieved.

*

That music's made of chance, he found,
ten years after the dance had claimed
his steps, its canny measure turning around
to fix him to the floor. That music maims,
he found, as seedy grandeur pinned him to a desk
high-piled with books, papers unread for years,
letters to which no answer would ever be sent,
the lamp hovering above his head
a menacing crown, more fire than light.
And there he sat, while the paper rustled away,
shedding the weave of his words like a blotted skin.

*

Did you never climb a three-bar gate
to pluck forbidden mangoes?
Did you regret the gash that opened
in your skin, wet with the hand-pressed
rawness of gathered juice?

He told a palmist he'd befriended
that he suffered the commonest of chosen things:
the need to make of sullen seed a tree.
Your tree will shimmer, its roots anchored in passion,

said the kerbside sage, but mind, it'll bend,
its branches heavy with poison fruit.
He saw that truth, and said: Not yet,
and stroked its prickly leaves.

Ghalib in the Winter of the Great Revolt
Delhi, 1857

The emperor's murdered grandsons hang
from the Gate of Peace like hushed bells
and rifles drill the sentenced air.
My neighbour, the flautist, slit his veins last night,
burning his prayerbook before he died,
true to a God of subtle tones
wasted on the deaf.

Ghalib writes to a friend:
All around us, the furies ride their burning horses.
It's as though Timur had broken Delhi's walls
again, his cinder-streaked soldiers heaping
pyramids of skulls in the streets,
an abacus for orphans to compute
the profits of betrayal, the penalties of defeat.

Cannon the only thunder, writes Ghalib, and no rain.
Gunners waving St George's flag
have driven the nobles from their charred mansions,
tethered the peasants to the surly river.
The coppersmith tapping at a dead branch
fills the vacant sky
with the privacy of his grief.

The friend, with a spy at his shoulder, writes back:
When did you become a poet of adjectives
roosting in the rafters of a broken house?
Ghalib, the owl must hide in the tamarind for now,
but the genies of havoc will go on furlough soon.
You say your ink-well is empty, but your dry quill
still claws at the fibres of the heart.

A pharmacist may drug himself with lyric,
Ghalib replies, and a tiger may vanish
in the rainforest of his hunter's dreams.
But the dry quill is a reproach and this raw winter

could be the living tomb of my song.
Send paper, friend, these are the last pages
of my journal I'm writing on.

Footage for a Trance
(for Shuddhabrata Sengupta)

The hours stop in my veins.
Evening falls, a spotted tissue
draped across dayglo streets.

The clocks go on marking
the time in another city

where the trains still run,
taking people home.

*

Over my shoulder, I see my country vanish
in a long unfurling of cornflower-blue sky.
My limbs are clear as glass.

The wind grazes my shoulders,
the animal buried in my voice
wakes up and growls.

Where I am is a boat without a pilot,
sculling through cold water.

*

Start again. There is no safety in numbers.
The sixty-four saints stand paralysed
in the authorised version of the legend.
No footnote explains the hunting songs
or the red skein curling downhill
in place of the river.

Script thrown away, I'm on my own.
The detectives will find me
when a rainbow prints itself
on the litmus sky at noon.
I clear my throat,
the movie stops.

*

The hours have stopped in my veins
but late-night travellers still rush past me,
through me, to reach the midnight express.
My country's been swallowed
by a sky darkening to cloud and sleep.

The sixty-four saints have formed a caucus
of havoc birds, the rainbow is a stanza
they refuse to sing. Close to the tympanum,
the horseshoe weather taps cryptic clues.
On every clock-face,
the hour hand and the minute hand
go on mating.

*

Wakeful, all eye, the havoc birds read
the scroll of earth unfolding,
every fleck a signal:
prey, home, danger,
hiding-place.

From a great height, each bird watches
its shadow falling
to its death.

*

I vanish, again, in the darkroom.
A lamp exposes
my heirloom bones.

On a park bench,
a gardener finds a surplice,
drooping, ravelled at the seams:

my skin, abandoned in flight.

A View of the Lake
Villa Waldberta

The man in white stands back to survey the landscape:
snow-melt just where he wants it and the crystal lake
an eye widening in a forest of viridian strokes.
Careful visitor from another planet, he probes,
then trails his brush across the canvas, a lull

before the sharp cobalt flick that unites water
with heaven; steps closer, dabs
at the palette, brush lighter than before,
the tempo languid, the man hardly there
except for the hand weaving images of itself.

So to renounce speed is his explicit purpose:
laying his knife aside, the man scrapes colour
from his sleeves, rests his brush; a pause
for breath, then circles back the way he came,
thawing aquamarine, stripping coats of umber,
dissolving velvet greens and speckled reds
until the canvas is down to the primer,
buff once more and void of sign
except for graphite smudges to mark
where cloud-hidden peaks will rise.

In the failing light, he lets the figures grow
again, the mountains and thickets, the clutter
that signals where the slang of boat and pier
has ruptured the grammar of leaf and wave:
his strokes are discreet ampersands that keep
the broken sentences of the district together,
gestures that compose an air more rarefied, an earth
more dense, a light more piercing than any the vista
that's squared in his picture window could offer.
He has the exquisite manners of a ghost

trained in an older school of grace:
he does not remind the present of its failures
or, returning to these haunts of persistent desire,
play the loud impresario of the prospect.
No, he calculates differently: the high, clear flute
tuned from the whistling breath of children lost
among the pines, the icon coaxed from dripping wax,
the reason distilled by the lame dancer
balancing on the wine-press of thought,
form his reward. He defers his signature for later.

Colours for a Landscape Held Captive

(in memoriam: Agha Shahid Ali, 1949-2001)

They never knew you, who only recall
your smashed golds and broken reds:
those flashing conceits, tropes of a night too dark

to spell out by the fading glow of words;
those surfaces that melted as you spoke,
laying bare depths in which we'd drown
without a pilot's full-throated voice
to bridge us to land. And as you sang,
a starburst of paisley moths lit up
our eyes behind closed eyelids, dark cells
unlit by thought of such a dawn.

You never meant to trap us in that country
without a post office, where boatmen and saints
trade stories to while away the days
of khaki captivity. No, Beloved Witness,
these were signposts you'd sketched
at the lake's treacherous edge, to break our fall
as we hurtled down the foothills of policy.
No, your smashed golds and broken reds
were never laments: not yesterday's colours
but tomorrow's they summon us to hope.
They never knew you, who only recall.

MEENA ALEXANDER

(*b.* 1951)

Born in 1951 in Allahabad into a Syrian Christian family, Meena Alexander was educated in Khartoum, in the Sudan, and at Nottingham University in Britain. As with many of the poets in this anthology, her first book *The Bird's Bright Wing* was published by P. Lal's Writers Workshop in Calcutta. She was 25 but the volume already carried her poetic signature: a mix of verse, fiction and memoir delivered in a high lyric register. She moved to the United States in 1979 and lives and teaches in New York City.

Indian April

I

Allen Ginsberg on a spring day you stopped
naked in a doorway in Rajasthan.

You were preparing to wash, someone took a snapshot:
I see your left hand bent back,
cigarette in your mouth,

metal basin set at your ankles,
heat simmering at the edges of your skin
in Indian air, in water.

Rinsed clean you squatted at the threshold again,
struck a bhajan on a tin can.

Watched Mira approach, her hair a black mass
so taut it could knock over a lamppost,
skin on her fists raw from rubbing chipped honeypots.

In the middle distance
like a common bridegroom,
Lord Krishna rides a painted swing.

You ponder this, not sure
if an overdose of poetry
might crash a princess.

Later in the alleyway you note
a zither leapt from a blind baul's fist.

William Blake's death mask,
plaster cast with the insignia of miracles.

In a burning ghat the sensorium's ruin:
a man's spine and head poked with a stick

so bone might crisp into ash, vapors spilled
into terrible light where the Ganga pours.

II

I was born at the Ganga's edge.
My mother wrapped me in a bleached sari,
laid me in stiff reeds, in hard water.

I tried to keep my nostrils above mud,
learnt how to use my limbs, how to float.

This earth is filled with black water,
small islands with bristling vines afford us some hold.

Tired out with your journals you watch
Mira crouch by the rough stones of the alley.
Her feet are bare, they hurt her.

So much flight for a poet, so much persistence.
Allen Ginsberg, where are you now?

Engine of flesh, hot sunflower of Mathura,
teach us to glide into life,

teach us when not to flee,
when to rejoice, when to weep,

teach us to clear our throats.

III

Kaddish, Kaddish I hear you cry
in the fields of Central Park.

He brought me into his tent
and his banner over me was love.

I learn from you that the tabernacles of grace
are lodged in the prickly pear,

the tents of heaven torn by sharp vines,
running blackberry,
iron from the hummingbird's claw.

He brought me into his tent
and his banner over me was love.

Yet now he turns his face from me.
Krishna you are my noose, I your knife.

And who shall draw apart
from the misericord of attachment?

IV

Holy the cord of death, the sensual palaces
of our feasting and excrement.

Holy, the waters of the Ganga, Hudson, Nile,
Pamba, Mississippi, Mahanadi.

Holy the lake in Central Park, bruised eye of earth,
mirror of heaven,

where you leap beard first
this April morning, resolute, impenitent,

not minding the pointed reeds, spent syringes,
pale, uncoiled condoms.

You understood the kingdom of the quotidian,
groundhogs in heat, the arrhythmia of desire.

I see you young again,
teeth stained with betel and bhang,

nostrils tense with the smoke of Manhattan,
ankles taut in a yogic asana, prickly with desire.

You who sang America are flush now with death,
your poems – bits of your spine and skull –

ablaze in black water drawing you on.
Allen Ginsberg your flesh is indigo,

the color of Krishna's face, Mira's bitter grace.
Into hard water you leap, drawing me on.

I hear you call: *Govinda, aaou, aoou!*

from Black River, Walled Garden

III

Last night in my bed in Peterborough
under a cherry-colored blanket
in midsummer as the moon beat down

on rough meadow grass,
the call of the hermit thrush in my ears,
I dreamt that childhood river:

black waters cutting and clashing,
wrists slit by raw sugar cane stalks,
a child crying to Jesus.

And how she fell:
ring after ring into the well,
the sore snare of it,

green ferns at the rim
slaking the bruise.
About her anklebone, a rope.

IV

Hurt makes us sing – a sweet foreboding.
Jacob and his angel, a muscular craze, one might say,
the ladder dismantled.

The two of them caught in a daze,
a summer's fever.

I will call this place Peniel.
Under the roaring blue
I come to you perpetually.

Whose words? Whose promise?
Am I a ghost, an aspect of an angel?
Who will bring him back to answer to me?

V

Now was that where I meant to go?
Or was I waylaid?
Call it anamnesis, living memory,

torchlit flesh.
At epiphany
the earliest Christians gathered

and over their heads
shot tongues of flame.
Raised by a fire altar,

you understand these things:
the need for human ritual,
plenitude of silence.

But also disorder of speech,
lives where drums beat
anarchic, implosive.

VI

I am a field of wild flowers
stitched without fortune,
grandmother wrote during her travels in China,

forty-seven-years old, my age,
five years from her end.

She sent back photos of herself in pale silk
next to the Great Wall, her friend Miss Hartley by her,
the two of them clasping a Bible.

What I miss about home
is the simplicity of our church services
and my little daughter combing out her curls.

Mother saved that letter
with its neat stepping scrawl.

VII

Did grandmother go into the room of books ever?
No, it was your grandfather's, hers was the rosewood
room, the one with the mirror you stared in.

You seemed in such a daze,
backwards running from the library,
slit your ankle at the bone against my mother's rice-pattern cup,

the one she brought home from Shanghai.
You were twirling it on your thumb.
You needed seven stitches, remember?

We had to get a basin for the blood,
one would have thought all the drains
in Mohenjo Daro were flowing!

VIII

Who could I tell about the library?
What grandfather did with fingers, lips, thighs,
within sight of Bibles, encyclopedias, dictionaries.

O books with seeing eyes!
I blacked it all away.

In the walled garden on hot mornings
I ditched ants from the love-apple tree
onto my belly and thighs,

lay still as they pinched and struck.
Afternoons I gazed into well water
watching a balloon child,

a Nowhere-Girl, her flesh striking
stone rings as she fell,
face tucked into a metal bucket.

IX

Somewhere a mirror smashed.
Ten thousand bits of glass
pierced my sight.

I drank sugar grains mixed with acid,
my hair stood on end.
Burning-Hair-Girl I called myself

just as I was sprouting it everywhere –
under my arms, between my thighs,
and my nipples grew large and brown as lakes.

At ten I swung in a tree, skin itching
as cinammon clouds skimmed the blue.
At eleven I paged through the book grandfather gave me,

pausing at Anna with her honey-colored hair,
the glint of metal in the railroad track
making her heart pucker and start,

till at the very end she fell –
a sentence of blood I could not spell.
Rain dimmed my eyes as I lay in the tree.

I felt the great storm lashing me.
My muslin dress crushed with hail
that pounded down –

a comfort after the shame of so much wet.
I shut my eyes, slid down,
down, into the merciful trunk of the tree.

X

That April of my life
when everything slowed down for me
I saw clouds drift

through the mirror in the rosewood room.
Grandmother's eyes in the portrait
made in her thirtieth year

started to smoke, lost coals,
when a fire is fanned.
Grandfather lay dying in his wooden bed.

They forced morphine into his veins
so he wouldn't bite
and tear the covering sheet to bits.

An old man's skin
hung on the bathroom hook
mouldy and flecked with rain.

The mint bush in the garden had tiny stains,
Love-apple leaves, rust holes.
His sweat seeped through the foundation stones.

I lay in a grave I dug in the earth.
I swayed in a cradle hung in a tree
and all of the visible world –

walled garden,
black river – flowed in me.

   XI

Must I stoop,
drink from those waters again,
reach a walled garden, memory's unquiet place?

Will I see a child under a tree?
Was she the one the poet traveler sought,
the sunspot in her thigh so hot

he was forced to cry
Prajnaparamita, burn with me!
Till the Indian Ocean and the salt waters of the Atlantic

rocked him free, the arms of the girl
a bent ship of longing,
her hair the skin of a muddied garden,

feverish source of ruin, as
over the anthills, leaves swirl
in an alphabet no tongue can replicate.

I see her as she skips to the garden gate,
What burns in me now
is the black coal of her face.

Shall I turn, make peace,
peace to the first gate
she will never enter again?

XII

The leaves of the rose tree
splinter and flee; the garden
of my childhood returns to the sea.

The piecework of sanity,
the fretwork of desire
restive bits and pieces edged into place

satisfies so little.
In dreams come calling
migrant missing selves,

fire in an old man's sleeve,
coiled rosebuds struck from a branch.
Our earthly world slit open.

MAMTA KALIA

(*b*. 1940)

Mamta Kalia was born in 1940. She published two books of poems in English, and more than 20 novels, plays, and short story collections in Hindi. She has said that the language she writes in depends on the city in which she lives. In Bombay she writes in English, in Allahabad she writes in Hindi; there are 'no transit problems' between cultures. In either language, the voice is striking – unembarrassed, ribald, so sharp it can be astringent. She currently lives in New Delhi where she writes in Hindi and English.

Against Robert Frost

I can't bear to read Robert Frost.
Why should he talk of apple-picking
When most of us can't afford to eat one?
I haven't even seen an apple for many months –
Whatever we save we keep for beer
And contraceptives.

Brat

Looking at my navel
I'm reminded of you, Mamma.
How I lay suspended
By that cordial cord inside you.
I must have been a rattish thing,
A wriggly roll of shallow breath.
You, perhaps, were hardly proud
Of your creativity –
Except for the comfort
That I looked like Papa
And not like the neighbour
Who shared our bathroom.

Tribute to Papa

Who cares for you, Papa?
Who cares for your clean thoughts, clean
                words, clean teeth?
Who wants to be an angel like you?
Who wants it?
You are an unsuccessful man, Papa.
Couldn't wangle a cosy place in the world.
You've always lived a life of limited dreams.

I wish you had guts, Papa;
To smuggle eighty thousand watches at a stroke,
And I'd proudly say, 'My father's in import-
                export business, you know.'
I'd be proud of you then.

But you've always wanted to be a model man,
A sort of an ideal.
When you can't think of doing anything,
You start praying,
Spending useless hours at the temple.

You want me to be like you, Papa,
Or like Rani Lakshmibai.
You're not sure what greatness is,
But you want me to be great.

I give two donkey-claps for your greatness.
And three for Rani Lakshmibai.

These days I am seriously thinking of
                        disowning you, Papa,
You and your sacredness.
What if I start calling you Mr Kapur, Lower
                Division Clerk, Accounts Section?

Everything about you clashes with nearly
                        everything about me.
You suspect I am having a love affair these days,

But you're too shy to have it confirmed.
What if my tummy starts showing gradually
And I refuse to have it curetted?
But I'll be careful, Papa,
Or I know you'll at once think of suicide.

Untitled

There he was flirting away
With the fastest would-be artist
While I was sulking on this New Year's Eve
When I asked him what he thought of loyalty
He laughed, 'don't expect dog's virtues from a full-limbed man'

Sheer Good Luck

So many things
could have happened to me.
I could have been kidnapped
at the age of seven
and ravaged by
dirty-minded middle-aged men.
I could have been married off
to a man with a bad smell
and turned frigid
as a frigidaire.
I could have been

an illiterate woman
putting thumb-prints
on rent-receipts.
But nothing ever happened to me
except two children
and two miscarriages

I'm Not Afraid of a Naked Truth

I'm not afraid of a naked truth
Or a naked knife or a naked drain.
That doesn't mean
I'm not afraid of a naked man.
In fact, I am very much afraid of a naked man.

After Eight Years of Marriage

After eight years of marriage
The first time I visited my parents,
They asked, 'Are you happy, tell us.'
It was an absurd question
And I should have laughed at it.
Instead, I cried,
And in between sobs, nodded yes.
I wanted to tell them
That I was happy on Tuesday.
I was unhappy on Wednesday.
I was happy one day at 8 o'clock
I was most unhappy by 8.15.
I wanted to tell them how one day
We all ate a watermelon and laughed.
I wanted to tell them how I wept in bed all night once
And struggled hard from hurting myself.
That it wasn't easy to be happy in a family of twelve.
But they were looking at my two sons,
Hopping around like young goats.
Their wrinkled hands, beaten faces and grey eyelashes
Were all too much too real.
So I swallowed everything,
And smiled a smile of great content.

DEBJANI CHATTERJEE
(*b.* 1952)

Born in Delhi in 1952, Debjani Chatterjee was educated in schools in Japan, Bangladesh, India and Hongkong. She moved to England at the age of 20 and worked in the steel industry, in education, and in community relations. She has written and edited some 40 books of prose and poetry. She lives in Sheffield, Yorkshire.

All Whom I Welcome Leave without My Leave

All whom I welcome leave without my leave,
Just as they come without invitation.
I am not their host, so why do I grieve?

Respite from sickness is a mere reprieve,
Death remains the final registration.
All whom I welcome leave without my leave.

While graying hair and shades of old age cleave
To me, those I love abandon station.
I am not their host, so why do I grieve?

Because I wear my heart upon my sleeve,
I stumble, prey to Death's revelation:
All whom I welcome leave without my leave.

A spectator's role I cannot achieve;
My life explodes in participation.
Though I am not their host, must I still grieve?

I writhe in every net that Fate may weave.
Wisdom accepts my human condition.
All whom I welcome leave without my leave;
I am not their host, so why do I grieve?

Words Between Us

Language breaks down and sounds have no meaning.
Words splutter, dialogues die in mid air;
you and I cross and there is no meeting.

Eyes do not glance, there is no encounter,
postures are hidden and gestures are bare;
language breaks down and sounds have no meaning.

Even masques expose the fading actor,
curtains are drawn but invite no fanfare.
You and I cross and there is no meeting.

We are less than strangers in theatre,
playing separate parts in solitaire.
Language breaks down and sounds have no meaning.

Silence replays the role of the jester.
No more are we one, no longer a pair.
You and I cross and there is no meeting.

Too many scenes have started to fester,
too many pauses are mimes that ensnare.
Language breaks down and sounds have no meaning.
You and I cross and there is no meeting.

JAYANTA MAHAPATRA

(*b.* 1928)

Jayanta Mahapatra was born in 1928 in Cuttack, Orissa, into a family of converted Christians. His father was an inspector of schools. Mahapatra taught physics for close to four decades in various government colleges. He began to write fairly late, at the age of 38, and won quick acceptance, particularly among American readers and editors. His melancholy lyric meditations favour the heartfelt over the ironic, which makes him unique among India's poets. And though he prefers not to live in a major Indian city, the Orissa of his imagination is a crowded place, corroded by monsoon rains and violence, where God's silence is 'deep and famous' and interrupted only by His laughter. Mahapatra has published 20 books of poems in English and English translation. He lives in Cuttack.

A Day of Rain

Once again, it has been a day of rain.
And I hear the flutter of light feet
on the warm earth, excited wings
loosening from the dark. There's
a summer hiding away behind the hills,

a haunting dream whose meaning
always escapes me,
like the sad shut tufts of mimosa,
hanging there tame and weeping
for the lost touch.
What thin air your face is now,
now that I touch it. Out here,
the stupid code of the crickets,
the wind's low whine; who knows
what's dying underneath
a growing blade of grass?
Or what habit palpitates
inside the dark pit of love:
art, ceremony or voice that lies
under my aimless hearing of the rain?

A Rain of Rites

Sometimes a rain comes
slowly across the sky, that turns
upon its grey cloud, breaking away into light
before it reaches its objective.
The rain I have known and traded all this life
is thrown like kelp on the beach.
Like some shape of conscience I cannot look at,
a malignant purpose in a nun's eye.

Who was the last man on earth,
to whom the cold cloud brought the blood to his face?
Numbly I climb to the mountain-tops of ours
where my own soul quivers on the edge of answers.

Which still, stale air sits on an angel's wings?
What holds my rain so it's hard to overcome?

Summer

Not yet.

Under the mango tree
the cold ash
of a deserted fire.

Who needs the future?

A ten-year-old girl
combs her mother's hair,
where crows of rivalries
are quietly nesting.

The home will never
be hers.

In a corner of her mind
a living green mango
drops softly to earth.

The Quest

Under the rain, beyond the walls,
I search for the lost inhabitants of my country.
Gleaming skulls of people I do not know,
those who died a violent death
at the hands of a God with noiseless thunderstorms.
It has become a ritual, this search
for history in which dignity neither comes nor goes.
I wonder why they continue to suffer, and why
this private unhappiness of mine
demands a certain quality in the people I like.
The sadness of crows flutters down into the light.
The rain comes nearer. A tiger of jaws.
Yearly floods turn into a genuine poetic achievement.
Weary steel plants keep on going through the night.
Even computers begin to understand our castes and prejudices.
The voluptuous figures of women in stone

only wish to save our feelings of love and freedom;
they are like old men who do not need their voices,
they have pulled them out of their throats
and hidden them away in their past.
I look into your eyes, trying to think
of newspaper headlines raising their hands
in a gesture expressing their inability to help.
The vicious assault on another young girl
progresses handsomely, breathlessly, without hope.
God still looks at me, his silence deep and famous,
the gaze of modesty touching earth and sky.
Searching for things in this land of rain,
I have really no intention of meeting inhabitants here.
And God? Do I have the need to create
another self whose laughter smothers my fears tomorrow?

The Moon Moments

The faint starlight rolls restlessly on the mat.
Those women talking outside have clouds passing across their eyes.
Always there is a moon that is taking me somewhere.
Why does one room invariably lead into other rooms?

We, opening in time our vague doors,
convinced that our minds lead to something never allowed before,
sit down hurt under the trees, feeding it simply because
it is there, as the wind does, blowing against the tree.

Yet time is not clairvoyant,
and if it has the answer to our lives, proud
in its possession of that potential which can change our natures,
beating the visions of childhood out of us,
the socialism and the love,
until we remain awkwardly swung to the great north of honour.
What humility is that which will not let me reveal the real?
What shameful secret lies hidden in the shadows of my moon?

All these years; our demands no longer hurt our eyes.
How can I stop the life I lead within myself –
The startled, pleading question in my hands lying in my lap
While the gods go by, triumphant, in the sacked city at midnight?

I Did Not Know I Was Ruining Your Life

Rain, all night.
All day.

It is clear
I would never reach home.

Something, one feels,
is sure to happen.

Just the chill
creeping across the floor.

Unreal Country

Rain grates in the silence. My son
walks in through the dim walls,
a strange map drawn by life.

It's as though, blind,
one goes on feeling for night.
And a lot of space I touch

that turns grandly into darkness.
His lost face, white enamel,
looks down at his feet

as if to say: Only the world
is left, and the rain
that hangs from the branches.

Searching for stars still, he asks:
What haven't you told me yet?
And through the dull suburbs

of his death, my old father
gropes his way back.
Yes, he seems to whisper,

overwhelmed by the defeat
in my eyes, hunger and earth
made the bones of one's breath.

I see them nod to each other,
suddenly in fear of the rain,
of the heart left behind.

A Hint of Grief

The rain is home, clinging
pitifully to the Orissa countryside.
Orioles turn on their wings of gold
where the sky falls into darker cloud.
Beyond the wood fence grow lotuses
and wild hyacinths of the wetness.
Again, from somewhere,
one calls back the love
of what one hungers to be touched by,
so I can call you by your name – Orissa,
as the wind returns again
for those empty voices it nurtures
in the thick-leaved mangoes and cashews,
and rain's frightened hands
drop the comic book of our history
onto the weathered stones.

KARTHIKA NAIR
(*b.* 1972)

Karthika Nair was born in 1972 in Kottayam, Kerala. Her father was an officer in the Indian Army and she spent her childhood and adolescence between Assam, Delhi, Kerala, Meghalaya and Uttar Pradesh, with stints for medical treatment in Calcutta, the United States and Australia. The health crisis that gives her poems their forward momentum and urgency is unnamed; and the reader looking for voyeuristic details, for 'a guided tour' or 'a ringside seat' of illness, will find only irony and an absence of self-pity. The selection below is from her first collection, which is forthcoming from HarperCollins India. She moved to Paris in 2001 where she works in arts management.

Zero Degrees: Between Boundaries

I met them first in a land where borders
get blurred; where day rises before night's end
and water morphs into high, brumal walls.
A warrior and a monk, two beings –
flanked by shadows that grow and roam at will –
cross-legged in thought, carving with four hands

arabesques on force, loss, fear – close at hand
– and some big runes – selfhood, death – that border
waking hours, and shape dreams against my will.
Their words whirl in unison to the ends
of still skies, etch a tale *of life being
pruned to papers; of puny men who wall*

*up futures, then watch unmoved as the walls
and roofs of egos tumble: sleight of hand;
nuke name, nation, calling – the very being
– then revel, leave the body on the border
of reality...* the words trail   jerk/end/
lost in this past, unsure of where they will

be sent next. The shadows step in, strong-willed,
free; spin stretch swallow space and bounce off walls.
Warrior and Monk rise and mirror, end
to end, their shadows who recede and hand
the stage over; drift to the near border
and then vanish like mythical beings.

I leave thoughts on belonging, on being
and the zeroth law that I wilfully
signed, and watch them – one compact, bordering
short; the other pale and spare – vault streaked walls
of culture and kinetic codes. Lock hands
embrace dodge thrust. The duet/duel ends

before I read which is which, if one's end
spells start elsewhere. Threat and trust were being
swirled in synchronised moves till just a hand
was seen, a smudge. Then Warrior's great will
and body juddered to a sudden crash; walled
by a stillness that steals through any border.

Monk departs, a worn being in his hands,
crooning of a day when borders and walls
will cease; midst white shells of spent words, I end.

Interregnum

Is it day where you are, or does the moon
loiter overhead, watching you like I
used to, tracing with an unsteady breath
those eyes, sleeping brows, the arc of a smile?
Do your hands still stray unbidden at night
angling to fold my beat within your heart?

It is an odd, wakeful creature, my heart,
tossing gravelly queries at the moon –
as though to smash the murky pane of night
and retrieve a name, a latitude I
seek: the exact location of your smile.
Delhi, Dhaka, I cite under my breath,

Bangkok, Beijing, or up north where the breath
scars the air still, white (like absence a heart):
Vostok, Yukon? Legends that made us smile
once, and contrail maps under a half-moon.
You had checked airline schedules while I
counted cash and clean socks that muggy night.

Your last letter said they woke you at night:
strands of memory that cut off a breath;
roving thoughts you cannot call to heel. I
find those in the mail, addressed to my heart,
dropped by the same russet-tinted moon
wearing faded love bites and a smug smile.

Free from nations and rules, that tramp can smile:
no trolled borders lie between her and night!
Not celestial travellers like the moon,
you and I fill up forms, plead, hold our breath;
cling to vagrant hope that an unknown heart
will relent, sign, scrawl ten digits. Then I,

decked in new, numbered dignity, yes! I
could indulge this tropism towards your smile;
rush across to you, blood back to the heart.
Swathed as one in the ample down of night,
we'd learn anew to synchronise the breath
of desire, and shut out the strident moon.

Till then, though, there is just the moon as I
carve with hushed breath the template of a smile,
sword to end the siege of night on my heart.

Visiting Hours

I *4 PM*

No, can't say I know you; nor recall a friendship
from nineteen sixty-six (they hadn't spliced me yet).
But you are family – that's what Achan let slip – ,

almost (his third cousin's...nephew back from Tibet?).
He said to welcome you, do take a ringside seat.
I'm here for the long haul – yes, that's the new gullet!

In vulcanised rubber – brick-red – to fight the heat,
woven firmly around what used to be my waist.
They'll unstitch me today; it's meant to be a treat.

Achan? He went to empty the bedpan in haste,
and Amma for a bath. She needs a real sheep dip
after sleeping on this floor – dirt flakes like dried toothpaste

– the last fifty-one nights. But this was no planned trip –
unlike yours – with pit stops, friends, and tea with gossip!

II *5 PM*

Is that your son, Ma'am? Yes, he is really smart
for not-quite-three-years-old, but he's trying to snatch
I.V. lines from the Port-a-Cath that fuels my heart.

I can see he is bored. It's sad he can't play catch
or explore autoclaves: they build wards with scant thought
for young visitors here! The doctor and his batch

of interns are coming (hard day? They look quite taut).
Hie, have the reports come? Drat, I've to unzip my chest?
Yes, do get rid of them, this solicitous lot

of teachers, toddlers, aunts – and a neighbour's house guest,
before the guided tour – complete with photos and chart
– you will begin on my sinking dune of a breast,

drilled with tube wells, watered. Will you say, *this won't hurt*,
or *it won't take long*: worn mantras you must impart.

You are late as usual. They'll soon call it a day:
disconnect the spent sun, transfuse the sky with sleep.
We get fifteen minutes. Must you walk all the way

from school to prove a point? Buses, ricks, your dad's jeep,
all shunned in favour of your newly-retrieved feet.
You're right, if I'd spent months yoked to a cast, I'd leap

like Bambi on a trip, turn cartwheels on the street.
Sorry I am scrappy – it's my sixteen-year-old
self, sprung free for the night – but it's so good to greet

someone without a smile! You don't need to be told
how kind it was to come; you aren't going to pray
for my young, shapeless soul. And when your hands enfold

mine, hennaed with heparin, it won't be to weigh
the pace of a stray pulse. Yes, I wish you could stay.

Snapshot on the Parisian Métro, or Landscape on Line 3

Hinged between symmetric hips
(mom and maybe young aunt, arms
caressing packages from Printemps), the little boy
gapes at a soft navel studded
with curved barbells, 4 mm balls.
Its owner pores over Bourdieu's *L'amour de l'art*;
by her side, a grizzled guitarist
thrums a familiar tune or two while a strapholder
swings wildly to the metro's heavier drums,
a Nokia 256 and the London
Stock Exchange welded to one ear.
And the woman in white silk
nuzzling a mottled bouquet
closes her eyes, and smiles
from République to Parmentier.

SRIDALA SWAMI

(*b.* 1971)

Born in 1971 in Mettur, Tamil Nadu, Sridala Swami was educated in a school founded by the philosopher J. Krishnamurti in Rishi Valley, Andhra Pradesh. One of the points of the school was to give its students the space and freedom to develop skills other than the academic. She is a freelance scriptwriter and editor, and has written three books for children. In the preface to her first book she writes that good poems 'tend towards silence'. The poems in this selection begin in the middle of what appears to be a continuing conversation with the self. They end just as quietly, without warning, in 'the sudden night' where 'a trumpet sounds our banishment.' She lives in Hyderabad.

Surviving the Fall Meant Using You for Handholds
(after Eric Fischl's Bedroom Scene #6, *oil on linen, 2004)*

Back striped black, suit striped white,
the wall just striped, the net just curved.
Crouched where the light comes from,
you see that there is no protection
in the downward curves of the net;
it is only a shroud over one half of the frame.
No comfort in the dark lines on her back
that could be wings; though they dip at the spine
like children's drawings of crows
in a deep blue sky, the lines will not lend
her wings.

He stands at the precise point where wall
meets wall, at the intersection of another
'V' that's going nowhere. Caught between
net and woman, objects weighing down the frame,
it appears that freedom would lie behind him,
in the empty spaces at his back. But look again –
the stripes on the wall spear him in place;
like X-rays, they pierce his insides.
Those might even be his bones
showing through, those white lines on
his suit.

His hands are clenched and white. He is looking
this way. Caught, unable to look away,
you slide like light off the window ledge
from where you were peeping. As you fall
you recall her hands bent at the elbows,
convenient handholds you did not take.

As the air rushes past, all is blue, white, blur.
A cocoon of sound. You remember
on the net in the room, caught, a little orange and yellow
that could have been flowers
or butterflies.

Cryogenic

Let's suppose it is the man who waits
for the woman to return.

Let's assume it's been twenty years,
or thirty.

In all that time, through all upheavals
and sorrows, and who knows, perhaps a few joys,

he holds himself ready for the moment
when she will return.

While she goes on adventures
and becomes lined with life,

or perhaps takes on large burdens
on behalf of many people,

he is perfect and cold.
He is waiting for her.

One day, triumphant, she returns
expecting to find many things changed

but some things, at least,
just as they were.

As with Odysseus, she thinks she will know him
by his old scars

and learn about him
by his new ones.

But in the twenty or thirty years she has been away
the world has left no mark on him;

nothing acquired, nothing changed.
He is just as she had left him.

Perfectly preserved,
he knows nothing.

What can he tell her about truth
or reconciliation?

Post Mortem

The brain in its jar floats and dreams:
streams of memory, consciousness preserved.
The two halves, like breasts, grieve
for the softness of skin   for the reserved
whisper of touch. All this has already happened

and will never happen again. The brain curls
itself up, hits glass, ricochets and remembers:
foetal, an echo of shape, a pearl
of desire – his body holding the other one
that burnt away and became ember.

There should be a question here. A 'how' or a 'why' –
a way to understand linearities. Instead, there are ridges
and convolutions, the repetition of blood beating,
the raising of hair along an arm when a finger follows
vertebrae down the spine.

Brain   body   umbilicus. Our bodies stretch
within and without to accommodate life. But
without you   without you   without you
I am only a dissonance, an object adrift, a wretched
longing for the pain of being alive.

Slip Dreams

One night his words slip under my dreams
and haunt me when I am awake:
'I know who you are. I have found you out.'
For several nights after that one
I clothe my dreams with nightmares.

He is a vulture in repose.
Evening comes and he watches me.
I show signs of failing.
I fall asleep, as I must.
From him there is no sound.

Once my dreams begin he enters,
dark as feathers and as dry and rasping.
If I ever had a face it is covered now
with his knowledge, with his eyes that
say, 'I see you as you really are.'

'What am I?' I want to ask
but I am afraid as much of knowing
the answer in dreams
as of forgetting it when I awake.
'Who are you?' I ask instead.

He is a vulture awake.
He devours me with his words.
The more he speaks the less I am.
I would like to say I am picked clean
but there is always the next night and the next and the next.

Lines on Water

The shore vanishes.
Under a lowering unfamiliar sky
the constellations reveal themselves
in short, incomprehensible bursts.
We are lost

to the waves, to the chasing spray,
the tossing horses
and to the country we have left behind.
To ourselves,
lost.

Ahead, a wild chase –
we don't yet know what
wealth: gold, ivory, pepper,
we hope.
I say, geese. Sheep. Dung.

On different shores now
we have drawn lines on the water
and this is where
the ink runs out:
where fingers darker than ours
clutch shiny glass beads

and where through the sudden night
a trumpet sounds our banishment.

Aftermath

A bloody moon tonight –
stained, solitary
and outcast.

The railway tracks gleam and glide
on their way to nowhere
with a memory

of voices. Once, even thoughts
clattered in time
to the trains' rhythms.

But tonight the moon is red
and the debris
remembers its shape.

It is the railway tracks
like slit throats
that grin at the empty sky.

All Music Is Memory

All music is memory:
a lone wind trapped in the chimes,
a window rattling dolefully
in time to the movement of the night.

If my life were stretched
across the drum of centuries
I might have time to discern
the pattern in the creaking of trees.

But destinies drown through time.
A million years are lost
and I try in vain to cup my hands
and hold a note, a scale, a song.

JERRY PINTO

(*b*. 1966)

Jerry Pinto was born in 1966 in Bombay into a family of Roman Catholics. His mother's family fled Burma for India at the time of the Japanese occupation and his father was a businessman. He was educated at the Government Law College, and has held jobs as a medical representative, a television script writer, and a school librarian. He works as a journalist and writer in Bombay.

House Repairs

All it took was the flick of chisel
And the bathroom wall came sighing down.
It wasn't quite what we had hoped for
But we took it for what it was:
One more act
In a prolonged dramaturgy
Of cement.

The new wall came up quickly.
Overnight, it was back in place
It was all that a new wall should be
Or so we hoped.

Only the next morning and the next
When, sleep-clogged, we lurched into it
We found it was our old wall.
With a suicide note still scrawled on it
With blood still fresh splashed on it.

We paid the masons anyway
And learned something about renovation.

Drawing Home

Were I to draw my home, I don't think
I would do it quite like this drawing of yours.
All these right angles and hinges bear no resemblance
To my memories of suddenness and curves, odd shapes
And our balancing act: four on a trapeze.
Still I don't resent your drawing.
I rather like it, in fact; this way of making coherent
Scenes of such randomness.
You could play one camera. I could be the other.
We could ask for a neutral third so that
Between the three of us, we'd miss nothing.
You could look for the big picture and I
For nuance. The third camera, full-frontal, unblinking,
Could mediate. We might arrive at something
Between your version and mine.

Window

What can you do with a window?
It will always remain four-cornered
Always be a savagery to the sky
Always offer enough room for only one head
Or one cloud.

There's nothing open about a window.

Rictus

The men who came to dress his body
Laid tender hands on his face.
Their first job, they knew, was to erase
That rictus of shock.

Death has a grim sense of humour.
One Saturday night, it tapped him
On the shoulder, handed him a toy.
Puzzled, he took it, shook it.
He rattled.

That dark red tub, my uncle's, has seen many uses.
It can tell you stories, mundane ones
And some perverse bloody horrors.
You will not wash him with detergent?
You will.

Mummy is in the next room.
I watch her between tasks. She does not react.
Mention coffins and her golden eyes do not flinch.
But rock salt and she asks: 'Why rock salt?'
'To absorb what flows out of the body.'

What flows out of his body?
Ordinary dreams and old fables.
A few riddles, a moral or two, some gaps,
The last fear.

'Wait one whole night,' he told us
'Before you bury me.' We did.
Was there something else, daddy,
Some other instruction? Something
We forgot?

ADIL JUSSAWALLA
(*b.* 1940)

Adil Jussawalla was born in Bombay in 1940. His jagged, rage-fuelled lines, particularly in
the poem 'Missing Person', embody the city in which he was born and where he continues
to live. Part skewed autobiography, part paranoid delusion, part politically incorrect socio-
sexual history, the poem is as relevant today – and as fresh and contemporary – as when it
was written. 'Once I was whole, I was all,' says its fragmented anti-hero whose bigotries
extend to everyone, gay, straight, black, white, brown, Hindu, Muslim, Christian, Parsi.
It's an extraordinary piece of writing from a nation where any utterance connected with
religion and sex is edited, or, more likely, banned.

Missing Person

I *Scenes from the Life*

> *A child may ask when our strange epoch passes*
> *During a history lesson, 'Please sir, what's*
> *An intellectual of the middle classes?*
> *Is he a maker of ceramic pots*
> *Or does he choose his king by drawing lots?'*
> *What follows now may set him on the rail,*
> *A plain, perhaps a cautionary tale.*
>
> W.H. AUDEN, 'Letter to Lord Byron'

1

House Full. It's a shocker. Keep still.
Blood crawls from a crack.
Keep still.
It's all happening.

It's a spear.
It's your saviour.
It's a quiet mirror with hair all over

born
to a middle-class mother.
God's gift for further reflection.

There's trouble outside:
crowds, stammering guns, the sea
screaming from side to side.

2

For The First Time On Your Screen
        MISSING JACK
    A slave's revolt and fall

His first cry with his mother,
his last look with a wall –
no round-up by sunset, no final corral –
his wit with his friends,
his seed with fugitive bodies
as settled as armchairs now
seething with other men's children.
No one believes   [jump cuts here
from mother to mistress and back]
his sepia distant or lurid recent
past.
Don't shut your eyes. It's only a movie.

'That speeding train –
It is my life.
Those are my hands –
split-ends of sabotage.'
Again and again, buttonholes friends
turned strangers, strangers friends:
'Believe, that's me on the screen –
through the stuttering dust, through the burst-open door.'
The running dog runs but they've put out its eyes.
'Once I was whole, I was all.
Believe, why don't you believe?'

Adil Jussawalla, Cuffe Parade, Bombay, 1997

3

A ~~~~~~~'s a giggle now
but on it Osiris, Ra.
An अ's an er...a cough,
once spoking your valleys with light.
But the a's here to stay.
On it St Pancras station,
the Indian and African railways.

That's why you learn it today.

Look out the school at the garden:
how the letter will happen
the rest of your life:
bright as a butterfly's wing
or a piece of tin
aimed at your throat:
expansive as in 'air',
black as in 'dark',
thin as in 'scream'.
It will happen again and again –
in a library in Boston,
a death-cell in Patna.
And so with the other twenty-five letters
you try to master now – 'cat', 'rat', 'mat'
swelling to 'Duty', 'Patience', 'Car'.

Curled in a cortical lobe (department of languages),
an unspeakable family gibbered.
'Where is their tape?' abroad, at a loss,
he asks. 'What does it say?'

'Wiped out', they say.
'Turn left or right,
there's millions like you up here,
picking their way through refuse,
looking for words they lost.
You're your country's lost property
with no office to claim you back.
You're polluting our sounds. You're so rude.

'Get back to your language,' they say.

4

They say,
'White hoodlums wreck your shop?

You've seen the moon dilate its drop
to full, you've seen
six yards of cloth clutched into a sewer,
childbrides bundled to a knot,
childbirth a bleeding bag,
and letting their people out like hair
onto a river,
squat temples weeping
till no fixed morning
for their lost daughters.

'Why drink up our debilitating drinks,
then look for fights? The word's about,
you've nothing left to say.
There's no finish to the work you work.
You sit at table grinding your jaws
against the teeming wheat you get.
Get back, go feed
your yowling country from an empty dish.'

Lost, running from acid to Marx,
he sees the world in twos
and says,
'Who helped me in a fashion
no longer function true.'
How had they helped,
plaguing his seed, carrying black tales
about his history, beating him with those dry
Christian sticks that crossed him yet?
Much more had to be cleared than
the mud thrown in a village well
if only to affix
his post-script to an unknown history.

'Let's sow that dump with TVs
while you search,' they say.
'Your programming's a mess.'

See Famines. See Wars. Their heaped-up dead
on the world's plate of gold, its food
ranged in sweet hills beside them.

A place for bones.

See Indians bite the dust,
streams of pent-up blood
bless their stones.

5

Lock up his hands.
His hands aren't there
and we know of no work they've done.

The blindfold now.
Much better, focus
his eyes on our rifles.

Have you dug out those flints,
his silly vernacular cries?
Nothing to speak of.

What was it our first file
accused him of? *It's missing.*
Start all over again.
Start: Missing Person.

6

Black vamps break out of hell,
rave up a cold hotel,
never touch him.
White faggots fall at his feet,
fuck up his central heat,
never feel him.
He panics. His friends
leave him for their wives
as much part of living
as the carry-cots, the lifts.
Shut out of the warm and furry,
not wanted in Lucifer's halls,
a fire on one flat plane he drifts.

7

In a brief clearing
above an underworld of headless roots,
he sees a tree divide its parts
to bird, insect, sky,
locked to its reflection
by its wrist.

Exile's a broken axle.

Goes back (to where
whose travels cannot home?)

goes back to where

a mirror shakes in recognition.

8

A mill of tubercular children
is what he wears.
The wretched of history storm into,
they smash
his house of ideas.

Who puffed up an Empire's sails
still fuel the big-power ships,
still make him fly
high to jet-setter fashion.
Blood tumbles down sleeves
hung upside down
to dry
in his flat.

He'll wreck himself yet;
docked in a bar with a criminal friend,
his shirt wrapping him like a wet
sail, his wood carcass breaking and burning
in mutinous sweat.

9

He travels the way of devotion
but no sky lights
his street.

A river of pills brings him no raft.
Death goes awash with wishing.

Cripples his own mouth then, sits
killing his tongue, sits
barred up behind his teeth.

Bright sparks
on the international back-slapping circuit
are picking up prizes like static.

He's for the dark.

10

God of our fathers,
of the broken tribe
and the petrified spirit,
why did you send us this horror?

Nothing we put in stayed put.
We put in the family history and prayers,
they flew out as comics.
Fed him grandmamma's custards, he spewed.
We poured in the tonics

but nothing sweetened his tongue.
He thrust it out
again and again,
the bloodied head of an arrow

made the girls run.

Drive your shafts through his neck.
Switch your hunting lights on.

For years we prompted his first
words, scolding the servants for theirs:
'Sweetie, say:
Let there be light, let there be us.'
We heard:

'Let there be dung.'

11

Heaven burns to ashes,
the masses crouch in prayer,
invitations to the waltz
return and flood
his famine with nostalgia.

China leaps. He ruminates,
a dinosaur in despair.
Saying,
'The masses in B minor are not known to fart.'
Fascists
leave their own in the air

in the halls of the nation.

As the underground runs, reassembles,
thinks of an earlier damnation,
thinks of how Orpheus' head
made straight for his heart and speared it
with the music of his future.
His trances grow. Its now
commando comrades butcher.

Their war-cries blot out his blinding.
Bad rhetoric rolls over his revolution's end.

His music a dribble of curses,
his wife a roof of tears each morning,

he abandons his friends.

12

In the fist of a rioting people
his rotting head.
A mirror fires at him point blank
and yells, 'Drop dead,
colonial ape,
back under an idealist spell.
Yes, you've made it to some kind of hell,
backslider, get liquidated.'

'Wait! You know whose side
I'm on,' he shouts,
'but the people, their teeth bright as axes
came after my stereo and cattle,
came after my bride.
I've said all my prayers.
O pure in
thought word and deed have I been,
delivering sun,
yet you gild street-urine –
theirs!'

So what's the scenario
for our two-bit hero
but sliding back further
into a gun,
but travelling on,
paling at riots and slaughter,
forgetting his family, rejecting his son,
men with raised arms, stripped of their skin,

passing him village on village,
seared in the blast of no food,
in the shock of no water?

13

Less time for kicks
except for those
aimed at the face and balls.
Less time for pricks
who dig into his time.
He faints and falls.
Less time less time
to suffer liberation in the end,
to freeze one lovely frame
and hide there for a while.
The sockets jag. Time's disjointed all.
But left enough to bear
the last attempts at compromise
as student posters patch a crumbling wall
to hide the botched affair,
to smile and smile and smile.

14

Bright angels – where?
          [the final scene: so choir]
so faintly heard,
so long and lost a pause
in this underthumbed compendium of joy
that's still his earth,
his shouts for law and order
won't shake the posse off;
its dogs
harry, attack,
are at his throat and back.
Watch his murder.

His cock, his ears, his eyes, his tribe
will have as penance. That won't make him sick.
The better to *feel* your love?
He coughs and kicks
with historical poisons,
bookdust, lies
that turn his words to sand.

(Say the nigger *does* exist. You'll save.
Smash his pride and enter.)

The trapped wrist says it all,
how barren branches fall,
how talents winter.

To break away. To stand
in steady confutation of the Law
is what the skunk demanded.
He stole his father's bread. He spat on him
and said, 'Your reign has ended.'

Students of Eng. Lit.,
still bunched round her merciful tit,
be up and about,
face more terror than you can take.
And this is how you will end:
Before the final fade-out, like an ad:

'Here is our smug little watch that's lost its hands.
Here is our own Bugs Bunny who acted funny...'

There in the dark with the dogs, in pieces,
your fucking fake.

And here's an announcement:
Hope
which periodically triggers
some men to act
and looses the bonds of the earth,
has set a bright tide revolving inside me, a door.
Give up your seats and join the cast of thousands,
revolve about his pieces too
(brown slaves, black vamps, white faggots,
deceivers, women who rend and claw)

and hear that head still singing...
O fallen throats that went down in a war,
O waters of the dark connection,
O pit of blood and knuckles,
Open, open up your jaws,

and hold me there – your missing person.

*We may thus conclude that this bourgeoisie in miniature that
thrusts itself into the forefront is condemned to mark time,
accomplish nothing. In underdeveloped countries, the
bourgeois phase is impossibly arid. Certainly, there is a police
dictatorship and a profiteering caste. But the construction
of an elaborate bourgeois society seems to be condemned
to failure.*

FRANTZ FANON, The Wretched of the Earth

1

No Satan
warmed in the electric coils of his creatures
or Gunga Din
will make him come before you.
To see an invisible man
or a missing person,
trust no Eng. Lit. That
puffs him up, narrows his eyes,
scratches him fangs. Caliban
is still not IT.
But faintly pencilled
behind a shirt,
a trendy jacket or tie,
if he catches your eye,
he'll come screaming at you like a jet –
savage of no
sensational paint,
fangs cancelled.

2

His hands were slavish;
but fingers burst out
from time to time
to point to a fresh rustling of tails
in the dustbin of history,
a new inflexion of sails
on the horizon.
His thoughts were bookish;
but a squall from the back of his skull
suddenly fluttered their pages,
making him lose his bearings,
abandon ship.
His cock, less rulable than his rest,
though fed on art-book types,

Hellenic forms,
plumped on libraries circulating
white bellies, white breasts,
with a catch in its throat,
jumped at nipples and arses
of indiscriminate races and classes.
His tongue,
his one underground worker perhaps,
bound by a sentence
pronounced in the West,
occasionally broke out
in a rash of yowls
defying the watch-towers of death,
police dogs:
a river of wild statistics;
or in riddles
crafted for cell-mates
aspiring to doctorates
from the Universities
of Texas, Bogotá, Bombay,
perspiring
students of socio-linguistics.

   3

Lacking the classical burst
of Achilles' tyre
or of Vidura's eye,

backboneless;

lacking the lyrical crux
of desert and wire
to pluck his heart in pain

whom Krishna rejected;

lacking the aboriginal's
throat, shafted with snakes,
whose songs bit to the quick;

touching his prick
from time to time
for moral support;

his adventures as flat as beaten tin
original only to the extent of
their extent

empty even of original sin

his women not worth a leaking bucket

inspite of the kingdoms
of skin he wandered in

still lacked the password
to Love's legendary valley's
shimmering anthems, past

his mountain of condoms.

4

To become a white dove,
homing to clefts of scripture, myth,
its shoulders rubbing buttock and breast
of all that gracious goodness
heaped on a temple's head
is why he flew to a guru. At home
with the serpent and the dope
for...
certainly not a yuga.
Five minutes? Five years?
What if forever?
Why this total abasement of sense,
this backward striding to light
with an outside-in people,
dead-eyed and hollow,
their seven-centred spines
burnt out
by...
what?
A gigantic Shiva-thrust?
A Black & Decker drill?

Blown away with a hearty laugh.

Was he the shout
of a new generation on the hill?
To become...
not the UN avatar
but Vishnu's
lion-with-missile –
to kill?

5

Few either/ors
in underdeveloped lands,
mostly alsos:
the also-rans
the also-mad
the also-so-sos.

Renaissance Europe (our one-time twin)
was non-specialist also.
We're the mix
Marx never knew
would make the best
Communists. Also

too fond was our hero of distinctions,
too consistently separated torso from torso.
Where did that get the Greeks?
You see,
we're *Das Capital*, a dried-up well
and a big *Mein Kampf*. Also.

6

He was the bloodied parts
that thumped the ground
around a rope that went into the sky.
He was a crowd of tourists
waiting for his own reappearance.
He was an eye in a maze
of its own making that I
could never catch.
He is what slipped out
from under a magic shroud, leaving
a knife pinned in a pumpkin head
to freeze a poor man's blood
behind a shock that said,
'He's acting out *my* life.
And I want more.'

What bit-parts, what a fall
for one we thought had gone
proud to adventure –
a local astronaut, no less.
How embarrassingly bad his re-entry
in drabs and dribbles,
meaningless symbols,

or that sudden tumult of blood
that messed us all.
Did he foul things up, up there?
It's not very clear.
Still...
does anybody here
know of a school of mystics,
a law of optics,
mathematics,
or even one of his odious
street-corner friends
to produce him before
his grieving wife,
our rifles,
or a criminal court of law?

7

My man, at the end of your tether,
gone,
even as,
against your words of glass,
stone-throwers mass,

tricksy with whisky and sin,
again and again you escaped
to hideaways nobody knew.

You had class

who Marx found
earth's wavering smell
determined to quit the earth.

In the unholy spin
of your new birth,
in new light-years of terror –

your rope dropped away, earth's gravity gone –

how much warmer my arms were at home;
mistrusting, my husband, my tomb –

tumbling through cavities of space,
your mind's gone,
onwards, rocketing
blind
with unloving error.

LAWRENCE BANTLEMAN

(1942-95)

Lawrence Bantleman was born in Pune. His father was an Indian Army officer who died in action. Bantleman was 15 and living in Bangalore when his mother died. He took a job in Calcutta, which he resigned in less than a year because his employers wished to send him to the 'cultural Siberia' of Cuttack, Orissa. From 1964 to 1967, he was the literary editor of a Delhi weekly, *The Century*. He published four books of poems and a play with the Writers Workshop, then emigrated to Canada. He died in Vancouver.

Graffiti (1962), where most of the poems in this selection are taken from, is a remarkably assured first collection for a writer who had not yet turned 20. In a letter to his publisher P. Lal, which served as a preface to the book, Bantleman wrote: 'I never went to college... I wanted to learn not to be taught; and I am agape at the immensity of the world through the peeled eye.' The letter also provided some perceptive self-appraisal. His poems 'are all contained in their last lines,' he wrote. '[R]emove my last lines and the whole poem flounders.'

Movements

Give the sea change and it shall change and not change.
Give the sea shift and it shall shift and not shift;
Although I have smelled spring's conversation
Yet I have seen the bare arms of the continent
Hairy with waves, and the teeth-marks of geology.

Some say geology's jazz age
Is played by the Interglacial Quartet,
And some have seen it
Itching in screes,
While others find a woman's leg
In trunks of trees
Marching to fife and drum.

But your hand moving in my hand,
Your body moving in my body,
Your mind moving in my mind,
Your soul moving in my soul,
Are simple things to write of:

What do I know of you?

Words

That mongrel summer of our god
we played, oh how we played, with words
and anagrams, discovering the broad
spread of the reversible was
Malayalam obversa sic; sic him, while
level was the perfect one, sic him, god
became dog, the bitch returned
as Rover your Alsatian and what
soul, exemplifying catechism sin, sports
coatwise Mediocre my Dalmatian?

Vegetable sellers, transmigratory
Hindu tomato yellers, men of spinach,
onion women, can you imagine someday shall
return as summer birds?
What of the vendors of words?
I hear them: crow crosswords,
vulture verbs, the albatross
of language circling the world's
end; oh the mute nouns, oh the day
of the sentence, oh the judgment of books
is far worse than wailing:

the birds are flying back,
the world is failing
the birds, even the black.

In Uttar Pradesh

The landscape stretches out its hands:
one is the plain whose distances
rise like hillocks in your palm.
The other is the sky, descending
like a hand descends on an insect.

The river beds are dry as the lines
read by a palmist in this handscape.

Here, the Aryans halted
at the street corners of history.
The event is remembered in every town

or village, poor or sad,
having a whitewashed temple stand
as a scarecrow for reality.

Reality is a big, black bird.
The wells hold equal parts of soil
and water as life holds myth and truth.
The land bears cane, a little rice,
millet; but the life
is only a bowl of polished rice
for thirty thousand gods.

Ghosts

You were not perfumed,
Yet stood
A delicate fragrance –
Smoking wood.

Your smell,
And soft wet earth
About your coffin
Being the birth

Of this cypress I shelter
Under in the rain:
From a farm wood smoke.
Wet earth here
And here you are again.

Septuagesima

The Friars eat the Fish and warn
Against the spiky centre bone
A soul may choke on should it scorn
Obeisance to God alone.
How lonely must be God alone?

The Bread has now, made from corn,
Been elevated with this grace,
'The harvest of construction rods

344

Will build new churches to our gods...
To Industry be praise.'

I've eaten Fish and in the place
Of centre bone a bomb
Smiles with a cherub's face.
Bless them who bleed their fellowman,
Bless them who war by mood,
Bless them who bathe their wounds again
To venture into blood:
And bless the ninth beatitude
Son of the Building Rod –
Render to Caesar and his good
The essences of God.

See now the Friars cut the Fish
While Fate stands back and smiles.
The irony of Easter morn,
The bleeding T, the woven thorn,
Now broken body, broken bone.
God must go down while Man goes on
To Easter and Christmas Isles!

D — to J —

I am blest with a love that is secret,
It opens like drying sand
Never to close or be fulfilled:
I suppose as a dying hand
Can still be read and granted length
Of life, I'll hope for love
Reciprocated – oh for strength
To remove it from the glove.

I am blest with a glory gurgling
Within, without my mask
Unchanging faces the changing eye
Of the world – but all I ask
Is a slight fit of lash on lid
To sanctify my task.
I am blest with no wooden burden;
But as Ghibelline to Guelph
It seems my love is certain –
I crucify myself.

I am blest, although am blest alone
Am content in that I've always known

I am blest with a love that is secret.

One A.M.

Listen to Time,
Old eater at his fruit,
Spitting seeds, the brute
Who has no brain or rhyme.

How artfully he moves,
Catpawing through a clock
And never stops to talk
But purringly he proves

With so much sound – no more
Than if you strain a ear
At one A.M. you hear –
The shutting of his jaw.

Gauguinesque

This is the last evening. In your way
I've made a liking for you
Where earlier you would not fit;
This last evening we sit
Opposite each other with
Tables made of coffin-wood between.
From where I write
The closed venetians let the twilight grey
Enter and die beneath electric light.
One week hence I shall be far away.

The greenery shakes, is sometimes still,
But is always green. The black tree trunks
In yesterday's thick rain have turned brown
Again. Voices fill the rooms they have to fill.
Chairs scrape. Typewriters talk in lead
On 'soul white' sheets (who talks of soul here?
Asks a voice within). All the noise

346

Ends as it begins. Should I be happy?
Should you say rejoice? Where I go
Voices and noises follow like we know.

E.V. RAMAKRISHNAN

(b. 1951)

Born in Kannur, Kerala, in 1951, E.V. Ramakrishnan is a translator and a critic. He lives in Surat, Gujarat, and teaches English at the University of South Gujarat. That state's periodic eruptions of sectarian violence are coded into poems where nothing is bucolic: cats are giants of doubt, an orchard is a place of menace and mystery, and a river will climb into a city in 'the full glare of the sun'.

Terms of Seeing

On our way home from school
We often spent hours in that abandoned
Orchard of mango, cashewnut
And tamarind trees, where each season
Had its fruit and each fruit tasted different.

There we raided the make-shift hideouts
Of bootleggers, and broke their buried
Mud pots. The crematorium in the corner
Revealed an occasional roasted vertebra.
Once we went further and discovered

A disused well, and peeped into its
Vaporous depths: the water smelt like freshly
Distilled alcohol. Through clotted branches
Of close-knit shadows floated white
Turtles with glazed, metallic shells.

Moving with a monastic grace, they looked
Knowledgeable, like much-travelled witchcraft
Doctors. If they cast a spell it was
Unintentional. As we bent down, their
Shaven heads rose and met a shaft of sudden

Sunlight at an angle, tilting the sun
Into the sea. Still the light lingered over the hill
Like an intimate whisper of something
Forbidden. By this time, the terms of seeing
Were reset: the well was watching us now.

Its riveted gaze pierced us and even went
Beyond us. In the dark cornea of the well
The white turtles moved like exposed optic nerves.
And as if a word was spoken, we stepped
Back into the world of gravity, in silence.

Stray Cats

They are not exactly homeless.
They are dissidents who have lost their faith
in furnished interiors, morning walks,
the cake and the cutlery.

When you have nine lives to live
you learn to take things in your stride.
You learn to stretch your body
at full length, and yawn at domestic
fictions. And for this reason

you figure in horror films
in the mandatory moment
between the flash of lightning
and the appearance of the ghost.
The light is darkish blue and you see
yourself in the iris of the burning
eye. The horror is in the seeing.
What you see is altered by the act
of seeing. The mystery does not stop
there. The seer is in turn altered
by what he sees. Having known this,
stray cats jump from roof to roof.

They monitor the world from treetops
and hold their weekly meetings
in the graveyard, like wandering mendicants.

And when they walk out of the mirror
of the sun and cross the crowded road
in a flash, for a shining moment,
they lurk in the light like a giant shadow
of doubt. Ill omens to those who cannot
see beyond what they see.

from For All Things Dying

2 *Falling Figures*

You have to look beyond the pigment
of paint to a point where the familiar falls away.

The trauma of the real cannot be tracked further.

Falling figures across the barbed wire
of a diagonal line: faces ignited
with the frenzy of fire-walkers.

A river is struck off the map with cranes,
pillars and dynamite. A mob with petrol
bombs moves deeper into the eyes of a man
frozen in fear, his hands folded.

This is how the linear world turns in on itself.
And this is when you long
for the script of the slanted rain on the plains
to tell you the difference between a prayer
and a false affidavit.

3 *Bikhubhai the Weatherman*

It is raining in the hills,
said Bikhubhai the weatherman.
But the sun was shining.

Don't go by the sun, he said.
The new moon means disaster.
The sea is bleeding. A boatman
saw scarlet fish circling his boat.

Bikhubhai dipped his palm in the river
and said, the sea is pushing inward.

In the full glare of the sun, the river rose
and climbed into the city.

And Bikhubhai went round in his boat,
shouting: Don't panic. The river will go back.
She is your guest just for a day.

There are things you don't even know
you know. Your body is a stranger

you see from a distance. A country
revealed through a satellite picture.

You inhabit only a part of it, its
periphery where pain manifests itself

as the pugmarks of a predator. It converses
with birds and water, strangers to you.

It knows how much can be held in two
hands. And legs need to be sturdy first.

The porous skin filters a humid world,
stays in a state of high alert. Its conscience

is clear. What you seek, the body found
long ago. It remembers what you've forgotten.

REVATHY GOPAL
(1947-2007)

Revathy Gopal was born in Bombay in 1947, a climactic year in Indian history that she would revisit in poems: 'That night / not all of us celebrated / freedom's tender blaze'. Like Salman Rushdie, her midnight's sibling, the historical fact of her birth year became raw material for the making of lyric narratives. Her gift was the ability to render complex subjects into short lines that covered much ground with a few quick strokes. Her first collection of poems *Last Possibilities of Light* (Writers Workshop) appeared a few months before her death from cancer. She died in Bombay.

Freedom!

That night,
not all of us celebrated
freedom's tender blaze, he said.

Was it the dust of departing armies,
or the blood-fog of partition,
or the smoke from fireworks
that seemed to darken our eyes?

And darkens them still, my father.
Lathis still rise and fall,
children still cry out in hunger.
Each day, somewhere a war ends
and begins again.

Loving one's country was never so hard.
Other fields seem greener, other skies more clear.
Too much blood blots out the sun,
too much history
shrouds the earth.

Frantic at fifty
with the din of the past,
we still seek messiahs
in a universe insensible
to our pain.

Just a Turn in the Road

Small towns named after big battles.
Chandernagar and Arcot,
Madras and Masulipatnam,
names from history texts
that send you to sleep in class.

Death under a tropical sun
comes in so many forms,
malaria and dysentery, syphilis and plague,
a tropical sun that drives men mad
and bullet wounds that fester.

European hostilities explode
a continent away and foreign blood
and bowels leak into Indian earth.
Here a fort is besieged and taken,
ships sunk, local rajahs bought and sold,
small accruals in a war that happens elsewhere.
Small men, mere Company-wallahs
like Clive and Hastings who seized their chance
and went down an uncertain road.

And here we are now, ruled by Macaulay's
Minute, not the Code Napoleon.
Shaped and made aware
by the blood and sinew
of the English tongue instead of
the froth and airy lightness of
s'il vous plaît and *je t'en prie*.

Picnic at the Zoo

Most of the cages are empty, now;
once there were civet cats, panther and jaguar,
even a family of white tigers from the Sunderbans
that made a splash of light in the infernal dark;
a black bear and a binturong
I remember particularly,
because of its droll name.
They died or were moved
to kinder climes, perhaps.
But when the kangaroos (strange import!)
died, one by one,
the local paper said they
probably pined away.

Somewhere between the orang-otan
and the peanut vendor,
she lies stricken in the dust,
Victoria, Queen Empress,
head averted in clotted rage
as pigeons strut
and cheeky boys clamber
on that capacious lap
from which once flowed
the long tedium of empire,
the unending reproach
of widowhood, somewhere
a haemophilic grandson;
and the men who walked away,
father, husband,
a recalcitrant son.

Seville

This is just a pretend city.
With its gaudy skies,
set on an endless plain,
where no trees grow and
where you can still hear
the cries of doomed men and
the clash of ghostly armies.
In the distance
a solitary knight droops towards you,
on his rickety mule,
to the steady drumbeat of Ravel's *Bolero*.

You have been here before
in stories read in childhood
and in dreams.
The skies whirl over your head
and the streets merge
one into the other.
How similar all the cities of Europe
appear! Hellenic ruins for tourists,
Roman arches for victorious
armies, and public squares,
and cemeteries
to honour the fallen.

Greatness existed here once,
in the dense dead air
of palaces and museums
named for kings long gone
or generals on horseback.

Back in the sulphurous air
of your third-world city, sometime
outpost of another empire,
in the missed beat between
cinema and coffee shop,
a sudden vision flares
of sun-washed cathedral and orange trees
in public gardens.

As the Crow Flies

You arrive early after peering
into several bedrooms on the way
and regurgitate the news of the day
in that startlingly familiar
and salacious tone
smirking and raucous.

I'd better have some rice ready
else that tone will turn
rancorous and I know you'd have
no compunction in letting
the neighbours know
what I'd rather they didn't.

Subterranean

Trying to begin again,
but this memory
with a long nose
pushes its way in,
untimely, unwanted.
Do you imagine a day
when we will meet
standing in a queue
or stepping over puddles
on a street corner?
And quietly without a flicker
we will find the flame
blown out
and the wax cools, spreads,
hardens on the surface.

Carved in Stone

I shall not be inconsolable. There will be other rooms, other faces, open spaces,
long stretches of time when I shall not even be conscious that you are not there.

I count the cost in concrete terms. You will not know my children's names, nor
I yours. That I may look at a photograph and remember my eyes looking at you
looking at me. That some green girl in love with herself will hold your life in
her hands.

I shall not say your name again, not even by chance.

One day, perhaps, love may die of disuse, left to rust in wind and weather.

Shapes

Mirror marks on wet glass,
finger-writing on steam,
hieroglyphs drawn by
the one who lives behind
the mirror, messages for me,
if I could only decipher them.
Communion of the lonely.

And when I spill milk I look
to see if the pattern spells anything,
meanings from the past or the future,
arrows shot into time
that will explain everything
I've missed.

Time Past, Time Present

I see
in this moment's intense scrutiny
the sleepless nights
that have brought us here.

There is a high wind, somewhere
a wild keening.
I know it from some other lifetime.

Look at me now, really look.
See me as I was, one last time.
Watch as I fall to earth.

SAMPURNA CHATTARJI

(*b.* 1970)

Born in Dessie, Ethiopia, in 1970, Sampurna Chattarji was brought up in Darjeeling, in the Himalayas, where her parents were schoolteachers. She has published a translation of Sukumar Ray's nonsense verse and several collections of Indian folk tales. Those books have a playfulness that is absent from her poems, in which something unnamed and impending is 'shutting out the light'. She lives in Bombay.

Still Life in Motion

I

The highway is a huddle of arms
around the girl. Cold prickling into
a pattern of needles on her legs,
bare in the 4 A.M. ride to
a place of calm, she has been told,
and musselled water.
Right now the city still streams
white around her ears, acrid,
tasting of too little sleep.
There is excitement between her legs
and a flask of coffee. Tell me when,
she says, teeth clattering, you want it.

II

The dawn seeps through a leak
in her sleep. Faltering,
they get off to check the air.
Barely begun and already
the puncturing of giddiness,
the grounding of the mad flight
she has foretold for herself.
The bristly boy at the shop
eyes her too-short skirt,
her naked feet, her jittery skin.
She buys water and a sweet
and wanders, distancing herself
from the two men by the car.
She finds a slice of sun
lying in front of the pump.
Before she can relish the trickle
of heat that caresses her calf,
it's time to go.
The water jostles in its sheath as she runs.

III

Too much water then.
She finds a public utility
where she can go in private.
The hiss of water
on neglected porcelain.
A lizard watchful on a wall.

IV

It grabs her, the pitcher,
incandescent on a wooden bench.
Perfectly shaped,
intoxicating and plastic.
Does it hold water, she thinks,
or the slow drip of drunken flowers.
It could be either.
Right now, it is innocent.
Still life of shocking green.
Plucked from the cluster
orange, green and yellow
that hangs efflorescent
from a hidden rope.
Emptily they sway.
The drawn one broods,
cursed with stillness,
pleading to be taken along.

A Memory of Logs

She understands nothing of this place,
and so it moves her.
The thought of faraway children
walking trancelike into the water
towards a hope of mussels.

She has married one of those children.
Tall, he walks beside her, boylike
in the memory of logs
that almost trapped him,
the old story made new
by the flitter of light,
the whisper of wood,
the wobble of the boat at her feet.

The timber factory sleeps.
Long ago,
a square patch of safety, rumble-bellied,
resisting the monotony of land,
tempted the boys to walk on water.
(And how must it have felt,
the lurch of shifting log,
solid melting into a panic of sunlight
snapping shut in a gridlock of fear?)

She feels the tug of tears,
certain as the hand that pulled out the boy
who sits beside her on this plank,
warm with sun, and ageing.

Crossing

Where the river tangles with the sea the island was born.
Too grand a word – island – for what takes a minute
from end to end and side to side, abrupt and beautiful.

No secrets scar this bareboned child lying exposed
under the sun, a thicket running down its spine.
Branches brought here by the silting tide, they say.

And now look at the way the mud clings, anchored
by its own untidy flotsam. So small and yet so burdened
by chance debris. A rip of plastic bag, a gash of tin.

Who comes here, she asks. People like you, they grin.
Abashed, she sinks herself in the wet blue embrace,
two sets of arms salt and fresh colliding

unreconciled and inextricable. The last of the seven bridges
hangs by itself. Impossible that she should have crossed it
in the dark and not drowned. The sky falls around her.

Are there rocks under this borrowed sand?
Does a rock lobster king hold this island afloat?
For thirty years the patient accretion of time, and then

the water turns to sand. What stops it from floating away
reborn as a spiny turtle, suddenly thirsty for land?
Watch out! they shout. She jolts. A purple oyster shell

lies buried beside her toes. How lovely, she says,
bending to fondle it. Only till you feel its bite, they say,
even sharper than the kitchen blade lying open

on the floor. Purple curls wicked with unshed blood.
Sorrow spurts unbidden, a taste on her tongue.
They have hidden the dead child behind their banter.

Back in the narrow boat, each couple silent on a plank,
a baby mullet leaps in and quivers on her palm.

Boxes

Her balcony bears an orchid smuggled in a duffle bag
from Singapore. Its roots cling to air. For two hours
every morning the harsh October sun turns tender
at its leaves. Nine steps from door to balcony and
already she is a giant insect fretting in a jar.

On one side of her one-room home, a stove, where she
cooks dal in an iron pan. The smell of food is good.
Through the window bars the sing-song of voices high
then low in steady arcs. With his back to the wall,
a husband, and a giant stack of quilts, threatening to fall.

Sleeping room only, a note on the door should have read,
readying you for cramp. Fall in and kick off your shoes.
Right-angled to this corridor with a bed, trains make tracks
to unfamiliar sounding places. Unhidden by her curtains,
two giant black pigs lie dead, or asleep, on a dump.

Everyday the city grows taller, trampling underfoot
students wives lovers babies. The boxes grow smaller.
The sea becomes a distant memory of lashing wave
and neon, siren to seven islands, once. The sky strides
inland on giant stilts, unstoppable, shutting out the light.

K. SATCHIDANANDAN

(*b*. 1946)

Born in 1946 in Kerala, K. Satchidanandan performs his poems – declaims rather than reads them, the words giving off an intense energy – in Malayalam and English. To listen to him is to be reminded that sound is the poet's primary tool, and that the sound of poetry prefigures the language and meaning. He has published 20 books of poetry and criticism in Malayalam and four in English translation. He lives in New Delhi.

Stammer

Stammer is no handicap.
It is a mode of speech.

Stammer is the silence that falls
between the word and its meaning,
just as lameness is the
silence that falls between
the word and the deed.

Did stammer precede language
or succeed it?
Is it only a dialect or a
language itself? These questions
make the linguists stammer.

Each time we stammer
we are offering a sacrifice
to the God of Meanings.

When a whole people stammer
stammer becomes their mothertongue:
as it is with us now.

God too must have stammered
when He created Man.
That is why all the words of man
carry different meanings.
That is why everything he utters
from his prayers to his commands
stammers,
like poetry.

The Mad

The mad have no caste
or religion. They
transcend gender,
live outside ideologies. We
do not deserve their innocence.

Their language is not of dreams but
of another reality. Their love
is moonlight. It
overflows on a full moon day.

Looking up they see
gods we have never heard of. They are
shaking their wings when
we fancy they are shrugging
their shoulders. They hold
even flies have souls
and the green god of grasshoppers
leaps up on thin legs.

At times they see trees bleed,
hear lions roar from the streets.
At times they watch Heaven
gleaming in a kitten's eyes,
just as we do. But they alone
can hear ants sing in a chorus.

While patting the air
they are taming a cyclone
over the Mediterranean. And with
their heavy tread they stop
a volcano from erupting.

They have another measure
of Time. Our century is
their second. Twenty seconds,
and they reach Christ; six more, they
are with the Buddha.

In a single day they reach
the big bang at the beginning.
They go on walking restless for
their earth is boiling still.

The mad are not
mad like us.

Genesis

My grandmother was insane.
As her madness ripened into death,
My uncle, a miser, kept her in our store-room,
Covered in straw.
My grandmother dried up, burst,
Her seeds flew out of the windows.
The sun came, and the rain,
One seedling grew up into a tree,
Whose lusts bore me.

Can I help writing poems
About monkeys with teeth of gold?

Gandhi and Poetry

One day a lean poem
reached Gandhi's *ashram*
to have a glimpse of the man.
Gandhi spinning away
his thread towards Ram
took no notice of the poem
waiting at his door.
Ashamed of not being a *bhajan*,
the poem now cleared his throat
and Gandhi glanced at him sideways
through those glasses that had seen hell.
'Have you ever spun thread?' he asked,
'Ever pulled a scavenger's cart?
Ever stood the smoke of
an early morning kitchen?
Have you ever starved?'

The poem said: 'I was born in the woods,
in a hunter's mouth.
A fisherman brought me up
in a cottage.
Yet I know no work, I only sing.
First I sang in the courts:
then I was plump and handsome;
but am on the streets now,
half starved.'

'That's better,' Gandhi said
with a sly smile, 'But you must give up this habit
of speaking in Sanskrit at times.
Go to the fields. Listen to
the peasants' speech.'

The poem turned into a grain
and lay waiting in the fields
for the tiller to come
and upturn the virgin soil
moist with new rain.

C.P. SURENDRAN
(*b.* 1959)

C.P. Surendran was born in Ottapalam, a small town in North Kerala, into a family of leftist intellectuals. His mother C.P. Parvathy was a short story writer and his father Pavanan a bureau chief with *Deshabhimani*, the official newspaper of the Communist Party of India before it split into Maoist, Marxist and Marxist-Leninist sub-parties. C.P. Ramachandran, a well-known editor and writer, was his uncle. The house he grew up in 'functioned like an underground shelter for the savagely persecuted Communists in the state'. This early life is recovered as background atmosphere in bitter and bitterly funny poems about Bombay, where he lived for many years, and, more recently, in a book of poems about his father's death. He lives in New Delhi and works as a journalist.

Milk Still Boils

He lies in bed, one hand
Thrown across his eyes. This,
He figures, is more like it.
He no longer thinks about her,
Or him. Just them.
And the postures they struck
Just before the milkman came.
In a minute he will be up
To put the milk on the boil
And no one the wiser.

A Friend in Need

He sits in a chair
Whose fourth leg
Is his. He loves
This chair. They used
To make love in it.
That was when the chair
Had four plus two plus two,
Eight legs. Days with legs.
There has been a lot of walking out
Since then. Now the chair's
Short of a leg. And he's lending his.

Curios

It's three in the morning.
The house rings with alarms,
There's someone leaning
On the doorbell.
It's her
After three years.
He lets her in,
Puts on some tea.
She lights a cigarette
With a match that might set
The house on fire.
She unpacks the weather
Which is New York.
They sit in silence.

The room turns into a museum of moods.

Family Court

At the Family Court
The lift wouldn't work.
So they walked up
Four flights

Of stairs and passed
On the fourth landing
Two toilets, one marked,
For Judges Only, and one,
For Others. They used
The first
But no one charged them
With Contempt of Court.

Later, they sat in the hall
With some 20 others,

People come together
To be separated.
The four fans in the hall
Big as windmills
Breezed past
Their several lives.

Late in the noon
An attendant
Called out their names
And led them into a hall
Where the judge
They met in the toilet said
They were no longer
Man and wife.

Conformist

First thing in the morning
He trips on the one chair in his room.
He opens the windows
And a teacup falls like a head axed.
The toothbrush slips from his fingers
And, then, the newspaper.
Too much gravity in here, he tells his cat,
And lies down on the floor.

from Catafalque

1 Post Natal

A room secreting smells.
Laundered linen
Breathing out camphor. Old Spice, old books, soap ghosting
Air with scent of pine. Blue ink gleaming thick in a vat of glass,
On the roll-top desk, the fat green pen on its side, run dry and smoking
Where it stopped. Lunar blips gilding the corner basin of water.
The floor waxed black verging on the brink
Of light, a dark pond mirroring the advance of the night.
Wet whiff of body wasting.

My father on the cot in white, straight as a corpse in a coffin,
The hours hushed about him in ambush, their scissor hands
Detonating memory cells like bombs at each intractable breath,
Burning synapses down like a bridge, weighting his tongue down
With speech slush.

Between flashes he wakes up blind, shakes a hand at the carnage
Laying him bare to the crib. Remembers neither the revolt
Of beginnings, nor the submission at arrival. Between birth
And death, there's nothing. Not even sorrow.
My father is a big baby, born today, gone tomorrow.

2 Eclipse

His fingers, like tendrils,
Coil the air about without a care.

His feet he carries after him,
Heavy, haphazard,
Like an afterthought.

His speech dies at birth.
If hyoid is a bone
He picked it clean a while ago.

He sits in a heap, wan, a smiling slave
To gravity
Pulling him down to the grave.

His eyes arrive at sight,
Slow, hesitant, strangely bright,
See the world in their left-over light.

3 *Favour*

Caught in the cross wires of a farewell sun
At the far end of a long, long passageway
He sits or stands, moves or pauses,
Comes or goes, as you please.
Clad or otherwise, he's naked
To the eye.
He is not here or the far there,
Where shadows sleep.

If you were a good son,
You'd hold to his head
A steady gun.

4 *Threshold*

The roses are on their own.
The grass spreads
Like water from an upturned urn.
Between mornings smudged blue like bruises
And evenings bubbling up like blood
Along broken arteries of the sky
The road narrowing through hedgerows,
Hens, fallow fields, darkening stream,
Slows towards home to halt
At my father's feet, far from town.
He clasps his hands over his head,
The softening crown.

And I see
His hands are no longer hard or brown.

SUJATA BHATT

(*b.* 1956)

Sujata Bhatt was born in 1956 in Ahmedabad and raised in Pune. She was educated in the United States, where she graduated from the University of Iowa's Writer's Workshop program. Her first book *Brunizem* (Carcanet, 1988) drew critical attention, both welcome and otherwise, for its extensive use of the Gujarati script interspersed with phonetic Roman and English translation. She continued the practice in several subsequent collections, countering charges of gimmickry with the argument that the use of Gujarati 'destabilises the authority of English within the poem'. Her best work, free of contrivance, makes effortless connections between the natural world and the subjective realm of the senses. She lives in Bremen, Germany.

White Asparagus

Who speaks of the strong currents
streaming through the legs, the breasts
of a pregnant woman
in her fourth month?

She's young, this is her first time,
she's slim and the nausea has gone.
Her belly's just starting to get rounder
her breasts itch all day,

and she's surprised that what she wants
is *him*
   inside her again.
Oh come like a horse, she wants to say,
move like a dog, a wolf,
           become a suckling lion-cub –

Come here, and here, and here –
but swim fast and don't stop.

Who speaks of the green coconut uterus
the muscles sliding, a deeper undertow
and the green coconut milk that seals
her well, yet flows so she is wet
from his softest touch?

Who understands the logic
behind this desire?

Who speaks of the rushing tide
                    that awakens
her slowly increasing blood – ?
And the hunger
              raw obsessions beginning
with the shape of asparagus:
sun-deprived white and purple-shadow-veined,
she buys three kilos
of the fat ones, thicker than anyone's fingers,
she strokes the silky heads,
some are so jauntily capped...
              even the smell pulls her in –

Looking Up

The hot air balloon convention floats
above our garden – weeks pass
but no one wants to come down.
At first the firemen stood by, ready
with their longest ladders,
their life nets and jumping sheets.
But now they've taken off
in their own, fire-red, hot air balloons:
Giant fireballs that dare to compete with the sun.
Who can look after the roses when the sky
ripples and throbs with so much passion?
Our neighbour's attic window glitters balloon-mad
and nostalgic for another life.
Yesterday's sunflower stares and stares.
The birch trees twitch restless
and can't get rid of their spores.
Only the children speak gently
as they collect snails
and line them up along the stone wall.

A Black Feather

This is the right half of my torso –
guarded by a black feather.

This is my grandmother's camisole –
examine the lace, the worn out buttonholes.

This is the left half of my torso –
invisible to all except the man who loves me.

This is my right breast, full
of a seventeen-year-old girl's memories.

These are the colours I know, the geometry
I must relearn, now after the surgery.

This is my left breast, hidden
by the way I am standing – hidden by violet shadows.

The buttons are lost – but look
I have sewn on new ones.

Sometimes in his haste he tore
the seams of my dress.

It was a raven he wished for
but only a crow's feather that I found.

This is the right half of my torso –
I let him unbutton the camisole.

This is the left half of my torso –
my heart was distracted by the light on the roses.

He touched the lace, the worn out buttonholes
and my breasts, still guarded by a black feather.

AGHA SHAHID ALI

(1949-2001)

Born in Srinagar and educated at the University of Kashmir, Srinagar, and, later, at the University of Delhi, Agha Shahid Ali moved to the United States where he described himself as 'Kashmiri-American' not Indian-American. He would on occasion let the pose slip: 'I never apologise, shameless little Indian that I am.' For Americans, he was an impossibly exotic figure: a self-professed product of three cultures, Muslim, Hindu and Western, and a permanent 'triple exile'. In contrast to the flamboyance of his personality, his subject was grief – for a vanished landscape or the death of a loved one – and his last book of poems *Rooms Are Never Finished* (W.W. Norton, 2001) was in large part an elegy to his mother, Sufia, who died of brain cancer. He would die of the same illness ('I will die that day in late October, it will be long ago'). The poems in this selections are woven like gauzes, with layered allusions – hidden or not – to a range of myths and literatures; and they are precise embodiments of form. He died in Amherst, Massachusetts.

Stationery

The moon did not become the sun.
It just fell on the desert
in great sheets, reams
of silver handmade by you.
The night is your cottage industry now,
the day is your brisk emporium.
The world is full of paper.

Write to me.

The Dacca Gauzes

> *...for a whole year he sought to accumulate*
> *the most exquisite Dacca gauzes*
> OSCAR WILDE, The Picture of Dorian Gray

Those transparent Dacca Gauzes
known as woven air, running
water, evening dew:

a dead art now, dead over
a hundred years. 'No one
now knows,' my grandmother says,

371

'what it was to wear
or touch that cloth.' She wore
it once, an heirloom sari from

her mother's dowry, proved
genuine when it was pulled, all
six yards, through a ring.

Years later when it tore,
many handkerchiefs embroidered
with gold-thread paisleys

were distributed among
the nieces and daughters-in-law.
Those too now lost.

In history we learned: the hands
of weavers were amputated,
the looms of Bengal silenced,

and the cotton shipped raw
by the British to England.
History of little use to her,

my grandmother just says
how the muslins of today
seem so coarse and that only

in autumn, should one wake up
at dawn to pray, can one
feel that same texture again.

One morning, she says, the air
was dew-starched: she pulled
it absently through her ring.

Farewell
(for Patricia O'Neill)

At a certain point I lost track of you.

They make a desolation and call it peace.

When you left even the stones were buried:

The defenceless would have no weapons.

When the ibex rubs itself against the rocks, who collects
        its fallen fleece from the slopes?

O Weaver whose seams perfectly vanished, who weighs the
        hairs on the jeweler's balance?

They make a desolation and call it peace.

Who is the guardian tonight of the Gates of Paradise?

My memory is again in the way of your history.

Army convoys all night like desert caravans.

In the smoking oil of dimmed headlights, time dissolved – all
        winter – its crushed fennel.

We can't ask them: *Are you done with the world?*

In the lake the arms of temples and mosques are locked
        in each other's reflections.

Have you soaked saffron to pour on them when they are
        found like this centuries later in this country
                I have stitched to your shadow?

In this country we step out with doors in our arms.

Children run out with windows in their arms.

You drag it behind you in lit corridors.

If the switch is pulled you will be torn from everything.

At a certain point I lost track of you.

You needed me. You needed to perfect me:

In your absence you polished me into the Enemy.

Your history gets in the way of my memory.

I am everything you lost. You can't forgive me.

I am everything you lost. Your perfect enemy.

Your memory gets in the way of my memory:

I am being rowed through Paradise on a river of Hell:
　　　　Exquisite ghost, it is night.

The paddle is a heart; it breaks the porcelain waves:

It is still night. The paddle is a lotus:

I am rowed – as it withers – toward the breeze which is soft as
　　　　if it had pity on me.

If only somehow you could have been mine, what wouldn't
　　　　have happened in this world?

I'm everything you lost. You won't forgive me.

My memory keeps getting in the way of your history.

There is nothing to forgive. You won't forgive me.

I hid my pain even from myself; I revealed my pain only to
　　　　myself.

There is everything to forgive. You can't forgive me.

If only somehow you could have been mine,

what would not have been possible in the world?

I See Kashmir from New Delhi at Midnight
(for Molvi Abdul Hai)

> *Now and in time to be,*
> *Wherever green is worn,...*
> *A terrible beauty is born.*
> 　　　W.B. YEATS

1

One must wear jeweled ice in dry plains
to will the distant mountains to glass.
The city from where no news can come
is now so visible in its curfewed night
that the worst is precise:

　　　　　　From Zero Bridge
a shadow chased by searchlights is running
away to find its body. On the edge

of the Cantonment, where Gupkar Road ends,
it shrinks almost into nothing, is

nothing by Interrogation gates
so it can slip, unseen, into the cells:
Drippings from a suspended burning tire
are falling on the back of a prisoner,
the naked boy screaming, 'I know nothing.'

2

The shadow slips out, beckons *Console Me*,
and somehow there, across five hundred miles,
I'm sheened in moonlight, in emptied Srinagar,
but without any assurance for him.

On Residency Road by Mir Pan House,
unheard we speak: 'I know those words by heart
(you once said them by chance): In autumn
when the wind blows sheer ice, the *chinar* leaves
fall in clusters –

             one by one, otherwise.'
'Rizwan, it's you, Rizwan, it's you,' I cry out
as he steps closer, the sleeves of his *phiren* torn.
'Each night put Kashmir in your dreams,' he says
then touches me, his hands crusted with snow,
whispers, 'I have been cold a long, long time.'

3

'Don't tell my father I have died,' he says,
and I follow him through blood on the road
and hundreds of pairs of shoes the mourners
left behind, as they ran from the funeral,
victims of the firing. From windows we hear
grieving mothers, and snow begins to fall
on us, like ash. Black on edges of flames,
it cannot extinguish the neighborhoods,
the homes set ablaze by midnight soldiers.
Kashmir is burning:

           By that dazzling light
we see men removing statues from temples.
We beg them, 'Who will protect us if you leave?'
They don't answer, they just disappear
on the road to the plains, clutching the gods.

4

I won't tell your father you have died, Rizwan,
but where has your shadow fallen, like cloth
on the tomb of which saint, or the body
of which unburied boy in the mountains,
bullet-torn, like you, his blood sheer rubies
on Himalayan snow?

        I've tied a knot
with green thread at Shah Hamdan, to be
untied only when the atrocities
are stunned by your jeweled return, but no news
escapes the curfew, nothing of your shadow,
and I'm back, five hundred miles, taking off
my ice, the mountains granite again as I see
men coming from those Abodes of Snow
with gods asleep like children in their arms.

The Floating Post Office

> *The post boat was like a gondola*
> *that called at each houseboat. It*
> *carried a clerk, weighing scales,*
> *and a bell to announce arrivals.*

Had he been kept from us? Portents
of rain, rumors, ambushed letters...
Curtained palanquin, fetch our word,
bring us word: Who has died? Who'll live?
Has the order gone out to close
the waterways...the one open road?

And then we saw the boat being rowed
through the fog of death, the sentence
passed on our city. It came close
to reveal smudged black-ink letters
which the postman – he *was* alive –
gave us, like signs, without a word,

and we took them, without a word.
From our deck we'd seen the hill road
bringing a jade rain, near-olive,
down from the temple, some penitent's
cymballed prayer? He took our letters,
and held them, like a lover, close

to his heart. And the rain drew close.
Was there, we asked, a new password –
blood, blood shaken into letters,
cruel primitive script that would erode
our saffron link to the past? Tense
with autumn, the leaves, drenched olive,

fell on graveyards, crying 'O live!'
What future would the rain disclose?
O Rain, abandon all pretense,
now drown the world, give us your word,
ring, sweet assassin of the road,
the temple bell! For if letters

come, I will answer those letters
and my year will be tense, alive
with love! The temple receives the road
there, the rain has come to a close.
Here the waters rise; our each word
in the fog awaits a sentence.

His hand on the scales, he gives his word:
Our letters will be rowed through olive
canals, tense waters no one can close.

Lenox Hill

(In Lenox Hill Hospital, after surgery, my
mother said the sirens sounded like the
elephants of Mihiragula when his men drove
them off cliffs in the Pir Panjal Range.)

The Hun so loved the cry, one falling elephant's,
he wished to hear it again. At dawn, my mother
heard, in her hospital-dream of elephants,
sirens wail through Manhattan like elephants
forced off Pir Panjal's rock cliffs in Kashmir:
the soldiers, so ruled, had rushed the elephant,
The greatest of all footprints is the elephant's,
said the Buddha. But not lifted from the universe,
those prints vanished forever into the universe,
though nomads still break news of those elephants
as if it were just yesterday the air spread the dye
('War's annals will fade into night / Ere their story die'),

the punishing khaki whereby the world sees us die
out, mourning you, O massacred elephants!
Months later, in Amherst, she dreamt: She was, with dia-
monds, being stoned to death. I prayed: If she must die,
let it only be some dream. But there were times, Mother,
while you slept, that I prayed, 'Saints, let her die.'
Not, I swear by you, that I wished you to die
but to save you as you were, young, in song in Kashmir,
and I, one festival, crowned Krishna by you, Kashmir
listening to my flute. You never let gods die.
Thus I swear, here and now, not to forgive the universe
that would let me get used to a universe

without you. She, she alone, was the universe
as she earned, like a galaxy, her right not to die,
defying the Merciful of the Universe,
Master of Disease, 'in the circle of her traverse'
of drug-bound time. And where was the god of elephants,
plump with Fate, when tusk to tusk, the universe,
dyed green, became ivory? Then let the universe,
like Paradise, be considered a tomb. Mother,
they asked me, *So how's the writing?* I answered *My mother
is my poem.* What did they expect? For no verse
sufficed except the promise, fading, of Kashmir
and the cries that reached you from the cliffs of Kashmir

(across fifteen centuries) in the hospital. *Kashmir,
she's dying!* How her breathing drowns out the universe
as she sleeps in Amherst. Windows open on Kashmir:
There, the fragile wood-shrines – so far away – of Kashmir!
O Destroyer, let her return there, if just to die.
Save the right she gave its earth to cover her, Kashmir
has no rights. When the windows close on Kashmir,
I see the blizzard-fall of ghost elephants.
I hold back – she couldn't bear it – one elephant's
story: his return (in a country far from Kashmir)
to the jungle where each year, on the day his mother
died, he touches with his trunk the bones of his mother.

'As you sit here by me, you're just like my mother,'
she tells me. I imagine her: a bride in Kashmir,
she's watching, at the Regal, her first film with Father.
If only I could gather you in my arms, Mother,
I'd save you – now my daughter – from God. The universe
opens its ledger. I write: How helpless was God's mother!
Each page is turned to enter grief's accounts. Mother,
I see a hand. *Tell me it's not God's.* Let it die.

I see it. It's filling with diamonds. Please let it die.
Are you somewhere alive, somewhere alive, Mother?
Do you hear what I once held back: in one elephant's
cry, by his mother's bones, the cries of those elephants

that stunned the abyss? Ivory blots out the elephants.
I enter this: *The Belovèd leaves one behind to die.*
For compared to my grief for you, what are those of Kashmir,
and what (I close the ledger) are the griefs of the Universe
when I remember you – beyond all accounting – O my mother?

VIJAY SESHADRI

(*b.* 1954)

Vijay Seshadri was born in 1954 in Bangalore and at the age of five went to Columbus, Ohio. His father taught chemistry at Ohio State and Seshadri's second book, *The Long Meadow*, centres on a prose meditation about his father's obsession with the American Civil War. His poetry makes use of tight, rhymed quatrains and blank verse and the elastic prose-like line evident in some of the poems in this selection. The tone is unashamedly American – in the long poem 'Lifeline', a new American vernacular is inventing itself: 'a gypo logger, scrounging / deadfall cedar for shake-bolt cords' – and if there are Indian references, as in 'The Long Meadow', they are intentionally separated from a context. Seshadri, a professor at Sarah Lawrence College, has worked as a commercial fisherman in Oregon, as a biologist with the National Marine Fish Service, and as a copy editor with *The New Yorker*. He lives in Brooklyn.

The Disappearances

'Where was it one first heard of the truth?'

On a day like any other day,
like 'yesterday or centuries before',
in a town with the one remembered street,
shaded by the buckeye and the sycamore –
the street long and true as a theorem,
the day like yesterday or the day before,
the street you walked down centuries before –
the story the same as the others flooding in
from the cardinal points is
turning to take a good look at you.
Every creature, intelligent or not, has disappeared –
the humans, phosphorescent,

the duplicating pets, the guppies and spaniels,
the Woolworth's turtle that cost forty-nine cents
(with the soiled price tag half-peeled on its shell) –
but, from the look of things, it only just happened.
The wheels of the upside-down tricycle are spinning.
The swings are empty but swinging.
And the shadow is still there, and there
is the object that made it,
riding the proximate atmosphere,
oblong and illustrious above
the dispeopled bedroom community,
venting the memories of those it took,
their corrosive human element.
This is what you have to walk through to escape,
transparent but alive as coal dust.
This is what you have to hack through,
bamboo-tough and thickly clustered.
The myths are somewhere else, but here are the meanings,
and you have to breathe them in
until they burn your throat
and peck at your brain with their intoxicated teeth.
This is you as seen by them, from the corner of an eye
(was that the way you were always seen?).
This is you when the President died
(the day is brilliant and cold).
This is you poking a ground wasps' nest.
This is you at the doorway, unobserved,
while your aunts and uncles keen over the body.
This is your first river, your first planetarium, your first popsicle.
The cold and brilliant day in six-color prints –
but the people on the screen are black and white.
Your friend's mother is saying,
Hush, children! Don't you understand history is being made?
You do, and you still do. Made and made again.
This is you as seen by them, and them as seen by you,
and you as seen by you, in five dimensions,
in seven, in three again, then two,
then reduced to a dimensionless point
in a universe where the only constant is the speed of light.
This is you at the speed of light.

The Long Meadow

Near the end of one of the old poems, the son of righteousness,
the source of virtue and civility,
on whose back the kingdom is carried
as on the back of the tortoise the earth is carried,
passes into the next world.
The wood is dark. The wood is dark,
and on the other side of the wood the sea is shallow, warm, endless.
In and around it, there is no threat of life –
so little is the atmosphere charged with possibility that
he might as well be wading through a flooded basement.
He wades for what seems like forever,
and never stops to rest in the shade of the metal rain trees
springing out of the water at fixed intervals.
Time, though endless, is also short,
so he wades on, until he walks out of the sea and into the mountains,
where he burns on the windward slopes and freezes in the valleys.
After unendurable struggles,
he finally arrives at the celestial realm.
The god waits there for him. The god invites him to enter.
But, looking through the glowing portal,
he sees on that happy plain not those he thinks wait eagerly for him –
his beloved, his brothers, his companions in war and exile,
all long since dead and gone –
but, sitting pretty and enjoying the gorgeous sunset,
his cousin and bitter enemy, the cause of that war, that exile,
whose arrogance and vicious indolence
plunged the world into grief.
The god informs him that, yes, those he loved have been carried down
the river of fire. Their thirst for justice
offended the cosmic powers, who are jealous of justice.
In their place in the celestial realm, called Alaukika in the ancient texts,
the breaker of faith is now glorified.
He, at least, acted in keeping with his nature.
Who has not felt a little of the despair the son of righteousness now feels,
staring wildly around him?
The god watches, not without compassion and a certain wonder.
This is the final illusion,
the one to which all the others lead.
He has to pierce through it himself, without divine assistance.
He will take a long time about it,
with only his dog to keep him company,
the mongrel dog, celebrated down the millennia,
who has waded with him,
shivered and burned with him,

and never abandoned him to his loneliness.
That dog bears a slight resemblance to my dog,
a skinny, restless, needy, overprotective mutt,
who was rescued from a crack house by Suzanne.
On weekends, and when I can shake free during the week,
I take her to the Long Meadow, in Prospect Park, where dogs
are allowed off the leash in the early morning.
She's gray-muzzled and old now, but you can't tell that by the way she runs.

Family Happiness

On our first date, I told my wife
I was a lesbian trapped in the body of a man.
Everybody says that now, of course,
on TV and radio, alternative media outlets,
tattoos and bumper stickers, but this was long ago, when
none but the brave (who deserve the fair)
would come up with something like that.
She smiled the pleased and goofy smile that flowers in her big eyes,
and I thought I had her.
Looking back now, though,
I can see her appraisal of me rounding to completeness.
I can hear her cognition firing.
She knew it. She knew even then
the truth it has cost me the aeons to acquire,
climbing and climbing the broken stairs:
I'm a man trapped in the body of a man.
I clutch the smooth walls and see through his eyes
the oil fires and containment units,
the huge clawed gantries strung out on the twilit polar horizon.
Through his alloyed ears, I hear
the objects of his scorn, his compassion, his hatred, his love
crying out and crying out.
Half my arms are his arms.
Half my face is welded to his face.
The other half mouths his clumsy ironies.
'Life is war,' he says.
'Tragic,' he says. 'Tragic.'
The simulacra are marching everywhere,
and deep in the caves the chimeras are breathing.

North of Manhattan

You can take the Dyre Avenue bus to where the subway terminates
just inside the Bronx
and be downtown before you realise
how quickly your body has escaped your mind,
stretching down the tracks on a beam
until the band snaps and the body slips free and is gone,
out the crashing doors, through the stiles,
and up the long chutes,
to burn both ways at once down the avenues,
ecstatic in its finitude,
with all the other bodies,
the bundles of molecules
fusing and dispersing on the sidewalks.
Ten to the hundredth power,
bundles of molecules are looking at paintings,
bundles of molecules are eating corn muffins,
crabcakes, shad roe, spring lamb, rice pudding.
Bundles of molecules are talking to each other,
sotto voce or in a commanding voice –
'I agree with you one hundred per cent, Dog';
'I looked for you today, but you'd already gone';
'I've left the Amended Restated Sublease Agreement on your desk';
'I'm going home now,
and you think about what you did.'
The ear grows accustomed to wider and wider intervals.
The eye sees shapes in the periphery
toward which it dares not turn to look.
One bundle is selling another a playback machine,
a six-square-inch wax-paper reticule
of powdered white rhinoceros horn,
an off-season-discounted ticket to Machu Picchu,
a gas-powered generator
for when the lights go out,
a dime bag of Mexican brown.
It is four o'clock in the afternoon.
The sunlight is stealing inch by inch
down the newly repointed redbrick wall.
She comes into the kitchen wrapped in the quilt
and watches as he fries eggs.
'After what just happened, you want to eat?' she says in disgust.
Will she or will she not, back in the bedroom,
lift the gun from the holster
and put it in her purse? The mind, meanwhile,
is still somewhere around Tremont Avenue,

panting down the tracks, straining
from the past to the vanishing present.
It will never catch up
and touch the moment. It will always be
in this tunnel of its forever,
where aquamarine crusted bulbs feed on a darkness
that looks all around without seeing,
and fungus, earlike, starved for light, sprouts
from walls where drops of rusted water
condense and drip.

Don't say I didn't warn you about this.
Don't say my concern for your welfare
never extended to my sharing the terrible and addictive secrets
that only death can undo.
Because I'm telling you now
that you can also take the same bus north,
crossing over against the traffic spilling out of the mall
and waiting twenty minutes in the kiosk with the Drambuie ad.
There. Isn't that better?
More passengers are getting off than on.
The girl with the skates going home from practice
will soon get off, as will
the old woman whose license to drive has been taken from her.
They will enter houses with little gazebos tucked in their gardens.
And then, for just a while, the mind will disembark from the body,
relaxed on its contoured plastic seat,
and go out to make fresh tracks in the snow
and stand and breathe under the imaginary trees –
the horsehair pine, the ambergris tree,
the tree that the bulbul loves,
the nebula tree...

Lifeline

As soon as he realised he was lost, that
in kicking around his new job in his head,
the new people he'd met, and how
he could manage a week in Seaside,
he'd stumbled past the muddy fork of road
that slithered down in switchbacks
to Highway 20, and now couldn't tell,
through rainclouds coarse as pig iron,

and about as cold, which languished
over each of the scarred mountaintops,
where west was, or east, or north,
or feel the sun's direction,
he stopped, as he knew he should,
and doubled back. An hour at the worst
would bring him to the International
inert in a ditch with its radiator
punctured, its axle broken, and blood
from his temple on the steering wheel.
He wished he'd never set eyes on that truck...
here he was, trudging like an idiot
through a thousand-square-mile dead spot
of Douglas fir, soaked to the bone
and hungry, with his head throbbing.
He wasn't up to this, he said to himself,
staring disconsolately outward
to the numberless ridges and valleys, singed
with the bitter green of the firs.
But why hadn't he reached the truck yet,
or at least somewhere familiar,
where he could get his bearings again?
He didn't recognise the ridge he was on.
He'd never seen this particular patch –
glinting with wild crocus prongs –
of clear-cut ground, torched and scarified.
Should he keep going, or return again?
There and then he made his third mistake.
Hearing, or thinking he heard,
deep in the valley below him plunged
in mist, a chain saw start and sputter,
he made off down toward the sound.
It would be a gypo logger, scrounging
deadfall cedar for shake-bolt cords,
or a civilian with a twenty-dollar permit
to cut firewood for sale at a roadside stand.
Either way, he could get directions
and hitch home by dark. Hours later,
night found him in a hollow, shouting
until he was hoarse for someone, anyone.
The weekend was almost here, and no one
at work would miss him before Monday...
He lived alone, idiot, he lived alone
and couldn't count on a single person
to send out an alarm. Those first hours
he spent shivering under a lip of rock,
wide awake, startling at each furtive,

night-hunting animal sound, each flap
of the raptors in the branches overhead.
On the second day he lost his glasses.
It happened like this: As he struggled
over the cryptic terrain all morning –
terrain that would seem, if looked at
from high above, from a helicopter
or a plane flying low enough to pierce
the dense, lazy foliage of clouds,
created, finessed, meticulously contrived
to amaze, like a marvellous relief map
of papier-mâché, revealing its artifice only
in the improbable dramas of its contours,
its extravagant, unlikely colors –
he had what amounted to a real insight.
All this was the brainchild of water.
Stretching back beyond the Pleistocene –
how many millions of years? –
imperial rain had traced without pity,
over and over again, its counter-image
on the newborn, jagged mountains
until the length of the coast had been
disciplined to a system on purpose designed
to irrigate and to nourish the soil.
He decided he'd follow the water down.
He'd use each widening tributary
like the rung of a ladder, to climb down
from his awful predicament, and soon
work his way to the ocean – though, of course,
long before that he'd run across people.
With this in mind, he came to a stream
heavy and brown with the spring runoff,
its embankment on his side steep
to the point of perpendicularity, thick
with brush, though on the other side
a crown of ferns tumbled gently down
to the next watershed. It seemed like
a good idea to cross, and farther on
he found a logged fir with a choker cable
still attached (it must have snapped
when they tried to yard the felled tree
to the road high above) straddling
the stream. A little more than halfway over
he slipped on the treacherous wood
and would have gone in but for the cable
which he lunged at just in time.
That was his lifeline, though flailing

to save himself, he knocked the glasses
from his head. Now they'd reach the sea
long before him, if he ever would.
He knelt down in the ferns, exhausted,
by fits growing determined never
to leave that spot. They'd find his bones
fifty years from now, clothes and ID
rotted away, a trillium poking through
his ribcage, a cucumber vine trellised
by the seven sockets in his skull.
The play of the thin, unending drizzle
on the overlapping leaves he sank below,
on the bark of the impassive trees
looming around him, grew indistinguishable
from the pulse turning loud in his head.
The ugly bruise on his forehead throbbed.
There were rents and gashes everywhere
down the length of his rain gear, which
let the mist and the dampness in.
Beyond a scant dozen inches, the world
looked blurry, smeared bright, unattainable.
Nothing in his life, up until then
(and if this had been pointed out to him
he would have acknowledged pride in it)
suggested that anything resembling
a speculative turn of mind cannibalised
the adequate, rhythmic, progressive
movements of his thoughts and feelings.
But, still, as almost everyone does,
he'd occasionally had inklings, stirrings,
promptings, and strange intuitions
about something just beyond the radius
of his life – not divine, necessarily,
but what people meant when they referred
to such things – which gave to the least
of his actions its dream of complicity.
Now he recognised, with a shock
almost physical, that those inklings
were just the returning, reanimated echo
(on a different scale but similar
to the echo we sometimes hear in our skulls
which leads us to the uncanny feeling
that an experience we're having is one
we've had before, at some other time –
but does anything ever repeat itself?)
of the vibrations his life made
bouncing off the things around him

sunk deep in their own being;
and that life, his life, blossoming now
in this daisy chain of accident and error,
was nothing more or less than what there was.
There was nothing hidden underneath this,
but it was small, so small, as the life
of his family was, his people, his species
among the other species – firs, owls,
plants whose names he didn't know –
all of them minute, and the earth itself,
its four billion plus years of life
just the faint, phosphorescent track
of a minute sea creature on an ocean
for the annihilating dimensions of which
words such as 'infinite' and 'eternal'
were ridiculous in their inadequacy.
He lay on his back inside the ferns
and listened to the rain's clepsydral ticking.
He tried to grasp – what was it? –
but it clattered away, that slight change
in the pressure binding thing to thing,
as when an upright sleeper shifts
just a little, imparting to his dreams
an entirely different train of meaning.
Beyond those clouds, the blue was there
which shaded to blackness, and beyond
that blackness the uncounted, terrifying
celestial entities hung suspended only
by the influence they had on one another.
And all of this was just a seed
inside a seed inside a seed...
So that when, finally, late the next morning
he half-crawled out of the woods, and came
in time to a wire fence in a clearing,
less than two feet high and decorated
with gleaming ceramic insulators,
which indicated that a mild current,
five volts at the most, ran through it
to keep the foraging animals off
the newly sown vegetable garden
enclosed inside its perimeter, and saw
beyond it the sprawl of the lawn,
the 4-by-4 parked in the driveway,
the Stars and Stripes on the flagpole,
and the house, he stopped paralysed.
The wind was blowing northwest, the clouds
were breaking up under its steady persuasion,

but, try as he did, he couldn't will
himself to step lightly over that wire,
and cross the garden's sweet geometry,
and go up to the door and ask to be
fed and made warm and taken home.
By that small fence, he sat down and wept.

ARVIND KRISHNA MEHROTRA
(*b*. 1947)

Arvind Krishna Mehrotra was born in Lahore in 1947, the year India became independent
and Lahore became a part of the newly formed nation of Pakistan. His family – caught up
in the enormous human dislocation that followed after Independence – abandoned Lahore
for the city of Allahabad, where his father set up a dental practice. His poems are coded
messages from the unconscious, but there is an exceedingly conscious hand that crafts them.
Initially misrepresented as a surrealist, he moved from the Beat-influenced extemporisations
of his late teens to a spare, controlled lyric line. His poems derive their power from what
they leave out as much as what they say, as if a host of ghost sentences stood behind each
one on the page; and he is a master of the short lyric of a dozen or fewer lines. Author of
three collections of poems and one of translations from the Prakrit, Mehrotra edited *The
Oxford India Anthology of Twelve Modern Indian Poets* (1991), possibly the most influential
collection of Indian poetry in English to date. He lives in Allahabad and Dehra Dun.

Genealogy

I

I recognise my father's wooden skin,
The sun in the west lights up his bald bones,
I see his face and then his broken pair of shoes,
His voice comes through, an empty sleeve.
Birds merge into the blue like thin strokes.
Each man in an unfinished fiction
And I'm the last survivor of what was a family;
They left in a caravan, none saw them
Slip through the two hands.
The dial spreads on the roof,
Alarms put alarms to sleep,
Led by invisible mules I take a path across
The mountains, my alchemies trailing behind
Like leather-bound nightmares;
There isn't a lost city in sight, the map I had
Preserved drifts apart like the continents it showed.

Arvind Krishna Mehrotra, Colaba, Bombay, 1997

II

My shadow falls on the sun and the sun
Cannot reach my shadow; near the central home
Of nomad and lean horse I pick up
A wheel, a migratory arrow, a numeral.
The seed is still firm. Dreams
Pitch their tents along the rim.
I climb Sugar Mountain,
My mother walks into the horizon,
Fire breaks out in the nests,
Trees, laden with the pelts of squirrels,
Turn into scarecrows,
The seed sends down another merciless root;
My alembic distills these fairy tales,
Acids, riddles, the danger in flowers;
I must never touch pollen or look
Into a watchmaker's shop at twilight.

III

My journey has been this anchor,
The off-white cliff a sail,
Fowl and dragons play near the shores
My sea-wrecked ancestors left.
I call out to the raven, 'My harem, my black rose,
The clock's slave, keeper of no-man's-land between us.'
And the raven, a tear hung above his massive pupil,
Covers my long hair with petals.
Only once did I twist the monotonous pendulum
To enter the rituals at the bottom of twelve seas,
Unghostlike voices curdled my blood, the colour
Of my scorpion changed from scarlet
To scarlet. I didn't mean to threaten you
Or disturb your peace I know nothing of,
But you who live in fables, branches,
And, somehow, icebergs, tell me whose seed I carry.

Continuities

I

This is about the green miraculous trees,
And old clocks on stone towers,
And playgrounds full of light
And dark blue uniforms.

At eight I'm a Boy Scout and make a tent
By stretching a bedsheet over parallel bars
And a fire by burning rose bushes,
I know half a dozen knots and drink
Tea from enamel mugs.
I wear khaki drill shorts, note down
The number-plates of cars,
Make a perfect about-turn for the first time.
In September I collect my cousins' books
And find out the dates of the six Mughals
To secretly write the history of India.
I see Napoleon crossing the Alps
On a white horse.

II

My first watch is a fat and silver Omega
Grandfather won in a race fifty-nine years ago;
It never works and I've to
Push its hands every few minutes
To get a clearer picture of time.
Somewhere I've kept my autograph book,
The tincture of iodine in homeopathy bottles,
Bright postcards he sent from
Bad Ems, Germany.
At seven-thirty we are sent home
From the Cosmopolitan Club,
My father says, 'No-bid',
My mother forgets her hand
In a deck of cards.
I sit on the railing till midnight,
Above a worn sign
That advertises a dentist.

III

I go to sleep after I hear him
Snore like the school bell;
I'm standing alone in a back alley
And a face I can never recollect is removing
The hubcaps from our dull brown Ford.
The first words I mumble are the names of roads,
Thornhill, Hastings, Lytton;
We live in a small cottage,
I grow up on a guava tree
Wondering where the servants vanish
After dinner, at the magic of the bearded tailor
Who can change the shape of my ancestors.

I bend down from the swaying bridge
And pick up the river
Which once tried to hide me:
The dance of the torn skin
Is for much later.

Canticle for My Son

The dog barks and the cat mews,
The moon comes out in the sky,
The birds are mostly settled.
I envy your twelve hours
Of uninterrupted dreaming.

I take your small palms in mine
And don't know what
To do with them. Beware, my son,
Of those old clear-headed women
Who never miss a funeral.

To an Unborn Daughter

If writing a poem could bring you
Into existence, I'd write one now,
Filling the stanzas with more
Skin and tissue than a body needs,
Filling the lines with speech.
I'd even give you your mother's

Close-bitten nails and light-brown eyes,
For I think she had them. I saw her
Only once, through a train window,
In a yellow field. She was wearing
A pale-coloured dress. It was cold.
I think she wanted to say something.

Where Will the Next One Come from

The next one will come from the air
It will be an overripe pumpkin
It will be the missing shoe

The next one will climb down
From the tree
When I'm asleep

The next one I will have to sow
For the next one I will have
To walk in the rain

The next one I shall not write
It will rise like bread
It will be the curse coming home

Approaching Fifty

Sometimes,
In unwiped bathroom mirrors,
He sees all three faces
Looking at him:

His own,
The grey-haired man's
Whose life policy has matured,
And the mocking youth's
Who paid the first premium.

The House

In the middle
Of a forest,
A house of stone.

Bats in the rafters,
Bat dung on the floor,
And hanging from a nail

A dentist's coat
Smelling pleasantly
Of chloroform.

Mud on his sandals
And smoke in his eyes,
On a railway platform

I saw him last,
Who passes before me
In the cheval-glass.

Scenes from a Revolving Chair

I

Day upon day, the outlook unchanged,
The long walk through elephant grass
In search of common speech. Sometimes
The nights are spent
In the middle of a borderless page,
And sometimes, unbroken clouds
Of late August darkening the frontier,
A wind rises in the octave branches.

II

The book lies open on two-voiced
Summer: the hawk-cuckoo's
Grey and white lines through hazeless
Air; overleaf, illuminated,
The copper-pod's long measures.
Standing like a bronze statue
In a public square, the city
Reads from the seasons.

III

After a heatwave and a night of storms
Have covered porcelain and rosewood
With a sheet woven with the threads
Of dust and rain,
A blue morning revives outside,
Offering to eyes what eyes cannot
Accept, unless a hand retouch
The unknowable picture.

IV

Without lifting their wings
The prey-birds climb
And fill the sky's dyed ground,
Throwing quilled shadows
Even as they move
Away from the eddying
River of consonants, the vowels that drown
Before leaden boats can reach them.

V

The moist-browed houses bury their dead
In unmarked valleys: the fanlight-eye
On which light does not fall,
The coping on which hard rain,
The bureau that will not be injured
By letters again. Steadily, for ever
Steadily, a sixty-year-old man
Blazes against a trembling wall.

ARVIND KRISHNA MEHROTRA

What Is an Indian Poem?

Here are two poems. The language of the first, which I have transcribed in the Roman alphabet, is not English. However, it uses English words – 'manager', 'company', 'rule', 'table', 'police', 'complaint' – that readers will recognise. If one keeps only the English words and erases the rest, the poem will resemble a Sapphic fragment:

> main manager ko bola mujhe pagaar mangta hai
> manager bola company ke rule se pagaar ek tarikh ko milega
> uski ghadi table pay padi thi
> maine ghadi uthake liya
> aur manager ko police chowki ka rasta dikhaya
> bola agar complaint karna hai to karlo
> mere rule se pagaar ajhee hoga

The second poem is a translation of the first:

> i want my pay i said
> to the manager
> you'll get paid said
> the manager
> but not before the first
> don't you know the rules?
> coolly I picked up his
> wrist watch
> that lay on his table
> wanna bring in the cops
> i said
> 'cordin to my rules
> listen baby
> i get paid when i say so

The language (it is more of a patois) of the first poem is Bombay-Hindi; that of the translation is American English. Both poems are by Arun Kolatkar. He was a bilingual poet who wrote in Marathi and English. 'Main manager ko bola', which was written in 1960, is part of a sequence of three poems, all written in the same patois. The sequence, which does not have a title, first appeared in a Marathi little magazine and subsequently, in 1977, in Kolatkar's first collection of Marathi poems. In English, Kolatkar titled the sequence 'Three Cups of Tea'.

Occasionally, Kolatkar translated his Marathi poems into English, but he mostly kept the two separate. Sometimes he wondered what the connection between them was, or if there was any connection at all. Kolatkar created two very different bodies of work of equal distinction and importance in two languages. The achievement, I think, has few parallels in world literature. What has a parallel, at least in India, is that he drew, in his work, on a multiplicity of literary traditions. He drew on the Marathi of course, and Sanskrit, which he knew; he drew on the English and American traditions, especially Black American music and speech ('cordin to my rules / listen baby / I get paid when i say so'); and he drew on the European tradition. He drew on a few others besides. As he said in an interview once, talking about poets, 'Anything might swim into their ken.'

Fortunately, in Kolatkar's case, we know something about that 'anything'. Kolatkar died in September 2004. Recently, while going through his papers in Bombay, I came across a typed sheet in which Kolatkar had put down a chronology of his life. In it, against each year, he gave the name of the advertising agency he worked for at the time (Ajanta, National, Press Syndicate); the area of Bombay he lived in (Malad, Sion, A Road); illnesses, if any; and the poems he wrote, both English and Marathi. That is how we know when he wrote 'main manager ko bola'. He also gave the names of the authors he read that year. Against 1965, he mentions the following: 'Snyder, Williams, Villon, Lautréamont, Catullus, Belli, Apollinaire, Morgenstern, Berryman, Wang Wei, Tu Fu, Li Po, *Cold Mountain*'. *Cold Mountain* is the title of a book of translations of the Chinese poet known as Han Shan (Cold Mountain), whom, incidentally, Gary Snyder had also translated.

'Art', Ezra Pound said, 'does not exist in a vacuum.' And Claude Lévi-Strauss, 'Whether one knows it or not, one never walks alone

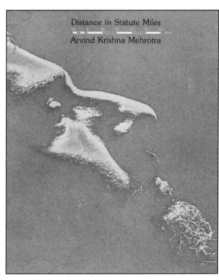

POETRY COLLECTIONS WITH COVER DESIGNS BY ARUN KOLATKAR

Arun Kolatkar's *Jejuri* (Clearing House, 1976) and Arvind Krishna Mehrotra's *Distance in Statute Miles* (Clearing House, 1982)

along the path of 'creativity'. Kolatkar's list of authors, which appears to be random, is in fact a capsule biography, a life of the life of the mind. Show me your books and I'll tell you who you are. It's a mind that could move with ease from 1st-century BC Italy to 8th-century China to 15th-century France to 20th-century America, while at the same time picking up the language spoken in the backstreets of Bombay, a slice of which he offers, without comment, in 'main manager ko bola'. But that said, the names of poets that appear in the list are not in themselves surprising. We were all reading the same or similar things in Bombay in 1965. There is, however, one exception to this, and that is Belli. Though his name belongs among the greatest in 19th-century European literature, he is known to very few, even in Italy. In the mid-60s, there was only one English translation of this poet around, and it's the one Kolatkar must have read. The translation is by Harold Norse and is called *The Roman Sonnets of G.G. Belli*. It has a preface by William Carlos Williams (a name that also figures in Kolatkar's list) and an introduction by Alberto Moravia. It was published by Jonathan Williams in 1960. What is striking about Harold Norse's translation is the idiom in which he translates Romanesco, the Roman dialect (perhaps not unlike Bombay-Hindi) in which Belli wrote his sonnets. Here is the opening sentence of Williams's preface:

> Gogol wanted to do the job, and D.H. Lawrence, each into his own language but they were written not into the classic language Italian that scholars were familiar with, but the Roman dialect that gave them an intimate tang which was their major charm and which the illustrious names spoken of above could not equal.

Coming to Norse's translation, Williams says:

> These translations are not made into English but into the American idiom in which they appear in the same relationship facing English as the original Roman dialect does to classic Italian.

'Three Cups of Tea' first appeared in Saleem Peeradina's anthology *Contemporary Indian Poetry in English* in 1972. The anthology was the first to represent the new Indian poetry in English, and 'Three Cups of Tea' has been a part of the canon since. I don't have a date for when Kolatkar made the translation, but I suspect it was made after 1965, after his discovery of Norse's Belli and the demotic American that Norse employs to translate Romanesco: 'If ya wanna be funny, it's enough to be / A gentleman.'

So there it is, your Indian poem. It was written in a Bombay patois by a poet who otherwise wrote in Marathi and English. It then became part of two literatures, Marathi and Indian English, but entered the latter in a translation made in the American idiom, one of whose sources, or, if you will, inspirations, was an American translation of a 19th-century Roman poet.

ARUN KOLATKAR

(1932-2004)

Born in Kolhapur, Arun Kolatkar was educated there and at the J.J. School of Art in Bombay. He wrote prolifically, in both Marathi and English, but his poetry appeared at decades-long intervals. His first book of poems, *Jejuri*, was published in 1976 when he was 44, making it possibly the oldest debut in Indian poetry in English. His first Marathi publication was a year later. There was no further publication in English until 2004, the year of his death, with the simultaneous appearance of two books, *Sarpa Satra* and *Kala Ghoda Poems*, from where the poems in this selection have been taken. *Jejuri* has gone into several reprints and continues to be bought and read by new generations of readers. A possible reason for its popularity may be the Kolatkarean voice: unhurried, lit with whimsy, unpretentious even when making learned literary or mythological allusions. And whatever the poet's eye alights on – particularly the odd, the misshapen, and the famished – receives the gift of close attention. He died in Bombay.

from Pi-Dog

1

This is the time of day I like best,
and this the hour
when I can call this city my own;

when I like nothing better
than to lie down here, at the exact centre
of this traffic island

(or trisland as I call it for short,
and also to suggest
a triangular island with rounded corners)

that doubles as a parking lot
on working days,
a corral for more than fifty cars,

when it's deserted early in the morning,
and I'm the only sign
of intelligent life on the planet;

the concrete surface hard, flat and cool
against my belly,
my lower jaw at rest on crossed forepaws;

just about where the equestrian statue
of what's-his-name
must've stood once, or so I imagine.

2

I look a bit like
a seventeenth-century map of Bombay
with its seven islands

not joined yet,
shown in solid black
on a body the colour of old parchment;

with Old Woman's Island
on my forehead,
Mahim on my croup,

and the others distributed
casually among
brisket, withers, saddle and loin

– with a pirate's
rather than a cartographer's regard
for accuracy.

3

I like to trace my descent
– no proof of course,
just a strong family tradition –

matrilineally,
to the only bitch that proved
tough enough to have survived,

first, the long voyage,
and then the wretched weather here
– a combination

that killed the rest of the pack
of thirty foxhounds,
imported all the way from England

by Sir Bartle Frere
in eighteen hundred and sixty-four,
with the crazy idea

of introducing fox-hunting to Bombay.
Just the sort of thing
he felt the city badly needed.

Arun Kolatkar, Wayside Inn, Kala Ghoda, Bombay, 1995

4

On my father's side
the line goes back to the dog that followed
Yudhishthira

on his last journey,
and stayed with him till the very end;
long after all the others

– Draupadi first, then Sahadeva,
then Nakul, followed by Arjuna and,
last of all, Bhima –

had fallen by the wayside.
Dog in tow, Yudhishthira alone plodded on.
Until he too,

frostbitten and blinded with snow,
dizzy with hunger and gasping for air,
was about to collapse

in the icy wastes of the Himalayas;
when help came
in the shape of a flying chariot

to airlift him to heaven.
Yudhishthira, that noble prince, refused
to get on board unless dogs were allowed.

And my ancestor became the only dog
to have made it to heaven
in recorded history.

5

To find a more moving instance
of man's devotion to dog,
we have to leave the realm of history,

skip a few thousand years
and pick up a work of science fantasy
– Harlan Ellison's 'A Boy and his Dog',

a cultbook among pi-dogs everywhere –
in which the 'Boy' of the title
sacrifices his love,

and serves up his girlfriend
as dogfood to save the life of his
starving canine master.

6

I answer to the name of Ugh.
No,
not the exclamation of disgust;

but the U pronounced as in Upanishad,
and gh not silent,
but as in ghost, ghoul or gherkin.

It's short for Ughekalikadu,
Siddharamayya's
famous dog that I was named after,

the guru of Kallidevayya's dog
who could recite
the four Vedas backwards.

My own knowledge of the scriptures
begins
and ends, I'm afraid,

with just one mantra, or verse;
the tenth,
from the sixty-second hymn

in the third mandala of the Rig
(and to think
that the Rig alone contains ten thousand

five hundred and fifty-two verses).
It's composed in the Gayatri metre,
and it goes:

Om tat savitur varenyam
bhargo devasya dhimahi
dhiyo yonah prachodayat.

Twenty-four syllables, exactly,
if you count the initial Om.
Please don't ask me what it means, though.

All I know
is that it's addressed to the sun-god
– hence it's called Savitri –

and it seems appropriate enough
to recite it
as I sit here waiting for the sun

to rise.
May the sun-god amplify
the powers of my mind.

8

As I play,
the city slowly reconstructs itself,
stone by numbered stone.

Every stone
seeks out his brothers
and is joined by his neighbours.

Every single crack
returns to its flagstone
and all is forgiven.

Trees arrive at themselves,
each one ready
to give an account of its leaves.

The mahogany drops
a casket bursting with winged seeds
by the wayside,

like an inexperienced thief
drops stolen jewels
at the sight of a cop.

St Andrew's church tiptoes back to its place,
shoes in hand,
like a husband after late-night revels.

The university,
you'll be glad to know,
can never get lost

because, although forgetful,
it always carries
its address in its pocket.

9

My nose quivers.
A many-coloured smell
of innocence and lavender,

mildly acidic perspiration
and nail polish,
rosewood and rosin

travels like a lighted fuse
up my nose
and explodes in my brain.

It's not the leggy young girl
taking a short cut
through this island as usual,

violin case in hand,
and late again for her music class
at the Max Muller Bhavan,

so much as a warning to me
that my idyll
will soon be over,

that the time has come for me
to surrender the city
to its so-called masters.

The Ogress

One side of her face
(the right one)
is human enough;

but the other,
where the muscles are all
fused together,

burnt perhaps,
or melted down with acid
– I don't know which –

is all scar tissue
and looks
more like a side of bacon.

*

The one-eyed ogress
of Rope Walk Lane
(one breast removed,

hysterectomised,
a crown of close-cropped
moth-eaten hair,

gray,
on a head half-covered
in a scarecrow sari)

has always been a kind
of an auxiliary mother,
semi-official nanny

and baby-bather-in-chief
to a whole chain of children
born to this street.

*

Give her a bucket filled with water,
a bit of soap
and an unwashed child

– the dirtier the better –
and the wispy half-smile
that always plays

on the good side of her face
loses
its unfinished look

without completing itself;
and she gets a wicked gleam
in her right eye

as she starts unwrapping her gift
– the naughtier the better –
and she is never so happy

as when she has
a tough customer on her hands,
and she has whisked

his nappy off
– like now
for example.

*

Soap in eye,
a furious, foaming boy
– very angry,

very wet –
cradled lengthwise
and face down

on her spindly legs,
extended jointly
and straight out before her,

she sits on the edge
of the pavement; facing the road,
sari pulled up to her crotch,

and her instruments of torture
within easy reach:
an empty, sky-blue plastic mug

bobbing up and down
gleefully
in a bucket of water.

*

As grown-up fingers soap him,
grab ass,
scrub and knead his flesh,

the headlong boy,
end-stopped by the woman's feet
pointing skyward,

nose down between her ankles,
and restricted
by her no-win shins,

is overrun by swirling
galaxies of backsliding foam
that collide,

form and re-form,
slither up and down
and wrap around

the curved space
of his slippery body,
black as wet slate.

*

She turns him on his flip side
and, face clenched,
he kicks her in the crotch;

starts bawling
and shaking his fists
at the world;

but she grabs both his feet
with one hand,
crumples his face,

pulls his ears,
tweaks his nose,
probes his nostrils,

twists his arms,
polishes his balls,
plays with his pintle

and hits him
with three mugs full
of cold water

in quick succession.

*

The water cascades down his sides;
it sluices down her legs
that form a bridge

over a lengthening river
of bath water
flowing down the kerbside

like frothing star-broth
that will be swallowed up
by a rat-hole

waiting for it
further downstream.

*

And, after the flood,
when the ogress lifts him up in the air
and sets him down

on solid ground
– dripping wet
but all in one piece –

feeling a bit like a little Noah,
bow-legged and tottering,
he stands,

supported by an adult hand
under an armpit,
but still

on his own two feet,
and a street-fighting man
already.

*

When the ogress throws
a towel over him
and starts drying him,

he nods unsteadily
– for he is still not quite able
to balance his head –

looks around
at the whole honking world
that has massed its buildings

menacingly around him
and he already knows –
what his response is going to be.

He points his little
water cannon
at the world in general

and (Right!
Piss on it, boy)
shoots a perfect arc of piss,

lusty
and luminous
in the morning sun.

Bon Appétit

1

I wish bon appétit
to the frail old fisherwoman

(tiny,
she is no more than just

an armload of bones
grown weightless over the years,

and caught
in a net of wrinkles)

who, on her way to the market,
has stopped

to have a quick breakfast
in a hole-in-the-wall teashop,

and is sitting hunched
over a plate of peas

– her favourite dish –
on a shaky table,

tearing a piece of bread
with her sharp claws

to soak it in the thin gravy
flecked with red chilli peppers;

and whose mouth is watering
at this very moment, I bet,

for I can almost taste
her saliva

in my mouth.

    2

And I wish bon appétit
to that scrawny little

motheaten kitten
– so famished it can barely stand,

stringy tail,
bald patch on grungy back,

white skin showing
through sparse fur –

that has emerged
from a small pile of rubbish nearby,

slipped once
on a bit of onion skin,

and, making its way
slowly but unerringly

towards the shallow basket
full of shrimps

that the fisherwoman has left
on the pavement

before entering the teashop,
has finally managed to get there,

raised itself on its hindlegs
to put its dirty paws

on the edge of the basket,
and kissed

its first shrimp.

ACKNOWLEDGEMENTS

The poems in this anthology are reprinted from the following books and other sources, all by permission of the authors or publishers listed unless stated otherwise. Thanks are due to all the copyright holders cited below for their kind permission:

Shanta Acharya: 'Bori Notesz' and 'Shunya' from *Shringara* (Shoestring Press, 2006); reprinted by permission.

Meena Alexander: 'Indian April' and 'Black River, Walled Garden III, IV, V, VI, VII, VIII, IX, X, XI & XII' from *Illiterate Heart* (TriQuarterly Books/Northwestern University Press, 2002); reprinted by permission.

Agha Shahid Ali: 'Stationery' and 'The Dacca Gauzes' from *The Half-Inch Himalayas* © 1987 by Agha Shahid Ali, reprinted by permission of Wesleyan University Press; 'Farewell', 'I See Kashmir from New Delhi at Midnight' and 'The Floating Post Office', from *The Country without a Post Office* by Agha Shahid Ali, copyright © 1997 by Agha Shahid Ali, and 'Lenox Hill' from *Rooms Are Never Finished* by Agha Shahid Ali, copyright © 2002 Agha Shahid Ali, all reprinted by permission of W.W. Norton & Company, Inc.

Kazim Ali: 'Gallery', 'Renunciation', 'Prayer', 'Night', 'Speech' and 'July' from *The Far Mosque* (Alice James Books, 2005); 'Vase', 'Flight', 'Two Halves', 'A Century in the Garden' and 'Four O'Clock' from *The Fortieth Day* (BOA Editions, 2008); reprinted by permission.

Lawrence Bantleman: 'Movements', 'Ghosts', 'Septuagesima', 'D— to J—' and 'One A.M.' from *Graffiti* (Writers Workshop, 1962); 'Words' and 'Gauguinesque' from *Man's Fall and Woman's Fallout* (Writers Workshop, 1964); 'In Uttar Pradesh' from *Modern Indian Poetry in English: An Anthology & A Credo*, ed. P. Lal (Writers Workshop, 1969); reprinted by permission.

Jane Bhandari: 'Steel Blue' from *Aquarius* (Harbour Line, 2002); reprinted by permission.

Sujata Bhatt: 'White Asparagus' from *Monkey Shadows* (Carcanet Press, 1991); 'Looking Up' and 'A Black Feather' from *Augatora* (Carcanet Press, 2000), all 'reprinted by permission of Carcanet Press Limited.

G.S. Sharat Chandra: 'Consistently Ignored', 'I Feel Let Down', 'Reasons for Staying', 'Vendor of Fish' and 'Rule of Possession' from *April in Nanjangud* (London Magazine Editions, 1971); 'Encircled', 'Friends' and 'Seeing My Name Misspelled I Look for the Nether World' from *Immigrants of Loss* (Hippopotamus Press, 1993); 'Brothers' from *Heirloom* (Oxford University Press, 1982); reprinted by permission.

Sampurna Chattarji: 'Still Life in Motion', 'A Memory of Logs', 'Crossing' and 'Boxes' from *Sight May Strike You Blind* (Sahitya Akademi, 2007); reprinted by permission.

Debjani Chatterjee: 'All Whom I Welcome Leave without My Leave' from *Albino Gecko* (University of Salzburg, 1998); 'Words Between Us' originally published in *A Little Bridge* (Pennine Pens, 1997); reprinted by permission.

Amit Chaudhuri: 'St Cyril Road Sequence 1, 2 & 5' and 'Nissim Ezekiel' from *St Cyril Road and Other Poems* (Penguin India, 2005); reprinted by permission.

Dilip Chitre: 'The First Breakfast: Objects', 'The Second Breakfast: Intimations of Mortality' and 'The Fourth Breakfast: Between Knowing and Unknowing' from *As Is, Where Is: Selected English Poems 1964-2007* (Poetryvala, 2007); reprinted by permission.

David Dabydeen: 'XIII', 'XVI', 'XVIII', 'XX', 'XXII', 'XXIV' and 'XXV' from *Turner: New & Selected Poems* (Jonathan Cape, 1994; Peepal Tree Press, 2002); reprinted by permission.

Mamang Dai: 'The Missing Link', 'Remembrance', 'No Dreams', 'Sky Song' and 'Small Towns and the River' originally published in *Fulcrum*; reprinted by permission.

Keki Daruwalla: 'The Poseidonians' and 'The Glass-Blower' from *A Summer of Tigers* (HarperCollins, 1995); 'Wolf' from *Landscapes* (Oxford University Press, 1987); 'Roof Observatory' and 'Map-maker' from *The Map-maker* (Ravi Dayal, 2002); reprinted by permission.

Kamala Das: 'The Descendants', 'Luminol', 'The Maggots' and 'The Looking Glass' from *The Descendants* (Writers Workshop, 1967); 'A Request', 'The Old Playhouse' and 'The Stone Age' from *Only the Soul Knows How to Sing* (DC Books, 1996); reprinted by permission.

Eunice de Souza: 'Poem for a Poet', 'Miss Louse' and 'This Swine of Gadarene' from *Fix* (Newground, 1979); Women in Dutch Painting', 'Pilgrim', 'She and I', 'The Road' and 'Unfinished Poem' from *Women in Dutch Painting* (Praxis, 1988); 'Outide Jaisalmer' from *Selected and New Poems* (Department of English, St Xavier's College, 1994); reprinted by permission.

Imtiaz Dharker: 'Purdah I' and 'Living Space' from *Postcards from god* (Bloodaxe Books, 1997); 'Object' from *I Speak for the Devil* (Bloodaxe Books, 2001); 'Its Face', 'Before I' and 'Dreams' from *The Terrorist at My Table* (Bloodaxe Books, 2006); reprinted by permission.

Vinay Dharwadker: 'Houseflies' originally published in *Ariel*; 'Words and Things' originally published in *Fulcrum*; 'Walking toward the Horizon' from *Sunday at the Lodi Gardens* (Penguin India, 1994); 'Life Cycles' originally published in *The Kenyon Review*; reprinted by permission.

Tishani Doshi: 'Countries of the Body', 'Pangs for the Philanderer', 'At the Rodin Museum', 'Homecoming', 'The Day We Went to the Sea' and 'Evensong' from *Countries of the Body* (Aark Arts, 2007); reprinted by permission.

Nissim Ezekiel: 'A Morning Walk' from *The Unfinished Man* (Writers Workshop, 1960); 'Night of the Scorpion' from *The Exact Name* (Writers Workshop, 1965); 'Two Nights of Love' from *Sixty Poems* (Bombay, 1953); 'Goodbye Party for Miss Pushpa T.S.', 'The Patriot' and 'Poet, Lover, Birdwatcher' from *Collected Poems* (Oxford University Press, 2005); reprinted by permission of Oxford University Press India, New Delhi.

Monica Ferrell: 'Walking Home' originally published in *Guernica*; 'In the Binary Alleys of the Lion's Virus' originally published in *New England Review*; 'Mohn des Gedächtnis' originally published in *PN Review*; 'Alexander Leaves Babylon' originally published in *PN Review* and *Tin House*; 'The Lace World' originally published in *Slate*. 'Des Esseintes's Last Book' originally published in *The Paris Review*; reprinted by permission.

Leela Gandhi: 'Sex', 'Homage to Emily Dickinson, after Pain', 'On Reading You Reading Elizabeth Bishop', 'On Vermeer: Female Interiors' and 'A Catalogue for Prayer' from *Measures of Home* (Ravi Dayal, 2000); 'Noun' and 'Copula' originally published in *Fulcrum*; reprinted by permission.

Revathy Gopal: 'Freedom!', 'Just a Turn in the Road', 'Picnic at the Zoo', 'Seville', 'As the Crow Flies', 'Subterranean', 'Carved in Stone', 'Shapes', 'Time Past, Time Present' from *Last Possibilities of Light* (Writers Workshop, 2006); reprinted by permission.

Anjum Hasan: 'Shy', 'To the Chinese Restaurant', 'March', 'Jealousy Park' and 'Rain' from *Street on the Hill* (Sahitya Akademi, 2006); reprinted by permission.

Gopal Honnalgere: 'The City', 'You Can't Will', 'A Toast with Karma' from *Zen Tree and the Wild Innocents* (Gray Book, 1973); 'Theme' and 'The Donkeys' from *The Fifth* (Broomstick, 1980); 'Nails' and 'How to Tame a New Pair of Chappals' from *Internodes* (Samkaleen Prakashan, 1986).

Ranjit Hoskote: 'Passing a Ruined Mill', 'Ghalib in the Winter of the Great Revolt', 'Footage for a Trance', 'A View of the Lake' and 'Colours for a Landscape Held Captive' from *Vanishing Acts: New and Selected Poems, 1985-2005* (Penguin India, 2005); reprinted by permission.

Adil Jussawalla: 'Missing Person' from *Missing Person* (Clearing House, 1976); reprinted by permission.

Mamta Kalia: 'Against Robert Frost', 'Brat', 'Tribute to Papa', 'I'm Not Afraid of a Naked Truth' from *Tribute to Papa and Other Poems* (Writers Workshop, 1970); 'After Eight Years of Marriage' from *Poems '78* (Writers Workshop, 1978); 'Untitled' and 'Sheer Good Luck' originally published in *Fulcrum*; reprinted by permission.

Subhashini Kaligotla: 'Lepidoptera' originally published in *Crab Orchard Review*, reprinted by permission; 'In Freezing Light the Chrysler Building', 'From The Lord's Prayer', 'How Versatile the Heart', 'How Xenophobic the Heart' and 'Ascent to Calvary' previously unpublished, printed by permission.

Kersy Katrak: 'Malabar Hill 4, 5 & 6' from *A Journal of the Way* (Writers Workshop, 1969); 'Ancestors' from *Underworld* (Writers Workshop, 1979); reprinted by permission.

Tabish Khair: 'Nurse's Tales, Retold' and 'The Birds of North Europe' from *Where Parallel Lines Meet* (Penguin India, 2000); 'Lorca in New York' and 'Monsters' originally published in *Wasafiri*; 'Falling' originally published in *Fulcrum*; reprinted by permission.

Deepankar Khiwani: 'Delhi Airport', 'Night Train to Haridwar' and 'Collectors' from *Entr'acte* (Harbour Line, 2006); reprinted by permission.

Arun Kolatkar: 'Pi-Dog 1, 2, 3, 4, 5, 6, 8 & 9', 'The Ogress' and 'Bon Appétit' from *Kala Ghoda Poems* (Pras Prakashan, 2004); reprinted by permission.

Gopi Kottoor: 'Penguins' and 'Old Time Friends' originally published in *Fulcrum*; reprinted by permission.

Jayanta Mahapatra: 'A Rain of Rites' and 'Summer' from *A Rain of Rites* (University of Georgia Press, 1976); 'A Day of Rain' and 'The Moon Moments' from *The False Start* (Clearing House, 1980); 'Unreal Country' from *A Whiteness of Bone* (Penguin India, 1992); 'The Quest' and 'A Hint of Grief' from *Shadow Space* (DC Books, 1997); 'I Did Not Know I Was Ruining Your Life' was published in *Fulcrum*; reprinted by permission.

Arvind Krishna Mehrotra: 'Genealogy' and 'Continuities' from *Nine Enclosures* (Clearing House, 1976); 'Canticle for My Son' and 'Where Will the Next One Come from' from *Distance in Statute Miles* (Clearing House, 1982); To an Unborn Daughter', 'Approaching Fifty', 'The House' and 'Scenes from a Revolving Chair' from *The Transfiguring Places* (Ravi Dayal, 1998); reprinted by permission.

Sudesh Mishra: 'Joseph Abela' and 'Suva; Skye' from *Diaspora and the Difficult Art of Dying* (Otago University Press, 2002), reprinted by permission; 'Sea Ode' and 'Winter Theology' appeared in *Fulcrum*, reprinted by permission; 'Pi-Dog 4 (Reprise)' previously unpublished, printed by permission.

Dom Moraes: 'Another Weather' originally published in *La Revue Bilingue de Paris*; 'At Seven O'Clock' from *A Beginning* (Parton Press, 1957); 'Visitors' and 'Absences' from *Collected Poems 1957-1987* (Penguin India, 1987); 'Two from Israel' from *John Nobody* (Eyre & Spottiswoode, 1963); 'After the Operation I, III, V, IX & XI' from *Collected Poems 1954-2004* (Penguin India, 2004); reprinted by permission.

K.V.K. Murthy: 'Just Dead' and 'Hospital Journal' originally published in *The Guardian Unlimited*, reprinted by permission; 'Martyr', 'Bookmark', 'Exhibit', 'Relocation', 'Signature' and 'Life Stilled' are previously unpublished, printed by permission.

Daljit Nagra: 'The Speaking of Bagwinder Singh Sagoo!', 'Look We Have Coming to Dover!', 'Singh Song!', 'Bibu & the Street Car Wife!' and 'My Father's Dream of Return', from *Look We Have Coming to Dover!* (Faber & Faber, 2007); reprinted by permission.

Karthika Nair: 'Interregnum' and 'Visiting Hours I, II & III' originally published in *Indian Literature*; 'Zero Degrees: Between Boundaries' and 'Snapshot on the Parisian Métro, or Landscape on Line 3' from *Distant Music* (HarperCollins India, 2008); reprinted by permission.

Rukmini Bhaya Nair: 'Genderole', 'Renoir's Umbrellas', 'Usage' and 'Convent' from *Yellow Hibiscus: New and Selected Poems* (Penguin, 2004); reprinted by permission.

Vijay Nambisan: 'Millennium', 'First Infinities 1, 2 & 3' and 'Dirge' originally published in *Fulcrum*; 'Holy, Holy', 'Madras Central' and 'Cats Have No Language' from *Gemini* (Penguin India, 1992); reprinted by permission.

Vivek Narayanan: 'Learning to Drown', 'Three Elegies for Silk Smitha' and 'Ode to Prose' from *Universal Beach* (Harbour Line, 2006); 'No More Indian Women' and 'Not Far from the Mutiny Memorial' originally published in *Fulcrum*; reprinted by permission.

Aimee Nezhukumatathil: 'Small Murders', 'One Bite', 'Making Gyotaku' and 'Dinner with the Metrophobe' from *Miracle Fruit* (Tupelo Press, 2003); reprinted by permission.

Bibhu Padhi: 'Stranger in the House' from *A Wound Elsewhere* (Rupa, 1992); 'Midnight Consolings' and 'Something Else' from *Painting the House* (Orient Longman, 1999); 'Sea Breeze 1 & 2' and 'Grandmother's Soliloquy' from *Going to the Temple* (Indus, 1988); reprinted by permission.

R. Parthasarathy: From 'A House Divided' (Ms.): 'Remembered Village', 'Under the warm coverlet my woman sleeps on', 'As you untie your long flowing hair in bed', 'It is noon: oak and maple fight', 'The fragrant breath of crab apple', 'Taj Mahal', 'At Ghalib's Tomb' and 'You, Amir Khusrau' copyright © 2007 by R. Parthasarathy; reprinted by permission.

Gieve Patel: 'Servants' and 'Post-Mortem' from *Poems* (Nissim Ezekiel Bombay, 1966); 'The Ambiguous Fate of Gieve Patel, He Being neither Muslim nor Hindu in India' from *How Do You Withstand Body* (Clearing House, 1976); Squirrels in Washington' from *Mirrored, Mirroring* (Oxford University Press, 1991); reprinted by permission.

Saleem Peeradina: 'Still Life' from *First Offence* (Newground, 1980); 'Landscape with Locomotive' from *Group Portrait* (Oxford University Press, 1992); reprinted by permission.

Jerry Pinto: 'House Repairs', 'Drawing Home' and 'Rictus' from *Asylum* (Allied, 2003); reprinted by permission.

E.V. Ramakrishnan: 'Terms of Seeing', 'Stray Cats', 'For All Things Dying 2, 3 & 9' from *Terms of Seeing: New and Selected Poems* (Konark, 2006); reprinted by permission.

A.K. Ramanujan: 'The Black Hen', 'Foundlings in the Yukon', 'Love 5', 'The Day Went Dark', 'To a Friend Far Away', 'Mythologies 2' and 'Second Sight' from *The Oxford India Ramanujan*, ed. Molly Daniels-Ramanujan (Oxford University Press, 2004); reprinted by permission.

Mani Rao: '1', '2', '3', '4', '5', '7' from *Echolocation* (Chameleon Press, 2003); '6' from *The Last Beach* (Asia 2000, 1999). Reprinted by permission.

Srinivas Rayaprol: 'Oranges on a Table', 'Poem', 'A Taste for Death', 'Travel Poster', 'Married Love', 'Middle Age', 'I Like the American Face', 'Life Has Been' and 'Poem for a Birthday' from *Selected Poems* (Writers Workshop, 1995); reprinted by permission.

Srikanth Reddy: 'Burial Practice', 'Corruption', 'Fundamentals of Esperanto' and 'Aria' from *Facts for Visitors* (The University of California Press, 2004); reprinted by permission.

Mukta Sambrani: 'The Insurgence of Color, or Anna Thinks Anne Carson Is God, No Smaller than Marx', 'Names Anna Forgets: Narayan, Vishwanath, Padmapani', 'What the Postman Might Translate' and 'Sashi, or How Moon Could Mean Sun' originally published in *Fulcrum*; reprinted by permission.

K. Satchidanandan: 'Stammer' from *Stammer and Other Poems* (Konark, 2005); 'The Mad' and 'Gandhi and Poetry' from *How to Go to the Tao Temple* (Har Anand, 1998); 'Genesis' from *Summer Rain* (Nirala, 1995); reprinted by permission.

Vijay Seshadri: 'The Disappearances', 'The Long Meadow' and 'North of Manhattan' from *The Long Meadow* (Graywolf Press, 2005); 'Lifeline' from *Wild Kingdom* (Graywolf Press, 1996); 'Family Happiness' originally published in *The New Yorker*; reprinted by permission.

Vikram Seth: 'Unclaimed', 'Love and Work', 'Ceasing upon the Midnight', 'The Gift', 'A Little Night Music' from *The Humble Administrator's Garden* (Carcanet Press, 1985); 'On the Fiftieth Anniversary of the Golden Gate Bridge', 'The Stray Cat', 'Things', 'Souzhou Park' and 'Qingdao: December' from *All You Who Sleep Tonight* (Vintage, 1991); 'The Crocodile and the Monkey' from *Beastly Tales* (Phoenix, 1991); reprinted by permission.

Ravi Shankar: 'Plumbing the Deepening Groove' and 'A Square of Blue Infinity' originally published in *Fulcrum*; 'Lucia' originally published in *No Tell Motel*; 'The New Transcendence' originally published in *Cake Train*; 'A Story with Sand' from *Instrumentality* (Cherry Grove, 2004); reprinted by permission.

Prageeta Sharma: 'On Rebellion', 'Blowing Hot and Cold', 'The Silent Meow', 'Birthday Poem', 'Release Me from This Paying Passenger' from *Infamous Landscapes* (Fence, 2007); 'Underpants', 'Ode To Badminton', 'Miraculous Food for Once' and 'The Fantasist's Speech on the Fifteenth of August' from *The Opening Question* (Fence, 2004); reprinted by permission.

Manohar Shetty: 'May' originally published in *Fulcrum*; 'The Hyenas' originally published in *London Magazine*; 'Stills from Baga Beach' originally published in *Shenandoah*; 'Moving Out', 'The Old Printer', 'Torpor' and 'Gifts' from *Domestic Creatures* (Oxford University Press, 1994); reprinted by permission.

Menka Shivdasani: 'Spring Cleaning', 'At Po Lin, Lantao', 'Epitaph' and 'No Man's Land' from *Stet* (Sampark, 2000); reprinted by permission.

Melanie Silgardo: 'Bombay', 'Sequel to Goan Death', '1956-1976, a Poem' and 'Stationary Stop' from *Three Poets* (Newground, 1978), reprinted by permission; 'Beyond the Comfort Zone 1, 2, 3, 5 & 9' previously unpublished, printed by permission.

K. Srilata: 'Two Stories' originally published in *Fulcrum*; reprinted by permission.

Arundhathi Subramaniam: 'To the Welsh Critic Who Doesn't Find Me Identifiably Indian' and 'Home' from *Where I Live* (Allied Publishers, 2005); '5.46. Andheri Local' from *On Cleaning Bookshelves* (Allied Publishers, 2001); all poems also from *Where I Live: New & Selected Poems* (Bloodaxe Books, 2009), reprinted by permission.

C.P. Surendran: 'Milk Still Boils', 'A Friend in Need', 'Curios', 'Family Court' and 'Conformist' from *Gemini II* (Penguin India, 1994); 'Catafalque 1, 2, 3 & 4' from *Portraits of the Space We Occupy* (HarperCollins, 2007); reprinted by permission.

Sridala Swami: 'Surviving The Fall Meant Using You for Handholds', 'Cryogenic' and 'Post Mortem' originally published in *Wasafiri*; 'Slip Dreams' originally published in *Kritya*; 'Lines On Water', 'Aftermath' and 'All Music Is Memory' from *A Reluctant Survivor* (Sahitya Akademi, 2007); reprinted by permission.

H. Masud Taj: 'The Travelling Nonvegetarian', 'Cockroach', and 'Approaching Manhattan' originally published in *Fulcrum*; reprinted by permission.

Anand Thakore: 'Departure', 'Creepers on a Steel Door', 'What I Can Get away with' from *Waking in December* (Harbour Line, 2001); 'Ablutions' originally appeared in *Fulcrum*; reprinted by permission.

Jeet Thayil: 'Malayalam's Ghazal' and 'The New Island' originally published in *Salt*; 'The Art of Seduction', 'Superpower' and 'You Are Here' originally published in *Fulcrum*; 'Poem with Prediction' originally published in *Wasafiri*; 'To Baudelaire' and 'The Heroin Sestina' from *These Errors Are Correct* (Tranquebar, 2008); reprinted by permission.

Ruth Vanita: 'Sita', 'Sisters', 'Swayamvara', 'Fire' and 'Effluence' from *A Play of Light: Selected Poems* (Penguin India, 1994); reprinted by permission.

INDEX OF AUTHORS

Boldface figures indicate work by the authors concerned.
Roman figures denote references to the authors or their work.